AF333695

THE OFFICIAL
1986
Miami Dolphins
Guidebook

by Lou Sahadi

Taylor Publishing Company
Dallas, Texas

Acknowledgements
The author wishes to express his thanks for assistance
in compilation of the material to: Michael Robbie; Eddie
White; Ted Plumb; Gayle Baden and Ann Laliotes.

Photographs courtesy of The Miami Dolphins and Dave
Cross.

Published in cooperation with The Miami Dolphins

ISBN: 0-87833-556-0

Printed in the United States of America

Design by Gerry Repp

Contents

The Winning Edge

JOE ROBBIE

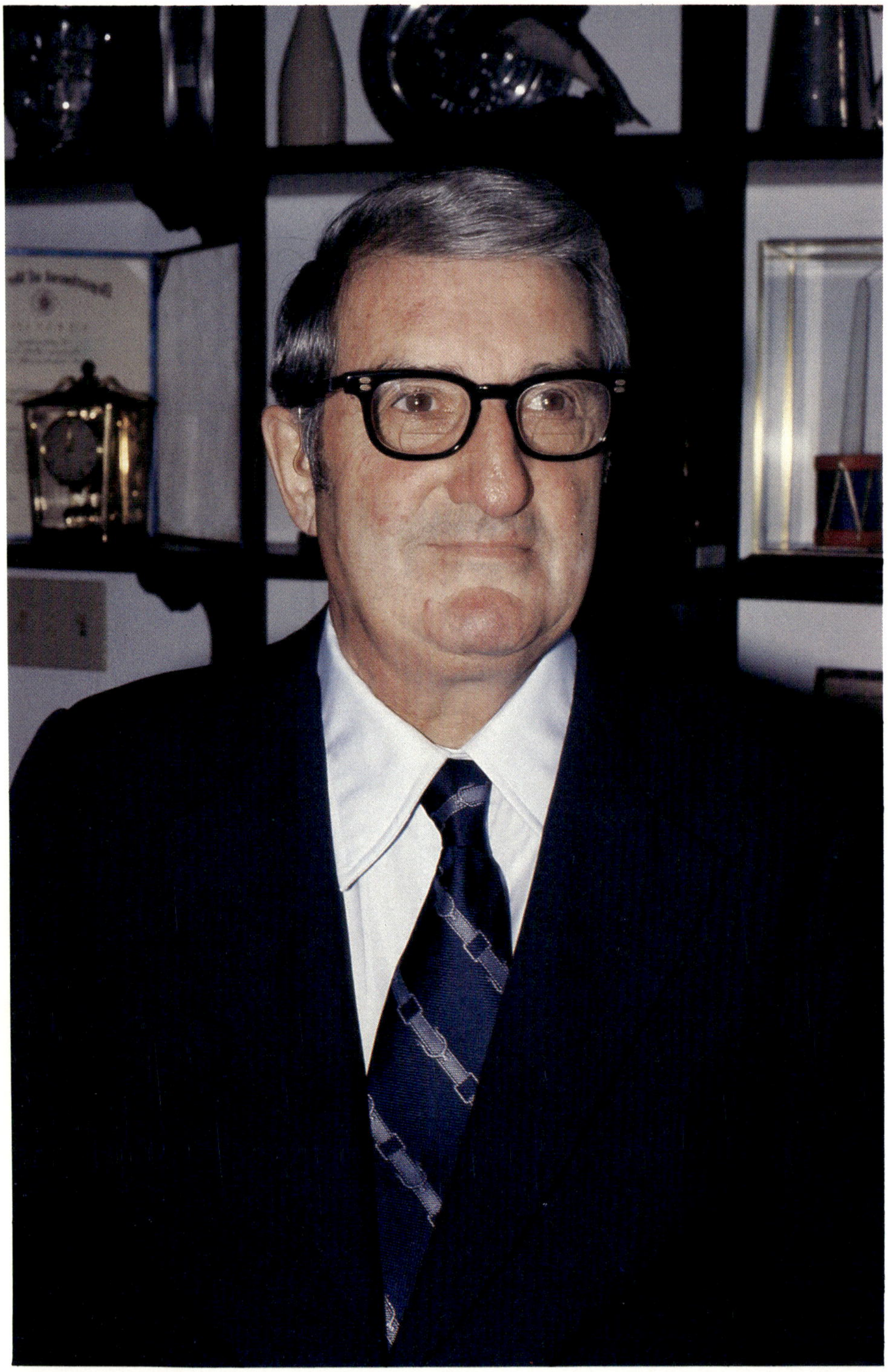

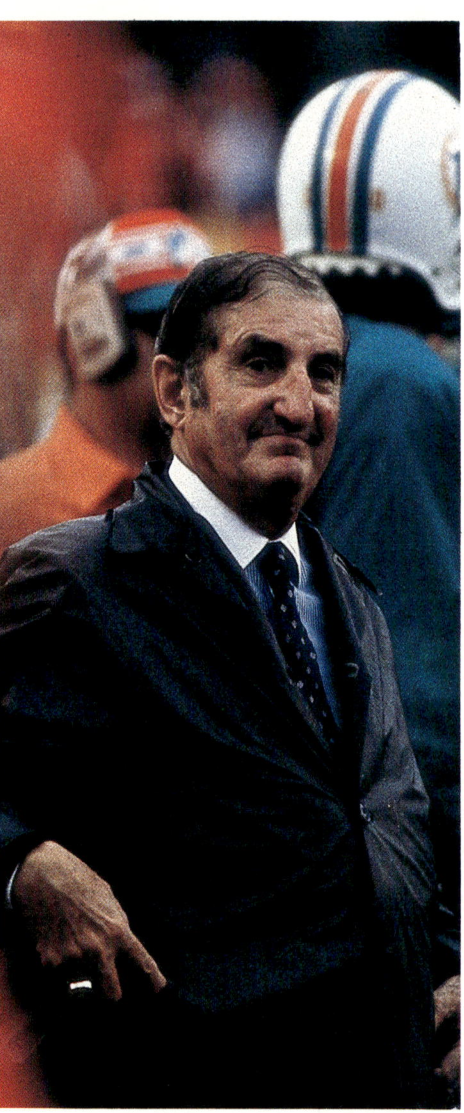

"If I were sitting on your side of the desk I would chase me right out of the office."

He can look back now. He can look back 20 years many of which were spent in anguish, of sleepless nights, endless travel and more meetings than Lee Iacocca ever had. Don't tell Joe Robbie about pain. He has endured more than he would ever mention, never one to complain simply because the dynamic Dolphins' owner never deals in negatives. It's probably why he has survived the early trauma during the formative years of the Dolphins to become one of the most respected owners in the National Football League today.

It wasn't easy. Robbie had to overcome financial woes, inner partnership betrayals, lawsuits, taunts and ridicule in first establishing and later developing one of the most attractive franchises in sports in an area that never had a professional team other than the ill-fated Miami Seahawks of the woebegone All America Football Conference days. Despite the uncertainties and travails of the first five years in Miami, the Dolphins saga turned into a storybook ending from a most inauspicious beginning.

Joseph Robbie, a successful lawyer in Minneapolis, Minnesota, never imagined that one day, in the summer of 1965, he would be sitting in a New York restaurant contemplating the choice of a coach for a professional football team. Politics, yes. But football? He had never dreamed of it.

Born in 1916 in Sisseton, South Dakota, Joe had a normal childhood. It wasn't until he was in college that he began to blossom. While at the University of South Dakota, Robbie was the National Collegiate Debating Champion of 1939—which perhaps explains why he can be so persuasive. One of his classmates in college was Joe Foss.

In 1942 Robbie married Elizabeth Lyle. After serving in the navy, he returned to get his law degree at South Dakota. He opened a law office in Mitchell and settled down to raise 11 children.

In 1948, Robbie was elected to the state legislature as a Democrat. Joe Foss, was also elected—as a Republican. Two years later, in 1950, they both ran for governor. Foss was defeated in the Republican primary; Robbie, the Democratic candidate, lost in the final election. After his defeat in the gubernatorial election, Robbie was appointed by the Truman administration as general counsel for the Office of Price Stabilization in Minneapolis, which serviced a four-state area—Minnesota, South Dakota, North Dakota, and Montana.

Robbie retained his taste for politics. He returned to private practice in 1953, and in 1956 he ran for Congress as the Democrat Farm Labor candidate. He lost a close election to incumbent Congressman Walter Judd.

Football did not occupy Robbie's mind in the early months of 1965. In January he was in Washington repre-

senting Hubert H. Humphrey on the Inaugural Committee, acting as the vice-president's liaison officer. After the January 20 inauguration of President Lyndon B. Johnson and Vice-President Humphrey, Robbie remained in Washington to complete any unfinished details. Never one to sit still for great lengths of time, Robbie flew home for a few days, jetted to New York to see the Floyd Patterson-George Chuvalo heavyweight fight, and headed for Miami for a short vacation.

Fulfilling such a tight schedule is typical of Robbie. He is not really relaxed unless he is doing something.

He has a quick manner of speaking, and he is amazingly convincing. He never hesitates to make a decision, and once he makes it, he never looks back. He never gets carried away in a conversation; he has made up his mind before the other person has finished talking. He manages always to keep one step ahead of the next person.

In many ways, Robbie is a charmer. Once removed from the rigors of his pressurized day, Robbie is warm and considerate. He possesses a quick wit, quite a change from his serious side, especially since his indefatigable drive makes him appear perpetually to scowl. Quite often he has been mistaken for Danny Thomas, the famous comedian. The two have been friends since 1959, when Robbie was appointed Minnesota state director of fund raising for St. Jude Hospital in Memphis, Tennessee, the institution Thomas founded to Aid Leukemia-Stricken American Children (ALSAC). Robbie has served on the hospital's board of directors ever since.

There had been strong rumors that the AFL was prepared to expand from its present eight-team structure. A businessman from Philadelphia who Robbie had represented wanted a franchise in that city. Robbie said that he would go straight to Foss, who was commissioner of the new league, and find out, and he later arranged a meeting with Foss for March 2 in Washington. This time the two did not talk politics. Foss told Robbie that the stadium in Philadelphia was under litigation. The right of the Philadelphia Eagles of the NFL to hold an exclusive lease on the stadium was being questioned. Foss was convinced that the litigation would take two or three years to process before a final judgment was given. In fact, he went a step further. He told Robbie to forget about Philadelphia. Foss advised him to persuade his client to apply for an AFL franchise in Miami. Foss said that Miami was the greatest potential open area for a professional football franchise.

The proposition sounded good. Robbie returned to Miami and discussed the possibility with his client, who would not commit himself. He disclosed to Robbie that he would be interested in obtaining the franchise but that he didn't want to advance any money for the months of work in promotion, legal representation, contacting all eight AFL owners, negotiations with Miami officials, and so forth.

Robbie decided to take on the project himself. As any good attorney would do, he did some research first. He learned that Ralph Wilson, the owner of the Buffalo Bills, had considered obtaining a franchise in Miami before settling on Buffalo, but Wilson had become discouraged. He was advised that Miami was not ready for professional football. He was informed also that the Orange Bowl would insist on a 17.5 percent rental, which would place too heavy a financial burden on a new franchise.

Later Robbie discovered that the NFL had ordered a survey of the possibilities of Miami's becoming a pro football city. The marketing report indicated that the city would not support professional football. In the area of sports, Miami had always been known as a college town. A number of friends advised Robbie not to seek a franchise in Miami, but he was undeterred. Robbie loves a challenge, and he was faced with one.

When Robbie called Mayor Robert High in Miami, he got an appointment immediately. High asked Robbie to meet him at the Miami Beach Auditorium, where he was to deliver a speech, saying that they could ride back together later. Professional football in Miami got its start in the back seat of a limousine.

Joe Robbie accepts the Lamar Hunt Trophy from Kansas City owner Lamar Hunt.

"Do you think that Miami should wait for an NFL franchise?" asked High.

"I would suggest that you take the first franchise available," replied Robbie. "With the NBC television contract secured by the AFL, it doesn't make much difference which league awards a franchise to Miami, just so long as the city gets professional football."

"That's a good point," agreed High.

"We have to move fast on this," cautioned Robbie.

"I'll tell you what," remarked High. "After my driver lets me off at my office, I'll tell him to take you to the City Hall so that you can talk to City Manager Melvin Reese. I'll telephone ahead and tell him to expect you."

"That's just fine," said Robbie.

"By the way, just what do you have on Vice-President Humphrey?" asked High.

"What do you mean?"

"Well, he took me aside at the mayor's conference and for 15 minutes he told me what great people you and Fred Gates are," said High.

"All he was doing was showing what kind of friend he can be," Robbie answered with a smile.

When the word got out that Miami was assured of a franchise, everybody, it seems, was trying to raise a group of investors. The beaches were deserted. After the sands had finally settled, there were five others legitimate groups besides Robbie's: the owners of Channel 7, Miami, led by Sidney Ansin; the Wometco Company, which owned Channel 4; Mitchell Wolfson and Jackie Gleason; the Golf-American Development Company; and a group from the Washington-Philadelphia area led by Bob Melnick.

But Robbie was the front runner. Then as he was preparing to fly to New York for the final presentation in July, he was faced with a crisis. The group of investors, assembled by George Coury of Miami, felt that the $7.5 million asking price was too high. Fortunately, Robbie had further financial support in Washington—he didn't have to go to the Treasury Department either.

At about 5:00 p.m. Foss dropped by. He told Robbie confidently that he felt that Robbie's group was in the favored position. He also disclosed that Lamar Hunt, chairman of the expansion committee, would discuss it

with him very shortly. Within the hour, Robbie got a telephone call from Hunt. He expressed the fact that the committee preferred the application that Robbie and Danny Thomas had signed. He wanted to talk further about it, and they agreed to meet in the Bull and Bear Room of the Waldorf. Robbie hung up and left for the Waldorf.

"Is Danny Thomas really serious about going into professional football?" Hunt wanted to know.

"He most certainly is," Robbie told him.

"I'd like to meet Danny and talk to him about it," remarked Hunt.

"Danny is entertaining at Lake Tahoe and can't possibly fly to New York," replied Robbie.

"Then I'll fly to see him," countered Hunt.

"When do you want to go?" asked Robbie

"Right away," snapped Hunt.

At a formal press conference on August 16, Robbie announced to the Miami press that he and Danny Thomas headed a group of investors who had officially been awarded the Miami franchise in the AFL. Commissioner Joe Foss made the formal announcement in Major High's office.

Later Danny had them laughing at a cocktail party at the posh Palm Bay Club. He posed with Joe Foss, not in the usual way, shaking hands and smiling, but sprawled out on the floor with a football propped on his nose.

"With a nose like this," exclaimed Thomas, "there is no way we can miss an extra point."

When someone inquired about the pin that Thomas displayed on his lapel, Danny said: "That's a pin commemorating the founding of St. Jude Hospital. In case you're not aware of it, St. Jude is the patron of hopeless cases. But it has absolutely no connection with the Miami team."

No single person was more familiar with the financial impediments of the new franchise than Robbie. He realized that he couldn't have a football man as the general manager because of the heavy concentration on business and financial affairs that the position requires. What was needed was working capital. Robbie had to concern himself with the paramount task of securing investors.

By December, Robbie had completed the formation of the delicate legal structure of the Miami Dolphins' ownership. He formed a partnership known as the Miami Dolphins, Ltd., by an agreement effective December 16. The original partners were: Danny Thomas, Robbie, Martin M. Decker, John H. O'Neil, Jr., George A. Hamid, Sr. and George A. Hamid, Jr. Robbie was the only individual general partner. Thomas appeared in ownership as the owner of a corporation known as Danny Thomas Sports, Inc. All the legal hodgepodge meant was that Robbie was the only person generally liable for all the debts of the partnership. The limited partners were limited in their liability to the amounts of their individual investments. In short, only Robbie had the noose around his neck. If the operation went bankrupt, the noose would be tightened, and the chair would be kicked out from under him.

Robbie was fearless despite the danger. Besides, he moves too quickly to get caught in a noose for long. He had been a fighter all his life. The first payment, $1 million, to the league was due on January 1, 1966. Already Robbie was faced with intense pressure. Inasmuch as he did not have a full complement of owners, he arranged a bank loan. That in itself required Robbie's resourcefulness. The club didn't have any assets to show as collateral. Robbie obtained the loan by pledging the season ticket revenue as the necessary collateral.

At the time, however, there wasn't any ticket revenue. It was not that nobody wanted to purchase tickets; the system was designed that way. Robbie would not accept any season ticket orders until February 1. If he had conducted a sale in 1965, while the club was still owned as a joint venture by him and Thomas, all the revenue obtained from down payments of season ticket subscribers would have been taxable on their personal income tax returns without off-setting expenses. To insure fairness, Robbie would not accept any orders postmarked before midnight on January 31. He wanted to provide an equal opportunity for the new fans. He received about 5,000 season ticket requests in the first mail, which ultimately resulted in the sale of approximately 12,500 seats.

Nobody expected the Dolphins to make any money that first year, and they didn't. Mainly due to the limited television revenue, the Dolphins lost more than $500,000 in 1966. Expenditures were high: Robbie had to spend over $1 million in the 1965 college draft to convince the fans in Miami of his seriousness in building a contender; and he spent close to $166,000 for free agents alone.

"At this point, I had more than 20 percent of the Dolphin ownership subscribed, so it was necessary to borrow money to meet the AFL payment in addition to the commitments of the partners," explained Robbie. "I left Miami for Minneapolis on New Year's Day to complete the loan that enabled the club to meet the payment. I am quite sure that there were certain persons who did not expect me back.

This dissident partner and the hangers-on were attempting to make it impossible for me to continue to operate the club. I wasn't about to let it happen. If they wanted to slug, I could slug too.

"I placed a mortgage on our family home in Minneapolis to help raise my own share. I flew to Los Angeles the next morning to see Danny Thomas and to pick up his share of the AFL payment. In the process of raising the million dollars, I not only mortgaged everything we owned, but I agreed to give up my entire interest in the Miami Dolphins without any reimbursement if I was unable to sell all of the unsubscribed ownership of the club on or before July 1, 1967, by refinancing. On January 31, 1967, the remaining unsubscribed equity was sold to W.H. Keland of Racine, Wisconsin."

With that hurdle crossed, another loomed. As Robbie tells it: "Keland assigned half of what he purchased to George M. Gillett, Jr. Gillett operated in

The late vice president Humbert H. Humphrey makes a point with Joe Robbie.

the capacity of a business manager for a few weeks, but he became mainly engrossed in attempting to purchase control of the club. Without my knowledge, he went to Danny Thomas and to Danny's tax lawyer and made an offer to purchase Danny's corporate interest in the franchise. Danny's lawyer recommended that he should sell.''

Robbie was hit on his blind side. He never expected it. He left Miami in a huff and grabbed a plane to Las Vegas. If Danny sold his share, Robbie would lose control of the club. But before he could look for another investor, he had another matter to settle. He had to meet Thomas in Las Vegas and ask him to give him the option to buy his stock. It was one of the longest nights that Robbie had ever spent. He had to wait until Danny finished his last show (and Robbie wasn't in a mood for laughs). Then he had to wait backstage while Danny and Myron Cohen swapped jokes for over an hour. Finally, he met with Danny behind closed doors. It was a stormy session, almost rupturing their friendship, lasting until 5:00 a.m. But in the end, Danny agreed to give Robbie the first option on his stock.

Again he survived. In the next few days, he convinced Keland to purchase Thomas's interest jointly and equally with him. They concluded a contractual arrangement in early June, clearly defining their respective rights and responsibilities within the partnership. At this point, Gillett joined a group to purchase the Harlem Globetrotters. In so doing, Gillett reconveyed the interest in the Dolphins that Keland had assigned to him, clearing the way for Robbie and Keland to purchase Thomas's stock in July. Ironically, Miami Mayor Robert High, who had helped Robbie to arrange the loan necessary to buy Thomas out and who had played such a key role in the founding of the Dolphins, died on the day that arrangements for the loan were completed.

Danny Thomas was out of professional football. Robbie, who his critics had predicted would be out too, was more of a force than ever. He was more than anyone—including a dissident partner, the Miami press, and a number of smug owners—could handle.

Robbie had still more miracles to produce. After 1967, there was 1968

and more financing for a club that was still operating in the red. In July of 1968, he secured a $550,000 loan from the O'Hare International Bank in Chicago. A short time later he met Philip L. Butler, senior vice-president of LaSalle National Bank in Chicago. In September, Robbie arranged a luncheon with Butler and Keland in order to explore a financing program for the Dolphins. Other LaSalle officers attended the meeting and expressed interest. Robbie presented all of the club's financial information for the first two seasons and the financial projections through 1975. The projections revealed that the club would turn the corner when the merger between NFL and AFL became effective in 1970, at which time, the Dolphins would earn a full share of the television revenue. LaSalle Bank was convinced that the forecast was valid and that a sound financial program could be established, based upon a revolving line of credit that would permit the club to draw funds as needed and reduce the loan balance as season ticket revenue and radio and television revenue were received. However, this mode of financing required the approval of the league.

In December the loan was ready to be consummated with full approval of the senior loan committee of LaSalle National Bank. The bank agreed to accept only Robbie's signature as managing general partner. It was also

agreed that Keland did not need to be personally liable for the note and the debt. However, since Keland was an officer in South Florida Sports Corporation (the successor to Danny Thomas Sports, Inc.), a corporate general partner, LaSalle required Keland's signature as a corporate officer to avoid any claim on his part that he had not approved the loan.

The loan was scheduled to close at

about the same time as the partners' capital contributions were due for their share of the annual payment to the AFL. Keland and O'Neil failed to make their payments. Keland did not appear for the closing, and it was impossible to close a loan without him, even though LaSalle Bank had expressed a willingness to help him finance his obligation. Robbie's suspicions were aroused.

Since the loan was not closed, Robbie had to borrow $45,000 from LaSalle to meet the payroll. A couple of days later, after he had returned to Miami, Robbie received a registered letter from Keland. It disclosed that Keland was assuming control of the Miami Dolphins. At the same time, Keland called a partnership meeting in Robbie's office. Keland's attorney asked Robbie if he would give Keland control. He might just as well have asked Howard Hughes to come out of hiding. Robbie declined. He turned the dispute over control to Commissioner Pete Rozelle, and a hearing on the issue was held during Super Bowl week, in January, 1969.

Nobody gave the New York Jets much of a chance against the Baltimore Colts in the Super Bowl that year. The Jets were 17-point underdogs, and a great many insiders figured that Robbie's odds were even more discouraging. But it was a week for the underdogs. Robbie won, and so did the Jets.

At the meeting, Robbie revealed to Rozelle and the owners his plan for financing the operations of the club until the dispute could be settled. It didn't take Rozelle long to render his decision. He ruled that Robbie had full and complete legal control of the club under the partnership agreement and all of the contracts relating to it, including the contract that Keland and Robbie had signed. Rozelle's ruling was based upon fact: Robbie had been the sole individual general partner, completely responsible for all of the debts of the partnership and for the daily operations of the club, and his authority had not been challenged until Keland failed to come up with his annual payment.

Strategy was obvious. Keland and O'Neil felt that Robbie would be unable to continue operating the partnership if they withheld their share of the money.

Both knew that there wasn't any cash balance to cover the daily operations. They also knew that LaSalle Bank was unwilling to close the loan for the revolving line of credit while the dispute was in existence. No bank wants to buy a lawsuit. However, Robbie was one step ahead of them at the teller's window. LaSalle was sold on the deal; in order to receive the loan, Robbie had only to obtain a favorable ruling from Rozelle.

When Rozelle ruled in favor of Robbie, Keland disclosed that he wanted to sell his interest in the club. Until three appraisers were appointed, under the procedure established, to fix the price of Keland's interests, Robbie was awarded the right to meet any offer that Keland might receive from outside investors. A date was established on which the appraisal figure would become effective if Keland did not receive a higher offer. Rozelle's ruling became final at the annual meeting in March. And in less than two months, Robbie was ready to move in. He was prepared to pay Keland several times more than the figure set by the appraisers, who took into consideration the substantial indebtedness of the franchise, including the debt to the AFL and the line of credit needed from LaSalle Bank ($2.5 million) to operate the club. Like all previous investors in the club who had pulled out—Danny Thomas, Martin Decker, Max Kampelman, George Hamid, Sr., and George Hamid, Jr.—Keland left with a profit.

With Keland out of the way, Robbie still was faced with a critical need for cash to keep the club solvent until the line of credit was properly established. So again, he headed for Chicago and an appointment with Philip Butler of LaSalle Bank.

"Phil, I need another $150,000," said Robbie, without mincing words.

"Another $150,000?"

"That's right," replied Robbie.

"Let me ask you something in all honesty," posed Butler. "What would you do if you were sitting on my side of the desk?"

"If I were sitting on your side of the desk, I would chase me right out of the office," snapped Robbie.

"Joe, you're unbelievable," Butler laughed. "I may be crazy, but I'm going to give you the cash."

Robbie obtained the loan, again unsecured, on his personal signature. He loaned the money to the Dolphins to meet operating expenses. The significance of the $150,000, together with the previously borrowed $45,000, is that Butler had authority to lend up to $200,000 without going to the loan committee. Butler went to the limit of his own authority to tide Robbie over. He was convinced that Robbie's projections were conservative and sound and that he had not attempted to paint too optimistic a picture.

Still, it wasn't until May 20, 1969 that Robbie could breathe easier after securing a loan at the First National Bank of Miami.

"This ended an anxiety about the financing of the Miami Dolphins," said Robbie. "We were now financially solid and stable even if heavily in debt. With the purchase of Keland's interests, I became the major owner of the club for the first time, although I always had had legal control.

"It should be remembered, nevertheless, that it was always erroneous for anyone to speak of himself as the major owner. A great many people don't realize this, but none of the investors in the Miami Dolphins has ever put up one cent to operate the club. None has ever been personally liable for any of the operating expenses or debts of the club. None has had any obligation to do anything except make his own annual payment of the debt to the AFL to acquire the franchise in the first place."

Robbie expected financial losses during the first few years. He also expected to lose on the playing field, although not as much as he did. The club improved its record in each of its first three years, but when the Dolphins compiled a disastrous 3-10-1 record in 1969, Robbie felt that a coaching

change was necessary. He had one more miracle to work; the hiring of Don Shula, the Baltimore coach who had compiled one of the finest records of any active coach in the NFL. It was an expensive prize, but Robbie plays for keeps.

"I decided at the end of the 1969 season to hire a new coach," disclosed Robbie. George Wilson had given us a satisfactory four years, but we had to move ahead. I also felt that we had invested in the best young talent in professional football. We seldom failed to sign a draft choice, we made solid trades, and we seemed to have undeveloped potential. I didn't seek Shula first. I wanted to sign coach Bear Bryant of Alabama, one of the greatest college coaches in history and a legend in his own state.

"When I returned to New Orleans, I learned that Don Klosterman had been named general manager of the Baltimore Colts. The thought occurred to me that it might not please an outstanding head coach like Don Shula to have a general manager employed to intervene in the chain of command between him and the owner. Most coaches aspire to hold the position of general manager. I thought about it all the way back to Miami. I had no idea that Shula would be willing to make a coaching change, and I couldn't even ask him because that would be a case of tampering; league rules prohibit such a practice.

"Shula called me, and I told him that he would have to obtain consent from the Baltimore owners before I could talk to him. He said that he would. He telephoned the next day and said that Carroll Rosenbloom was in Tokyo but that Steve Rosenbloom, Carroll's son, had given him permission to see me. Steve told Shula that Baltimore would not stand in his way. Shula and I arranged to meet two days later in Washington. His lawyer joined us, and we discussed the Miami situation generally. We came to no conclusion.

"When Shula returned to Baltimore, he reported progress at the meeting and asked permission to see me in Miami for further talks. Permission was granted. We met and made additional progress, which he reported to Klosterman and Steve Rosenbloom. I then had a tax man stop in Baltimore to discuss the tax aspects of the proposed deal, and he reported to me by telephone. I then arranged for Shula and his lawyer to meet me in Miami on February 18. We still had not reached any agreement, but we were getting close.

"Once again Shula received permission from Steve Rosenbloom to see me. We met in a negotiation session that lasted from late morning until 4:00 p.m., and Shula agreed to become head coach of the Dolphins. I signed the contract and left Shula and his lawyer, David Gordon, and returned home. I had to call commissioner Rozelle and the Colts, and I had to locate George Wilson so that I could tell him my decision."

Despite all the mutuality, Rozelle later ruled that the Dolphins were tampering with Shula, who was under contract to Baltimore. He penalized the Dolphins by taking away their 1971 first-round draft choice and awarding it to Baltimore. It was a strange decision.

"It never occurred to me either then or now that if a person under contract is told that he can discuss entering a new contract with someone else, the someone else need to ask permission to talk to the person under contract," remarked Robbie.

"Commissioner Rozelle agreed that Shula had obtained permission from the Baltimore Colts to talk to me, but he held that I need permission to talk to Shula. Think about that one for a while. Shula could talk to me, but I couldn't talk to him."

If the Dolphins survived the loss of a first-round draft choice, if they survived the uncertain and shaky early years—and they did both—it was because of the tenacity of one individual: Joe Robbie.

Florida Governor Graham brings a smile to Joe Robbie's face.

DON SHULA

The drive is always there. It is endless. During the season it consumes him. In the off season it still remains, although not quite so visible. The drive is what sets Don Shula above the rest of the NFL coaching hierarchy. It is part of his psyche, the one that enables him to have a winning edge. Whatever the rest of the components are in the coaching structure, make no mistake that the winning edge begins with Shula and filters down to his aides. He has the numbers to prove it: a 23-year record of 255-99-6, the best of any active coach in the NFL. Only George Halas, who coached for 33 years has more. Yet, there is more: a 17-0 season in 1972, the first ever in league history; a phenomenal two-year record of 32-2 that included Super Bowl victories in 1972 and 1973; the youngest coach to reach the Super Bowl three straight years and the youngest ever to win 100 games. It's a lifetime of accomplishments already.

When he first arrived in Miami to take over a sagging franchise in 1970 after seven years in Baltimore, Shula thought the cocktail parties would never end. Everyone wanted to meet the new Dolphin coach who had had so much success at Baltimore. Even Shula had not expected such a reception, but Miami is a society town. Miami is one big magnum of champagne, and when you're the new kid in town, everybody wants to pour you a glass.

Dorothy Shula likewise got caught in the social whirl. Most of the Shula children were still in school in Maryland and Dorothy's immediate concern was finding a house big enough for the family. In between plane trips and dinner parties, Dorothy would go house hunting. On one Saturday her plans called for her to accompany her husband to Gulfstream Park. Although her husband had not yet won a game for the Dolphins, the officials at the track had named a race in his honor, the Don Shula Handicap, and Shula had been asked to make a presentation to the winning jockey. By the time the races were over, Dorothy had picked five winners in a row, and she's no horse player. That alone should have been an omen of what the Dolphins' fortunes would be.

Shula had work to do and began putting together a new coaching staff. The first assistant he signed was Bill

Arnsparger as head defensive coach. Shula and Arnsparger go back a long way. In 1964 the two had been at Baltimore and in 1959 were assistants at the University of Kentucky. Shula was delighted to get Arnsparger. A former back in college, Shula always had a high regard for defense; and Arnsparger, who molded the Colts together as a crack defensive unit, was one of the best in the business.

To complete his staff Shula named Howard Schnellenberger as head offensive coach, renewing a relationship that the two began at Kentucky. He also added former pro lineman Monte Clark, in his first season as

coach of the offensive line; Mike Scarry, a scout for the Los Angeles Rams in 1969, San Francisco 49ers and Dallas Cowboys', defensive line; and Carl Taseff, a former Shula teammate at John Carroll University. The only Dolphin coach whom Shula retained was Tom Keane, who started with the club in 1966.

In addition to learning the new coaching staff and its demands, the players had to learn a new system. No one in Miami really knew what kind of a taskmaster Shula was. Shula insisted that he was no miracle worker. The only way he could attain success was through hard work and sweat—plenty of sweat. He had to make the players

respond to him and his methods while at the same time eliminating a losing atmosphere that had prevailed around the club.

At the same time Robbie was expecting results, and Shula knew it. He had been hired to develop a winning team and that's all Robbie thought about.

"I just hope you will give Don Shula time to produce a winner," said a fan to Robbie one day.

"Sure will," smiled Robbie. "He's got all summer."

Shula is a meticulous organizer, and things were very different from previous years in his first training camp, the veterans soon learned when they arrived. Like a general, Shula had special sleeping arrangements for his troops at the two-story dormitory. On the first floor he billeted the offensive players, and on the second, the defensive players. He arranged for the coaches to be on the same floor as their teams. In that way they would be available for any questions by the players, day or night. He also had a theory about rooming individuals. He had quarterback Bob Griese together with wide receiver Paul Warfield and the offensive guards with each other so that they could talk over their assignments. Shula's room was next to Griese's and Warfield's. Shula left nothing undone.

The players knew where Shula was coming from during his first training camp. It's just that the players' strike that summer gave Shula an obstacle he never planned on. When the strike was settled, Shula was ready for the veterans. The first day on the field Shula put them through three workouts. Some of the veterans couldn't believe it. Jim Kiick, who thought he was in good shape when he reported, soon had other ideas.

"I'm tired," sighed Kiick as he dragged his body off the field after a night session. "I'm in good enough shape for George Wilson, but I don't know about Don Shula."

Miami soon learned. In his first season, Shula dramatically turned the team around. The Dolphins finished 10-4, quite an achievement for a first-year coach with a new staff and system in transforming a team that was 3-10-1 the year before into a playoff contender. It was only a hint of what would develop in the next 15 years. The Dolphins suffered only one losing season, 6-8 in 1976, the only one in Shula's storied career. In 22 years of winning, he'll never forget that solitary losing season. He's made certain that it would never happen again and it hasn't.

''I like to think that I'm intense and driven,'' said Shula. ''Once the season starts, you have to be totally dedicated to the job, there's no other way. I'm fortunate that Dorothy understands it. She's been there when I haven't, and she's been just outstanding in raising the kids and substituting for some of the things I should've been doing. There are many benefits to a head coach's job, but the loss of family life is one of the negatives.''

But when does the season start for Shula? Where is the myth separated from the man? He is already established as a coaching legend. Winning does that. Yet, with all his success over the years, he is up for review every Sunday essentially victimized by his unparalled success. George Young, the general manager of the New York Giants, who had formerly been the Dolphins' director of pro scouting and a close Shula friend since Baltimore, explains it easily enough.

''He's already more of a myth than a man in the minds of many fans, and he has to compete with his own legend every Sunday,'' pointed out Young. ''To coach in the NFL is to be wounded—often. And Shula has a lot of wounds. He moans and groans like everyone else, but he's adjusted to adversity better than the others. That's why he's survived so long.''

The success that Shula has achieved and what Young talks about is awesome. In 1985, the Dolphins won the AFC Eastern championship for the fifth consecutive year. Miami has either won or shared the divisional title 13 times in 16 years under Shula and have appeared in the playoffs 12 times. Overall, in 23 years of coaching, Shula's teams have won 10 or more games 18 times. His drive to succeed is relentless. How does he achieve it?

''I believe my strong points are preparation, organization and transmitting my knowledge to the people I'm responsible for. A lot of coaches have all the answers on the blackboard Monday morning. I want to have the answers on Sunday afternoon. I believe firmly in discipline. I'm very demanding.

''My flaws? Sometimes I'm overanxious and impatient. Also, sometimes I'm too demanding, but there's a fine line. Sometimes I have to get on a player during the course of a game. Sometimes a player is not naturally aggressive and the thing that makes him aggressive is getting ticked off at me. If that's what it takes, fine.

''The important thing is not what Don Shula knows or what any of my assistant coaches know. The important thing is that we can transmit to the people we are responsible for. They're going to be tested on Sunday after-

noon, and the fact that we win on Sunday afternoon indicates that we are getting through to them. That's what coaching is—the ability to transmit information.''

That, too, is part of the winning edge which Shula likes to refer. It is conceivable that he developed the winning formula as a child growing up in Painesville, Ohio. Often he would play cards with his grandmother. Whenever he'd lose, he'd run out of the house upset with himself, hide underneath the porch and cry. It tells something about the man. Even in a friendly game of cards, winning was the important thing.

It was only natural that Shula carried his penchant for winning to the football field when he got older. He had thoughts of attending Notre Dame, but the influx of veterans following World War II readjusted his thinking to John Carroll University in Cleveland. He played two ways, as a running back and a defensive back. One of his thrills was gaining 125 yards in helping John Carroll upset Syracuse in 1950. In 1951, Shula found himself as the only rookie on Paul Brown's defending NFL champion Cleveland Browns and was later joined by Taseff. Two years later, both were involved in the biggest trade in NFL history, a 15-player transaction that sent both players to Baltimore. Shula played cornerback for four years at Baltimore and closed out his playing career in 1957 with Washington before turning to coaching.

He began at the college level, first as an assistant at Virginia in 1958 and then at Kentucky in 1959. It didn't take the talented Shula long to rejoin the NFL. A year later, he was hired by George Wilson in Detroit as the Lions' defensive coordinator. In his three years there, the Lions were 26-13-1. Shula was ready for a head coaching job. His break came in 1963 when he replaced Weeb Ewbank at Baltimore. At the age of 33, Shula became the youngest head coach in NFL history. He learned how important training camp really was after his first season.

''When I first became the head coach at Baltimore, after being a player there, the big mistake I made was in assuming too many things about the veteran players who were also great players,'' recalled Shula. ''I was now in the position of coaching a quarterback like Johnny Unitas who was a much better player than I ever thought of being, and I didn't put him and the other great veterans like Gino Marchetti through the preparation in classroom that I should have made them do, feeling that they've been through it all and knew it all.

''After that first year, I went back to basics in all areas with rookies and veterans. That way no one could say we didn't cover what they were supposed to know. Coaching is also a learning experience and I've tried to learn from all and copy none. Everyone I played or coached under were different types, and I learned from them while still being myself. I've never gone out and tried to be Paul Brown or Blanton Collier or George Wilson. They satisfied my great thirst for knowledge, my searching and looking to find out the what, how, and the why.

''I've tried to learn from everyone I've been exposed to, but I've also been very conscious about doing things within the framework of my personality. I don't want anyone to ever think that I'm trying to act like somebody else, but I'd be pretty stupid not to learn things from men I've played under or coached against.

''To me, coaching is finding out what makes an individual play to the best of his ability. I have to understand how best to motivate each and every one, and of the 45 players I'm going to be responsible for each year, there are no two alike. Some are not naturally aggressive and I have to do something to make them aggressive. It could be yelling and screaming. It could be a kick in the pants. But that's the wrong approach on those who can't handle that treatment.''

Through the years Shula's thinking has not changed. He transmits his philosophy down to his players, focusing on the quarterback which he feels is the most important position, not only in football, but any sport. The three he has been associated with, Unitas, Griese and Marino, all had different characteristics which Shula studied and then shrewdly revolved his offensive thrust around each's abilities. Somehow, one gets the feeling that he knows Marino will be the best of all.

''I've always been a coach who tailored my offense around the people who I've had to work with,'' disclosed Shula. ''In Baltimore with Unitas, we weren't known for ball control. When I came to Miami, I didn't try to take my offensive philosophy and jam it down Bob Griese's throat. Instead, I sat back. We didn't really gain an identity offensively until halfway through that first season.

''I've been accused of being a conservative, grind 'em out kind of coach because that was the style of my teams in 1972 and '73. It's just we had a wide open, explosive passing attack with Unitas. Griese was a different kind of quarterback. By the same token, I didn't try to force Griese's style on Marino when he came along.

''Marino is so amazing you wonder why he doesn't get even more credit. It all comes so naturally to Danny, you never even wonder how he does it all. He just does it and nothing is ever out of place. Quarterback has got to be the most difficult position in all of sports. All that responsibility, mentally and physically. You've got to be so smart, so tough. And a great athlete to beat the pass rush. And of course, a good arm.

"What other position in all of sports makes the demands that quarterback does? Nothing compares with it. And Danny has just stepped in and done it in such a natural way. Right from the time he stepped out on the practice field, it's been nothing but upbeat excitement. It was evident from the beginning we were dealing with a real talent. When he makes up his mind to throw the ball, he really uncorks it. It's boom …the release and the throw.

"The only question in my mind was how smart was he? He didn't test well. But we've never seen that to be a problem on the field. I think the thing that helped get him ready is that I made him call his own plays right from the start in training camp his rookie year. He learned our system, took over the offense and called his own plays."

Shula is much the same. Once train-ing camp begins, he takes over with a daily regimen that includes a 17-hour day. Although he lives a short distance from the team's St. Thomas training facilities, Shula moves right in and directs his operations like a field general. He literally eats and sleeps football. His credo is to lead by example and nobody does it better.

> **❝I believe firmly in discipline. I'm very demanding.❞**

"Once you get up in the morning you know there's a lot of work ahead of you," maintains Shula. "You just throw yourself into it. There's no feeling sorry for yourself. At the beginning of the season you don't say to yourself, 'We can't win every football game.' I believe you go out every day trying to win and every week trying to win. You set a goal to be the best, and then you work hard every hour of every day, striving to reach that goal. If you allow yourself to settle for anything less than number one, then you're cheating yourself."

"We never let an error go unchallenged. Uncorrected errors will multiply. Someone once asked me if there wasn't a benefit in overlooking one small flaw. I asked him, 'What's a small flaw?'"

This attention to every detail is a Shula trademark. In the 16 years he has been in Miami, the Dolphins have been the least penalized team in the NFL. It is a criteria Shula demands of his players and expects them to main-

tain year after year. Yet, in his early years, Shula was a fiery individual on the sidelines. He remembers getting hit with a penalty himself, and of all times, in a Super Bowl game against Dallas.

"Things were going so bad that I was a bundle of frustration on the sideline," recalled Shula. "It seemed like every time the officials drew the penalty flag out of their pockets and threw it, it was always against the Dolphins. Even though I'm a mild-mannered person on the sideline during a game, I was getting a bit upset. I never say anything to the officials unless I get worked up this way. It got so bad that I tell this story: Somewhere during the fourth period I reached the point of being angry. Every time the official threw the flag, I made my anger known. One time after we were penalized, I yelled quite loudly. The official turned, pointed his finger at me, and said:

'Shula, if you open your mouth one more time it is going to cost you!'

"Things were going so badly that the last thing I would want to happen was for me to say something on the sideline that would cause the official to penalize me. As he turned to walk away, I noticed that one of our players was slightly out of position. Being frustrated because of our lack of performance, I yelled at him.

'Hey, you dummy, move over.'

"Hearing that the official whipped around. He thought I was yelling at him. He came storming over toward me, took the flag out of his pocket, and threw it at my feet in front of 80,000 people. I then calmly explained to him that I wasn't shouting at him, but yelling at one of my defensive backs. He accepted my explanation. However, now he, too, was embarrassed. He had already thrown his flag to indicate a penalty."

'Well, it's down. I've got to call it on you.'

'Coaching from the sidelines.'

"What? Coaching from the sidelines. I never heard of that penalty."

'That's what it is…coaching from the sidelines.'

"What's the penalty?"

'Let's see, coaching from the sidelines is a five-yard penalty.'

'This proves that you're stupid. It's a fifteen-yard penalty.'

'Shula, for your coaching…five

yards!''

Since those days, Shula has admittedly mellowed somewhat, although he still stalks the sidelines looking terse with that icy stare during the heated moments of a game. If he sees something wrong he still yells, leaving nothing undone.

> **❝If I'm remembered for anything as a coach, I hope it's for playing within the rules.❞**

"I guess you can say I've mellowed some," smiled Shula. "I've learned to control myself. I enjoy coaching. If I didn't, I would quit. The game has changed. The players have changed. I work hard to keep abreast. I still get excited every season. The closer I get to the stadium, the faster I walk. I get the butterflies, I get the anxiety and I get the excitement before the game that I've had all through my coaching career. As long as that's there, I want to continue to coach and do things that I enjoy.

One thing Shula definitely enjoys is taking a family vacation before the rigors of training camp demand his time. Such time can have it's lighter moments. Like the time several years ago when the Shulas vacationed in Maine. The Dolphins had appeared in two straight Super Bowls and Shula was a household name.

"We were driving through this little town one night looking for something to do," recalled Shula. "We saw a movie that started at nine o'clock. There were only a few people in the theater, but as we walked down the aisle, they started applauding. I told Dorothy, 'I can't believe it. They recognize me all the way up here!' When we sat down, a man came over and shook my hand. I asked him, 'Are you a Dolphins fan?' The guy said, 'I don't know what you're talking about. I came over to thank you for coming, because the manager just announced that if we didn't get at least 10 people in the theater pretty soon, he wasn't going to show the movie.'"

Shula will always remember that night and at the same time wonders how he will be remembered when he finally leaves the sidelines after all these years.

"If I'm remembered for anything as a coach, I hope it's for playing within the rules," said Shula. "I also hope it will be said that my teams showed class and dignity in victory or defeat."

He'll be remembered for a lot more than that…

DAN MARINO

back from his nightmarish first quarter to throw for 332 yards and three touchdowns in a 38-35 overtime loss. The defeat notwithstanding, the Dolphins did indeed find a quarterback. His teammates realized it after just that one game.

"I'm sure he was jittery," said Moore. "He could have succumbed to the pressure and gone into a shell, but he didn't. He kept believing in himself and the guys around him and worked his way out of it."

Marino explained his performance easily enough. It was as if nothing fazed him.

"I couldn't worry about the first quarter," explained Marino. "If you start thinking about the past, about your interceptions, you'll throw more."

Marino's performance justified Shula's opinion of him and he never goes overboard on rookies. He knew Marino, however, was special.

"He has a toughness about him, a real desire to win," exclaimed Shula. "It just shows you what his capabilities are. He's a winner because he's not afraid to lose. He keeps gunning it and sometimes bad things happen, but he's got that confidence that something good will happen the next time. You never see him hang his head after he throws an interception. He'll come off the field and ask, 'okay, what did I do wrong?' Sometimes he already knows. The thing is he never gets down and his teammates respect that."

"Coach, all I want is to be the best quarterback in the NFL and I'll do whatever you want me to do to be that."

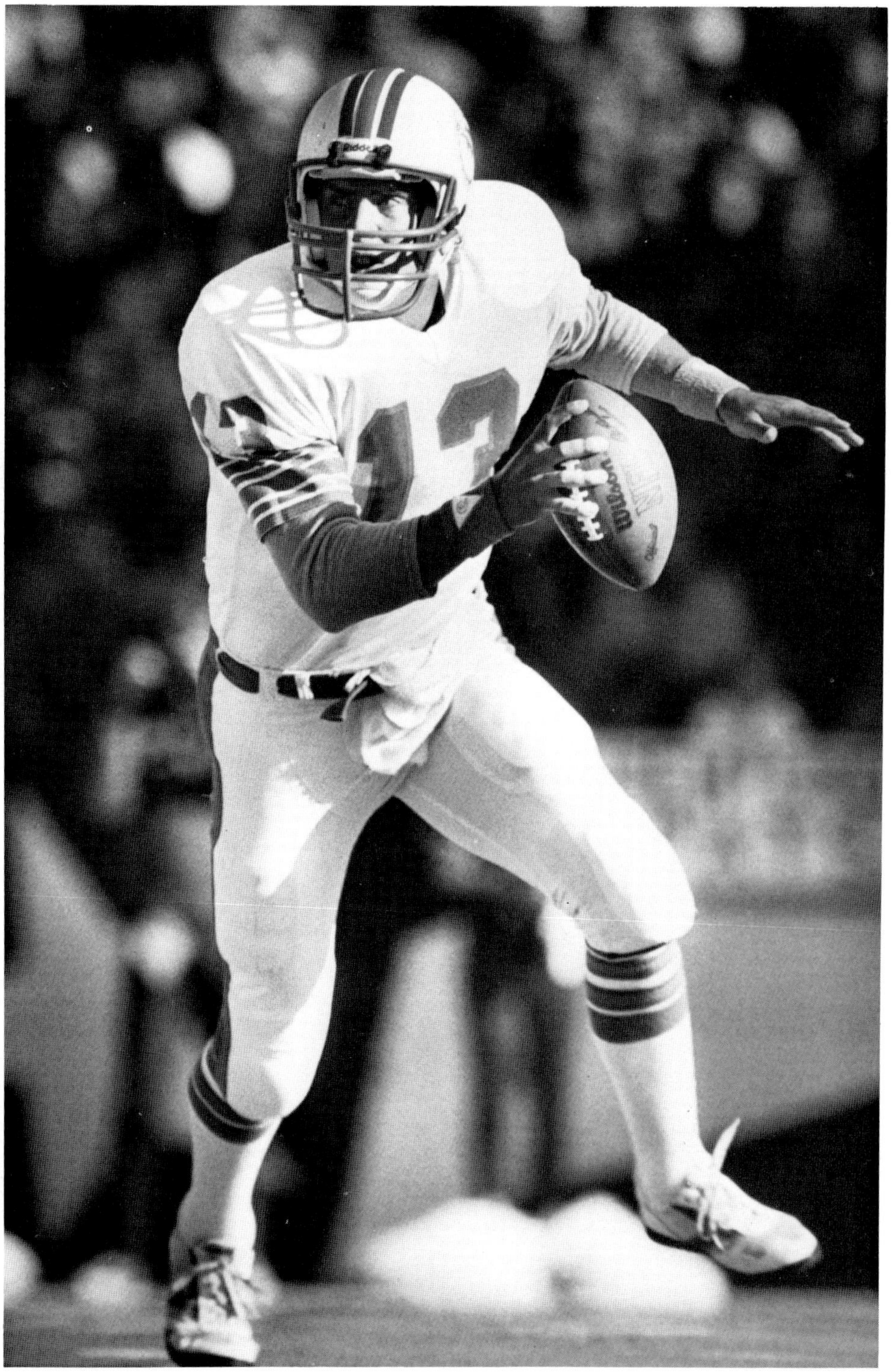

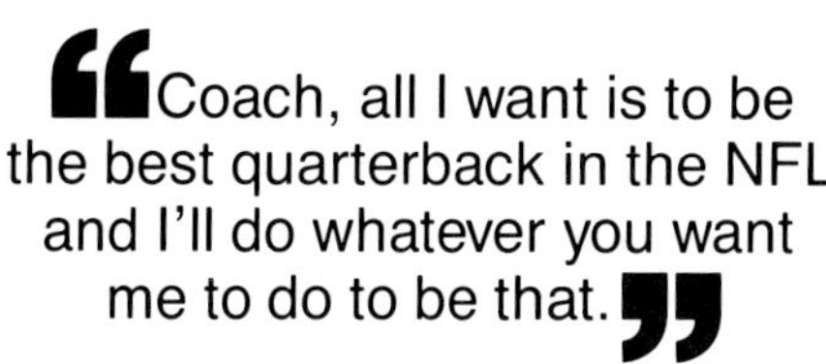

Besides Shula, Marino has a valuable ally in Don Strock who has been the Dolphins' quarterback in residence for 14 years now. Strock is a student of the game from his spot on the sidelines and helped Marino to progress even quicker in overcoming some of the nuances that result from inexperience on the professional level.

"He had to work on getting a better touch on his passes," pointed out Strock. "He didn't have any serious trouble with any of his passes. He just had to learn that there was a big difference between the deep throw, the slant-in throw and the quick check-off throw."

Marino took the Dolphins to the playoffs his first season and Miami had a franchise player for the next 12 years. His second season in 1984 should be carved in stone. Marino lit up the sky across the entire nation with a performance that may never be duplicated. When historians glance through the NFL record books, they are certain to pause and ponder an accomplishment that almost could be equated with America's first moon shot. It was that exciting. Just look: 382 completions;

.642 percent of completions; 5,084 yards; 48 touchdowns and only 17 interceptions. The Marino phenomena that season elicited an average of 40 requests a week for interviews and his face appeared on every major sports magazine. Amazingly, Marino kept a low profile.

"The records are nice, but I don't really dwell on it," he shrugged. "I play with a lot of emotion and that's the way you have to play this game. I really feel that every time we get the ball we are going to score. That may sound cocky, but you have to have confidence in yourself. If you don't, you just aren't going to get the job done. It's the same with all those people who make me out to be a hero. I'm in a position where there's a lot of recognition paid. I'm honored by the attention but I'm just one of several guys who had a good season here."

The streets of Pittsburgh and a close family upbringing have kept life in perspective for Marino who could easily bask in the bright lights reserved for glamour quarterbacks. In Pittsburgh's sports haven, a downtown spa called Froggy's, or in Ft. Lauderdale's fashionable Roland's, Marino is looked upon as one of the boys. He prefers it that way rather than the artificial tinsel of a Hollywood image. It's simply not Marino's style. He much prefers the laid back life.

"He just doesn't like to talk about himself," said Strock. "We'll just sit around bulling about a lot of things when we go out for a beer. We'll sit around with Bruce Hardy and Dan Johnson and Joe Rose and talk about golf or basketball or somebody we can pick on in the next game. There's always somebody."

Marino just shrugs.

"I'm not a playboy or anything like that," emphasized Marino. "I enjoy the extra things like making appearances, but I never want to get too involved. You start thinking about that and you loss sight of what you really have to do. I know the reason I've had these opportunities is because I'm a quarterback on a winning team. That's what it's all about. If I let that get away from me, this image stuff won't mean a thing. Football is number one. It has to be. And for me, that's where the fun is.

> **"All I know is I'm having fun."**

"You have to draw the line somewhere. I don't mind doing interviews, but I need some time to myself. Actually, I don't think I'd be too interesting to follow. I go to the movies, I watch TV. I'm a pretty typical guy."

No typical guy could have done what Marino did in 1984. After that Herculean season, whatever critics there were, waited to see what Marino would do in 1985. Surely, they couldn't expect him to repeat his performance. That would be asking the impossible of anybody. Even Shula never entertained such thoughts. He is wise enough to know it was only one season and each new one brings other challenges.

"Improve, I just want him to maintain," stressed Shula. "Dan is an exceptional talent. He has the quickest arm I've ever seen and he makes ev-

Gatorade
Gatorade

erything seem so natural. I find myself comparing him to Unitas and I didn't think I'd do that with any quarterback, much less a second-year one.

"Marino is a dropback passer who enjoys attacking and going after the coverage. I really enjoy him. He has his own style. What you're seeing is the personality of Dan Marino let loose. He's very competitive. On the practice field, he immediately goes toward the receiver after a pass. It's a natural thing for him to communicate. He's the first one downfield after a touchdown to congratulate the receiver.

"I used to talk about Nick Buoniconti's tremendous reactions. It never took long for the thought to go from his head to his feet. Marino's like that in that it doesn't take long for the thought to go from his head to his feet to his arm. He has a natural knack with cadence. He'll go on the quick count to try and draw people offside like Griese did, or he'll go on the long count. He doesn't even think about it.

"He makes quick decisions and has that great peripheral vision. This is a trademark not only of outstanding quarterbacks but running backs and receivers as well. He doesn't bring the ball up and throw with that long arm action. It's just boom, and the ball is gone with a tremendous whip of the shoulders. He gets his whole body and legs into it. Boom!"

Marino developed his quick release at an early age. His father, who drives a newspaper delivery truck in Pittsburgh, worked with him whenever he could. As early as the fourth grade, Marino had visions of being a quarterback and later developed into an excellent baseball prospect until a knee injury his sophomore year in college sidelined him. The injury has since given him trouble and even after a couple of operations has to wear a special brace on his right knee for protection which curtails his mobility, and all the more reason he has to get his passes off quickly.

"My dad emphasized throwing without any wasted motion," recalled Marino. "He'd tell me to throw from my ear and not wind up. When you're younger, you don't have the arm strength to stand and throw like that, but he said if I worked on it right away I'd be able to throw it a lot better once I got bigger and stronger. He made me

practice the right way."

In 1985, Marino got off slowly. He missed most of training camp and when the season began, he wasn't that sharp. He needed practice time to work with his receivers on touch and timing. His progress was further impeded when Mark Duper got hurt in the second game of the season and missed seven weeks which meant that Mark Clayton would attract double coverage every game. At one point, the Dolphins were 5-4 before Marino shifted gears and went on a roll that produced seven straight victories and the Eastern Division championship.

> **"** I play with a lot of emotion and that's the way you have to play this game. **"**

Naturally, he couldn't emulate his record-shattering year of 1984. But what quarterback in the NFL wouldn't grab the numbers Marino put up: 336 completions; .593 percent of completions; 4,137 yards; 30 touchdowns and 21 interceptions. The numbers didn't get past Marino. He merely looked at the season differently.

"It's obvious that I didn't have as good a season statistically as last

year," offered Marino, "but I think I'm a better quarterback. I wouldn't call it tough. It's been a good season for me personally and for the team. I learned a lot of things that will help in the future. It helps when you're playing in games when you have to win. I don't think things were as bad as people made out early in the season. Teams weren't beating us; we were beating ourselves."

Strock couldn't have agreed more. He was verbal in praising Marino.

"Stats aren't everything," said Strock. "Marino is better than he's ever been. We're talking about a guy who walked in and took us to the playoffs his first year, the Super Bowl his second year, and had us in the AFC championship game his third. I've looked in some history books and never found that. Danny was great the day he got here and keeps improving. What does that say about him?"

Strock is not alone in his accolades of Marino. His golden receivers just love him.

"It's like playing with a legend," smiled Clayton. "Dan Marino is a legend in his own time. What more can you say about the guy?"

"One day he's going to throw for 700 yards in one game," added Duper. "And you know what? It's not going to surprise anybody!"

Even the stoic Shula is ecstatic.

"What this guy has done, I want to stand up and applaud," remarked Shula.

Still, Marino isn't completely satisfied. He still want to improve, which says something about his leadership qualities.

"My strong point as a quarterback is that I've always been able to make the throws that were necessary to this team," said Marino. "My weakest point is that I want to learn. I want to get better, learn from my mistakes.

"It's funny how things work out. I still remember draft day, wondering why so many teams were passing me by. I was disappointed and hurt, then I get the call from Miami. Now here I am starting and winning. I don't know if it's fate or what. Maybe if I had a better senior year at Pitt I wouldn't be here, I'd be someplace else. Maybe I'd be on the bench. Who knows? All I know is, I'm having fun."

Winning does that...

THE OFFENSE

Ever since Dan Marino took charge midway through his rookie season in 1983, the Dolphins haven't had to worry about the quarterback position. What concerned Don Shula most before the 1985 season began was his running game. As he reflected about his squad's accomplishments following a season that just fell short of his goals, Shula is still seeking the same improvement in his ground offensive.

"We wanted to improve our running game and I don't think we did that," disclosed Shula. "There are a lot of things that have to be done to make us a better football team. It's obvious from the way we struggled that we have to improve."

Yet, there are many who look with wonderment at what Shula accomplished last year. Some say it was the finest year of coaching in his illustrious 23-year career, one in the wake of holdouts, an inordinate amount of injuries and even tragedy in the form of the death of a player's wife.

The running game begins with Tony Nathan. The eight year veteran is one of the most versatile backs in the NFL, one who is immensely overlooked. Even though he has never had a 1,000 yard season, Nathan's career average of 4.8 yards a run is one of the highest in the league. He has had only one 100-yard game simply because never once has he carried the ball 20 times. Yet, he is also valuable in catching passes out of the backfield, having a lifetime total of 325, an average of 47 a season.

In 1985, Nathan had one of his finest seasons. He not only led the Dolphins in rushing with 667 yards, averaging less than nine carries a game, but he was tops in receiving with 72 for another 651 yards. Combined, it added up to a 1,318 yard season. He is invaluable as a third down receiver looking for the first down to keep a drive going.

"I guess recognition will come to me in due time, but I don't think it has yet," sighed Nathan.

Shula certainly appreciates him. After all, that's all that really matters even if Nathan hasn't gone to the Pro Bowl once.

"Tony Nathan is a money player," remarked Shula. "He has been making big plays for us all his career. I can't say enough about Tony. He's an exceptional runner, more of a pick-and-choose type than a slasher or breakaway threat. He has great vision and great quickness, and when he gets to the hole he makes quick decisions. It doesn't take long for thoughts to go from his head to his feet, and he'll block when he doesn't have the football.

"But the thing he probably does as well as anyone in the league is catch the ball coming out of the backfield. We have a lot of plays where he has the option of breaking in or breaking out, and he makes very intelligent decisions. It's a split-second timing thing where he has to anticipate what the quarterback sees. That's hard to work on, you just have to have the instincts to do it. He's one of the rare guys with the ability to do it."

Tony Nathan: **"I guess recognition will come in due time, but I don't think it has yet."**

Nathan had to work for his success. At Alabama, it was unheard of for a running back to catch a pass in Bear Bryant's way of thinking.

"There's a feel for how a defender is playing you," said Nathan. "If you can read him, he'll tell you where the open spot is. You get to the point where you see and react instantly because you've done it so often. It's a spur of the moment thing. When you see it you have to hit it. If you get caught thinking too long, you'll hesitate too long and by then it's too late to hit the open route."

Nathan keeps it all in perspective. He considers himself a blue collar guy on a team with such glamour types as Dan Marino, Mark Duper and Mark Clayton. He'd like to contribute more, but has a handle on what his role is.

"I'd like to contribute more if I can, but there are a lot of individuals in there, and everybody's wanting the football," explained Nathan. "Everybody can't get their hands on it at the same time. I'm more satisfied than I was. This has been the best offense I've been involved with here. It's very explosive, and we put a lot of points on the board."

Nathan is often paired in the backfield with Woody Bennett, a fullback type. He, too, is another back who goes beyond the statistical chart in the Dolphin scheme of things. He almost goes unnoticed for the things he does which are not measured by yards.

"What Woody Bennett has taken on is the identity of the H-back," explained Shula. "We've been using him a lot in the double wing, double tight end. He's been moving up and utilized as a blocker and a pass receiver. Although I know he'd like to have the ball more, we just feel the things we're doing with him is the best way for us to be the most productive offensively."

Like all big fullbacks, he would rather run the ball. But like everyone else in the Shula system, he acknowledges his participation as a role player.

"It's been working out well for me but I'd still rather run the football," admitted Bennett.

Bennett got his break when Andra Franklin went down with an injury two years ago. This time he made the most of his opportunity after having been discarded in Canada and let go by the New York Jets in 1983. He's learned to combat adversity.

"I've always said my life is like a book," replied Bennett. "There's been so many ups and downs, so many highs and lows. I don't know if too many other players who have gone through this. One thing always seems to hold true. I've always been able to weather the storm."

With solid play from both Nathan and Bennett, it was difficult for Joe Carter to get much playing time. What held back the second year speed burner was that he got injured just before the 1985 season opened and was on injured reserve for six weeks. When he came back, he saw action primarily on special teams for the next eight games. Shula had plans of using him more until his training camp mishap.

"We had high hopes for Joe based on the great camp he had," acknowledged Shula. "He gave us some real quickness and then he had the injury. We'd been looking for a way to juice up the running game and for somebody to spell Nathan."

Carter can run. He was clocked at 4.37 in the 40 at Alabama, which is fast on anyone's stop watch. What the clock didn't measure was his acceleration. In his rookie year in 1984, he turned in a 105-yard game, the first Dolphin runner to do so since 1982.

"It's been a pretty tough adjustment from college to the pros," revealed Carter. "It's been a lot of work getting prepared and I have to concentrate more on the passing game."

In a projected effort to strengthen the team's running game, the Dolphins drafted two runners in the 1985 draft, Lorenzo Hampton, a halfback on the first round and Ron Davenport, a fullback on the sixth round. Hampton primarily gave Nathan a breather. Like all rookies, he had adjustments to make and actually got off to a slower start than anticipated.

"Our backs switch off in so many different situations that we really don't get the feel you would like in a game," remarked Hampton. "Each week I got a little better. I'm an impatient person, so trying not to rush is hard. It's a mental thing. Sometimes I tend to overreact to my mistakes. When you make mistakes, you've just got to forget them and do your best the next time out."

At the end of his first year, Hampton rushed for 369 yards. He was outstanding on kickoff returns, averaging 22.7 yards a run.

Davenport established himself as the club's short yardage specialist. Not only did he finish with 370 yards, but he led the Dolphins in touchdowns with 13, just one less than Marcus Allen and Curt Warner, both of whom were number one draft choices, had in their rookie seasons. Admittedly, Davenport was inconsistent throughout his college career and a reason why he wasn't drafted until the sixth round.

"I had a problem with my state of mind," confessed Davenport. "There were so many distractions that sometimes I let it get me down. I really have to concentrate on something to get my intensity high. Something like short yardage. But I've improved my intensity. I just have to get better about it. I think I should be automatic in short yardage. It's not that far to go and even if you don't et a good block you should be able to fight and make it."

While Marino is the catalyst at quarterback, Don Strock is the constant. How else can you describe someone who has been with the Dolphins for 12 years and is invaluable on the sidelines in helping to determine play selections? He is in a sense the Dolphins' quarterback in residence, having been through nine playoffs, three Super Bowls and the only member of the Dolphins with a Super Bowl ring on his finger. For the most part, his visibility is

Lorenzo Hampton

detected when he trots on the field to hold the ball for Fuad Reveiz's kicks. Other than that, Strock has no kicks of his own.

"I have no complaints," grinned Strock. "There are a lot of players in this league who would love to play behind Marino. I'll do whatever it takes. I'm a team player and it's a joy to be a part of this team."

Even though he has started only 20 games in 11 years, and just five since 1980, Strock is paid up insurance. Shula, for one, appreciates having Strock around all these years.

"He came up under Griese and like Griese, he has a thorough understanding of the game," said Shula. "He's also a very intelligent player. He's been through a lot of situations, and we use his knowledge in several ways. When we have the ball, he watches everything that's going on through a quarterback's eyes. He picks up little things, like a defensive lineman shifting more to one side, or a cornerback coming up an extra step. Then he and I talk about what's working for us and what isn't, and we discuss it with Marino when he comes off the field. Between us we decide what plays we want to use."

Making use of wide receivers Mark Duper and Mark Clayton is like throwing gasoline on a fire. They are that hot and that explosive, like 5-9 sticks of dynamite. It's no wonder that Miami has the deadliest deep passing game in the NFL. Duper has been around a year longer. He was the Dolphins' number two draft choice out of little Northwestern State Louisiana where basically he was a track star and had a 4.28 clocking in the 40 yard dash. He didn't catch a pass his first year in Miami, having appeared in only two games. But all the while Duper was learning. He played only two years in college and caught only 24 passes in his senior year. In reality, his speed earned him a track scholarship, but Shula detected that he could instinctively catch a football when he first saw him at an NFL tryout session in Detroit.

"He was catching a lot of balls in the middle of the field and that told me he had soft hands," recalled Shula. "But then there was this one ball, slightly underthrown, that he sort of leaned back for and caught right over his head, rather than turn and slow down.

Ron Davenport

A guy who could make that kind of adjustment, plus those hands, he was eye catching."

Duper calls his first season in Miami a nightmare. He doggedly worked hard in the off season with receiver coach David Shula to improve. He spent long, hot days listening to Shula and running one pattern after the other.

"One day I told him I could beat him in a 20-yard sprint, which is ridiculous," said Shula. "He beat me, but not by much. Afterward I said, 'All right, how would you do it in a real race? Show me a track start.' He got down and blew off the ball so fast, people were oohing and aahing."

Duper became a pro receiver that summer of 1983. When the regular season ended, he became the first Dolphin receiver to go over a 1,000 yards. His 51 receptions netted 1,003 yards, an average of 19.7 a catch, and 10 touchdowns. He did it all starting only in 11 games. In 1984, Duper was even better. he caught 71 passes for 1,306 yards. When Clayton showed the way with 73 receptions for 1,389 yards, the two became the first set of receivers in NFL history to produce over 1,300 yards in season. Still, Duper looked for improvement.

"If you've think you learned everything there is to learn, it's time to quit," believes Duper. "I can still get better. I recognize that. If I caught 120 balls, it wouldn't mean there wasn't room for improvement. It's a learning game. Every day that you are out there, you pick up something."

Unfortunately, Duper couldn't improve on what he did in 1983 and 1984 because of a fracture in his left leg. It happened unknowingly in the opening game of the 1985 season. He played the entire game against Houston with soreness, which remained in his leg at practice the rest of the week. On the first play against Indianapolis, he knew something was wrong.

"I thought my leg was just sore and I could run the soreness out," disclosed Duper. "I ran a route and cut on it and it felt real bad. I tried to line up for a few more plays and then I told Marino I couldn't do it. I got out of there as quick as I could."

Duper missed the next seven games. He didn't return until the 10th game of the season. Still, he managed to catch 35 passes for 650 yards, an average of 18.5, tops on the squad. Just being back in the lineup, although he wasn't completely 100%, enabled defenses to stop double covering Clayton. Yet, no one will forget Duper's return against the New York Jets. Miami was struggling with a 5-4 record and a loss to the Jets would drop them three games out of first place with only six regular season games remaining. With only 49 seconds left, the Jets were ahead, 17-14. Duper went deep on a fly pattern, reached up and tipped the ball, then grabbed it with one hand for a 60-yard touchdown pass that gave the Dolphins a 21-17 victory, one which turned the season around.

"Dupes has tremendous hands," exclaimed David Shula. "I'd say about 70 percent of getting a receiver to catch the ball with his hands is getting him to believe he can do it. If he doesn't, his hands will be tense and the ball will bounce off them. I don't know anyone who has more confidence in his hands than Dupes. Marino can throw him a rocket and he doesn't even think about it. It comes naturally to him."

Clayton was a sleeper that the Dolphins landed on the eighth round of the 1983 draft. Despite a fine senior year, his biggest claim to fame was that he could leap over a ping pong table lengthwise. He never doubted that he could play football even though he never had spectacular statistics at the University of Louisville to support him. When he wasn't drafted on the first round, he promptly turned off his television set, went out and played basketball, and didn't return until about 10 o'clock that night when he got a phone call from the Dolphins.

"I was determined to prove then wrong," said Clayton about being picked so low. "I have that self-confidence."

Like Duper, Clayton didn't turn the NFL upside down his rookie season, not with six receptions in 14 games. His biggest notoriety that season was that he and Marino broke into the starting lineup together the sixth week of the 1983 season.

However, before the 1984 campaign, David Shula worked diligently for 10 weeks with Clayton, Duper and Marino. It paid off once the season began. Clayton utilized his amazing 38" vertical leap to set an NFL record of 18 touchdown passes.

"The problem my first year was that I couldn't get the coaches to have confidence in me," claimed Clayton. "That's what I knew I had to change before the 1984 season."

Clayton never lost confidence in his ability. He just wanted the opportunity to play, and when Tommy Vigorito went down with an injury in 1984, Clayton got his chance and hasn't been out of the lineup since.

"Every time I've talked about doing something, I've always done it," remarked Clayton. "I honestly don't think there's anything I can't do."

With Duper out for most of the 1985

Mark Duper

Mark Clayton

season, Clayton attracted the attention of opposing defenses by being double-teamed. Still, it didn't prevent him from making 70 receptions, just missing his second straight 1,000-yard season with 996. Yet, all Clayton wants is to improve.

"I could block better, run patterns better, concentrate harder on catching the easy balls," said Clayton. "There's always room for improvement. If you're content staying where you are, what's the use of going out there trying to be the best? You always have to set your goals higher."

Some defensive backs around the league are intent on keeping Clayton from getting better. They even go so far as trying to verbally intimidate him during a game.

"I don't talk until someone talks to me," emphasized Clayton. "I don't like getting into verbal wars out there, but I'm not going to let anyone just say something to me without saying something back."

Don Shula: **"We wanted to improve our running game (1985 season) and I don't think we did that."**

Nat Moore is as quiet as Clayton is verbal. Ironically, because of the rapid success of both Clayton and Duper, Moore has added a couple of years to his NFL life span. At 35, Moore is beginning his 13th year in Miami, and actually had his best season in seven years in 1985. Moore caught 51 passes, seven for touchdowns, that totalled 701 yards. From 1974 through 1979, Moore was the team's top receiver, averaging 43 receptions and 700 yards per season. Now he is looked upon as a possession receiver.

"There comes a time in your career when there will be someone younger than you, quicker than you and faster than you," reasons Moore. "Back many years ago I was the man. I was the game-breaker. At that time we had a run-oriented offense where now it's

Woody Bennett

pass-oriented. The real difference is that I can be a possession receiver and catch as many balls as I did while being a game-breaker in a run-oriented offense."

How long can Moore continue? A year, perhaps two? He almost quit before the 1985 season but a talk with Shula convinced him to play.

"The one thing you don't want to do is overstay your welcome," said Moore. "If you can't produce on the field it doesn't make a lot of sense to come back. I felt the last couple of years I've made the most of every opportunity given to me. I feel I can still do that.

"When you get to my level, my age, you realize youth takes precedence. When you got guys like Duper and Clayton, you look forward to just coming in and replacing them. At this point in my career I don't want to play 16 games, play every down. If I was being replaced by guys who didn't have more talent, it would be a difficult adjustment. With Duper and Clayton, it's very easy to accept. Sometimes I find myself being a fan. I get so worked up watching them."

Some teams are lucky to have one good tight end. The Dolphins are fortunate in that they have three, Bruce Hardy, Joe Rose and Dan Johnson. Hardy had his finest season in 1985 while Johnson and Rose were slowed by injuries. Hardy had a career high 39 receptions for 409 yards.

"Hardy is such an aware player," said Shula. "A lot of times you think just because he doesn't have great speed he's not going to get open. You see it every day in practice. He's always open. He's always in a position where the quarterback has somebody to throw to. He just has a great knack for finding the holes and beating the man coverage."

Rose came up with only 19 receptions, but four were for touchdowns and his 306 yards averaged out to 16.1 yards a catch. He didn't appear to suffer any ill effects from a 1984 shoulder injury and appeared in every game last year.

"I got more publicity over the shoulder injury than anything else I've done," reflected Rose upon his decision not to have surgery. "What I thought was a minor decision turned into something major. I just hope people realize that I can do other things than get my shoulder hurt. We all have a role. I think I've accepted mine. If I'm called on, I'm going to do my job.''

Johnson's injuries plagued him to the point that he pulled down only 13 passes last year. It brought back memories of 1984 when he played the entire season with a flak jacket to protect cracked ribs, yet managed to catch a career high 34 passes.

''We think Dan has the potential to become one of the best in the league because he gives you the combination of blocker and receiver at tight end that you're looking for,'' said Shula.

Johnson agrees.

''There's no question I can become a better player, perhaps the best tight end in the league,'' acknowledged Johnson who answers to the nickname of Boomer. ''I've had that nickname ever since I was a year old learning how to walk. I would get up to start walking and then run into the TV, then get back up and run into the table again, knock chairs over, then fall and the whole floor would shake.''

In case Marino needs any more targets to throw to, he has Tommy Vigorito, Vince Heflin and Jim Jensen to zero in on.

Over the years, defenses have learned that it isn't easy to zero in on Dwight Stephenson. Fact is, they go out of their way to avoid the perennial All-Pro center who was drafted on the second round from Alabama in 1980. It's just as well because Stephenson, the fulcrum of the offensive line, hasn't shown any weakness in his six years in protecting Dolphin quarterbacks. He hasn't missed a game during all that time and a reason why the quarterbacks can't complain about being sacked.

''I think the nicest compliment I ever got, at least one that meant a lot to me, was when Coach Bryant said I was the best center he ever coached,'' disclosed Stephenson. ''That was only his opinion, though. But I appreciated it. I don't think I ever got the big head because of it. I'm sure if I had, somebody would have straightened me out right away.''

Instead, Stephenson is straightening out anybody who comes his way. There is no question he is a deterrent when opposing defenses exert a rush.

Nat Moore

Roy Foster

"We use an unusual blocking system because of him, because he can always go one-on-one," pointed out Marino. "And that system is why teams can't blitz us."

The efficiency level at which Stephenson operates almost goes unnoticed. He's that smooth and that quiet to a point of being lower than low key.

"I don't have to be seen," contends Stephenson. "I don't need glamour. Maybe that's why I like playing center. You can't be easily rattled to play there; and it's very hard to get me mad. I believe in what Coach Bryant used to say: 'Minimize I.' "

Yet, there is no minimizing the praise Shula has for Stephenson.

"He's not a holler guy," said Shula. "He's not a rah-rah guy. He has just gained the respect of everybody and that's how he has gained the leadership role he has. Dwight has really emerged as one of the dominating centers in the league. He's strong, he's quick, and he's a tremendous competitor. Very intense. He goes all-out on every play."

Still, Stephenson makes certain that he doesn't fall into the comfort zone.

"I don't want to get to the point where I think I'm good, where I get overconfident," confided Stephenson. "I do want to keep working, to get better every game."

With the exception of Stephenson, the Dolphin offensive line was decimated by injuries last season. Ed Newman and Cleveland Green went down, Eric Laakso had to call it quits, and Jon Giesler gamely played in 13 games even though he couldn't practice all week. One other, who escaped injury, Ray Foster, emerged from under Bob Kuechenberg's shadow to earn All-Pro honors in only his second year as a starting guard.

"There was a lot of pressure trying to fill the shoes of a 14-year veteran who was in and out of the Pro Bowl all his career," admitted Foster. "I just wanted to help this team do the best it could do. I had a couple of shots at starting that I simply blew. I didn't rise to the occasion but Coach Shula stuck with me. He gave me another shot and let me come around.

"I really had no doubts that I could do it. But you still had to do it on the field. I felt plenty of pressure. I was

Dwight Stepenson

replacing a legend, a guy who is going to be in the Hall of Fame. I could tell people were sensing that I wasn't going to be able to cut it, that I couldn't possibly fill the shoes of the great Bob Kuechenberg."

He did and now Shula is hoping that the injury cloud won't appear overhead in 1986 like it did last year.

"We had a lot of injuries that kept us

from being as good as we wanted to be and that probably hurt us in the running game," analyzed Shula. "It's remarkable that we did as well as we did with the injuries that we had. It's a tribute to John Sandusky, our offensive line coach, and to the players who filled in when they were called upon."

That's what it takes to win…

HUGH GREEN

He looks like something out of Star Wars. The plastic shield gives him an ominous look. It covers most of his face, yet somehow the coal black eyes burn through. With or without the additional facial protection, that resulted from an automobile accident, his menacing look enables him to stare down an opponent. Around the league he is known as Laser Eyes. It only underlines Hugh Green's mission, which is to seek and destroy. Al Davis would love him.

The trade that brought the aggressive linebacker from Tampa to Miami last fall could go down as one of the greatest in Dolphin history. Years from now, Dolphin watchers can analyze its results. When Don Shula orchestrated the dramatic deal for the All-Pro linebacker, it was the equivalent of landing Dan Marino on offense. The honest fact is, Miami's draft occurred on October 9 long before the NFL's May lottery.

It was no secret that Miami's defense was shaky even before the 1985 season began. Once the campaign got underway, there was no denying it. A rash of injuries added to the woes. The Dolphins needed an impact player to position them for the playoff run. Shula had always looked for someone like Green in the college draft but could never get one. Quietly he learned that Green was unhappy at Tampa. Shula's mind began accelerating. He studied the draft prospects for 1986 and found no one in Green's class. He decided to go after Green and got him for a number one and number two draft choice.

"I would to the same thing again in a second," exclaimed Shula. "He's a pretty good number one draft choice. If I was sitting here on draft day without a Hugh Green and could give up two draft choices to get him, I'd do it right now. You're talking about a totally committed football player. He plays defense the way Dwight Stephenson plays offense."

For Green, there could be no other way. He has been aggressive ever since he was a kid learning to survive in Natchez, Mississippi. He wanted to grow up quickly and miss the unhappiness he faced as a youngster. He never knew his father who left home before he was born. At the age of six his mother died and left him bewildered about life, looking around and finding no one. An aunt, Lucy Berry

tried to pick up the pieces of the youth's broken life and put it back together. It would take a lot of patience on Lucy and her husband Eltee's end. Not only were their children grown and out of the house, but they had an angry child to raise.

"When my mother died, it bothered me," revealed Green. "I went to my aunt's and I was old enough to realize that she wasn't my mother. I always called her 'Aunt,' but never quite accepted the situation until I was lots older, maybe 16 or 17. Finally I learned to love her as my mother. I realized this lady did a lot of different things for me. Finally, I started calling her Mom."

Up until then it was hard. There was quite a bit of hostility pent up in the youngster. Every other child he played with had a mother or a father. It gnawed at Green and one day he decided to run away from home.

"He couldn't have been 11 or 12," remembered Lucy. "There was some problem with a neighbor's boy and him. I think they broke a tape recorder or something. Next thing I know, Hugh didn't come home. It turns out that he slept overnight in a bus somewhere. We had gone to the police and the next day they saw him. They were

chasing him all over but he kept running away from them. Nobody could catch him."

However, he couldn't run forever. Shortly afterward, a policeman caught up with him. The first thing he asked Green was his age. Green never hesitated in answering.

"Thirty-five," snapped Green as if wanting to rush past his childhood to adult life.

The policeman brought him to the station and called his aunt and uncle. Before they left, another cop at the station house offered some advice.

"One of the policemen asked him if he ever thought about football," recalled Lucy. "He told him it might be better for him than running away."

Slowly, Green began to think about football. He liked the physical part and who knows maybe one day he would be good enough to be a pro and make a lot of money. Suddenly, life began to look better to Green. Still, his uncle taught him that money was hard to come by. He was a construction worker who labored hard, saved his money and inflicted discipline on Green.

"Growing up, he taught me to say just what's on your mind," said Green. "He said you might as well learn now, things don't come easy and nothing is free. He made me come up the hard way. If I asked him for a nickel or a quarter, he made me borrow it and pay him back. It took me a long time to understand."

When he got to North Natchez High School, Green went out for football. It didn't take him long to quit. In his fast world of wanting to be an adult, he never knew the meaning of patience. He wanted everything then and now.

"I was a freshman and the coach had talked me into coming out," disclosed Green. "However, when I did, I saw that they had an 11th grader playing in front of me. I didn't want to sit on the bench, so I quit. But not long after that, the guy flunked out and they asked me back. I started every game after that."

He rushed to stardom. Although he was small as defensive players go, Green was good. He was good and he was tough. Defense allowed him to hit people, to release his aggressions. Green liked nothing better than popping a ball carrier. Controlled violence gave life a new meaning to Green. He played to win. When his team lost, Green took it personally. He already lost enough in life. Football was a new start.

A lot of college coaches felt that Green was too small. However, an assistant coach at the University of Pittsburgh was quite impressed with Green. Pittsburgh was one of a dozen colleges interested in a runner across the river at Pascagoula, Mississippi named Raymond "Rooster" Jones. He earned his nickname because he was the fastest thing to hit Pascagoula since the automobile. After viewing hours of video tape on Jones running by everyone, the Pitt coach noticed that he was always caught by the little linebacker from Natchez. Both Jones and Green ended up at Pittsburgh.

It didn't take long for Green to make an impression there. He made an impact the first day he lined up on the practice field. He ran and hit, going all out on every play. By the time Pitt opened the 1977 season, Green earned a spot in the starting lineup. However, in the opening game against Notre Dame, Green watched the first play from the bench. Instead, Mike Lenosky lined up for the first play. On the second one, Green replaced him and never missed another play the rest of his college career. He was an All-American for three straight years beginning as a sophomore, won the Lombardi Trophy and finished second for the Heisman Trophy his senior year. Is it any wonder that they retired his jersey at Pitt?

"Nobody in college football could block him," claimed Jackie Sherrill who coached Pitt at the time. "There was no question who was the best football player in the nation his senior year. Hugh Green is the best linebacker in the history of college football. It got to the point where we wouldn't let him practice much for fear he'd hurt one of our guys."

Every pro team knew who Green was by now. Tampa Bay didn't have to think twice about making him their number one selection in the 1981 college draft. For the next five years, Green played for the Buccaneers the only way he knew how, to win. Twice he made All-Pro, in 1983 and 1984, but the Bucs didn't win enough. Twice Green got a taste of the playoffs, and both times Tampa Bay got eliminated. There was no way Green could console himself because winning is where it's at for him.

"It wasn't only the absence of winning that got to me," said Green. "It was the absence of giving 110%. It was like a losing cause. It kept me emotionally down in so many ways. I had always felt I was the kind who gave full effort. I didn't know if I could still do that.

"You get to the point where you say you're having a great year, but you look in the win column and see nothing there. You look at yourself and say, 'Am I doing all that I can to help the team? Losing hurts."

It hurt so much that on October 2 Green failed to show up for practice. He was giving Tampa Bay a message, just as he had done 13 years ago as a kid in Natchez. The Bucs were responsive to the point that Green had made in wanting out of Tampa. That's when Shula made his move. He doesn't miss much on or off the field. He instructed Charley Winner, his Director of Pro Personnel, to contact Tampa Bay immediately. He made Winner call a second time the following day. The deal simmered over the weekend and by then other teams were in pursuit of the golden Green. By Monday, Shula dealt directly with Tampa Bay. By Tuesday night, Shula had closed the deal for Green.

"I went home about 10:30 feeling pretty good," said Shula.

So did Green.

"I never thought I would end up in Miami," he admitted. "But I'm happy to be here. I don't want to talk about what happened in Tampa. I feel that all of that is behind me now, and I want to start over, start from scratch, with a team that can win. I made it to the first round of the playoffs twice with Tampa Bay and lost twice. I wanted so much to play in a championship game, in a game where the pressure is tremendous."

Still, the transition from Tampa Bay to Miami wasn't easy even for a player of Green's magnitude. It took Green about a month to feel comfortable in the Miami defensive scheme. And Green had to work hard to accomplish what he did in that short period of time, putting in extra hours of practice to the point that he even missed having dinner with Dan Marino one night. The mental part was heavy for Green in that he was learning his third defensive philosophy in the same year. He had mastered the Tampa Bay scheme, then had to learn the one introduced by Leaman Bennett before the 1985 season and finally had to cram the intricacies of Chuck Studley's system.

Marino tried to help Green during this trying period by having him move in with him.

"Learning the basics was one thing, feeling comfortable was another," confessed Green. "It took time. I had to be patient. But I never lost confidence that I could do the job. Mentally it was tough, trying to adjust to a system that's already developed. It was frustrating because I knew I was going to make mistakes. But you realize the position you're in with a new system and all you can do is learn.

"Yet, I felt then that things weren't working out the way they should and I was pushing myself too hard to learn. Finally, things worked out for me because the coaches didn't push me. I learned the defense the way I should. It took time to learn the defenses and the personnel. Until you do, you end up not being the athlete they knew you as, but you can't let the change frustrate you. You just have to work harder.

"We played Tampa the second game I was here and people wondered how I could go right out and do that to my old teammates. Miami had always been our archrivals, but I had to reverse roles. It wasn't difficult. I'm a football player. I'm paid to do a job. Logos shouldn't affect a person. But I was lost that day. I didn't know what we were doing. It was the worst game I ever played."

However, a month later, Green got a game ball. Strangely, it was the first one he had ever received, not that he wasn't deserving of any previously. It's just that the University of Pittsburgh and Tampa Bay have a policy of not issuing game balls. When he was given the ball after the Jet game in which Miami won, 20-17, Green was thrilled.

"The guys gave me that ball because I think it was more or less that they were behind me and appreciated what I was doing," reasoned Green. "I think it meant more than me playing well. It showed the support and confidence they have in me."

By the end of the regular season, Green had finished his 10 game campaign with 58 tackles, five sacks, one interception and two forced fumbles. Quite encouraging after a slow start. As he had done in his previous years in Tampa, Green bought $1,413 worth of tickets for the final game of the sea-son for 80 underprivileged youngsters to attend as his guests.

Green relished being a guest in Marino's house. He admits that being such helped make his transition to the Dolphins that much easier. It allowed Green and Marino to spend a lot of extra hours talking football.

"Dan and his parents, we're like family," explained Green. "It's good for me to have someone like that. We talked a lot, especially the early part of the week. He'd talk offense and I'd talk defense. We talked about how different guys looked on film."

Yet, Green didn't let his friendship take preference on the field a year earlier. Marino remembers it well.

> **❝I feel like my best games are ahead of me.❞**

"When we played Tampa in an exhibition game he blindsided me," disclosed Marino. "I had a bruise for a long time afterward. And, he likes me, so just think what he does to people that he doesn't like."

It's just that Green comes by his aggressiveness naturally and will never change.

"I've always competed, and things have turned out the best for me," contends Green. "You always go full speed and the odds are that life will work out to your benefit. I go full out in practice. Some guys don't like it but that's me. If I don't crush somebody on a play, I'm disappointed. Let's be truthful. Fans like the sport because of the violence—which is also why I like it.

"You never know when things will end. That time may seem far ahead of you, but then, like that, it's over. If you're a man, you go out and work your whole life so your kids will be proud of what you accomplished. You have to show those kids how hard you've worked because they have to know you don't get nothing easy in life. That's the way life is. If I hadn't been like this, if I hadn't gone full out, I wouldn't be where I am. I wouldn't be the person I am.

"I'm not happy my mom died. But if she were alive today, I don't think I'd be where I am. My mom's death changed my whole life. I grew up without a mother, father, brothers or sisters. That's a challenge for anyone. I grew up within myself. I had to accept responsibility at an early age. I solve my own problems. I set my own pace. I don't depend on anyone else for answers."

The Dolphins are going to depend on Green a great deal more in 1986. Now that he's learned the system, he can be used in a variety of ways.

"We're going to make every effort to take advantage of Hugh's great ability," said Shula. "He's an excellent blitzer and an excellent man-to-man coverage guy and we didn't have time to get into enough of that last season."

It will be up to Studley to make Green more of an impact player. He's anxious to do so, too.

"The possibilities with Hugh are almost unlimited," offered Studley. "I think the difference this year compared to last year will be noticeable to the guy on the street. He's a very unusual player in that he's an excellent blitzer and he's also probably our best coverage outside linebacker.

"In our anxiety to get him into the blitz you say, 'gee, I'd like to have him in coverage.' You find yourself in a situation where you throw him one way, the play goes the other way and he's sort of wasted. You'd like to have him blitzing, playing the run, covering man-to-man all at once. What we'd like to have is about 11 Hugh Greens.

"When you come in in the middle of the year, there are experiences you're not going to get. Hugh likes it here. He likes our scheme of defense. He likes the fact that we know he can be an impact player. We'll be devising ways to use him like that."

Green can't wait.

"A lot of people keep asking me how much better I can get this season," remarked Green. "I've thought a lot about that. Well, I feel I can be a lot better. I think that will be evident from the beginning. I feel like my best games are ahead of me. I don't plan on letting anybody down."

That'll never happen simply because Hugh Green has never let himself down...

THE DEFENSE

They were a colorful bunch. They buzzed and they stung and they succeeded in writing a new chapter of lore in Miami's book of defense that for a time brought back memories of the fabled No Name defense of the 1970's. The defense in the 80's was called the Killer Bees as in Kim Bokamper, Doug Betters, Bob Baumhower and A.J. Duhe. It's just that time and injuries have taken away the sting the past two years.

Duhe is gone. Baumhower, Bokamper and Betters have been wracked by injuries. Baumhower was hit the hardest, Betters the least and Bokamper somewhere in between. At the age of 31, Baumhower is staring at a serious comeback in 1986. The veteran nose tackle never played a down in 1985, sidelined the entire campaign, a victim of ankle and knee surgery. It was a frustrating time for the five time Pro Bowler. He tried to make it back the middle of the '85 season, but his knee betrayed him. It wasn't completely rehabilitated.

"The thing about being injured is that it's like being invisible," said Baumhower. "You don't feel like a part of the team. Your mind starts to play games with you; you feel like people are ignoring you."

No nose tackle lasts very long. The position is extremely demanding physically. On every play there is contact. On every play there is a pounding by one and often two offensive protectors. Baumhower always found a way to keep coming.

"I'm not complaining," he remarked. "I know this comes with the territory. Every nose tackle knows he's going to get banged on in every game. But I don't ever think about it. If you're going to worry about getting hurt all the time, you don't belong in the game."

Baumhower grew into the position. Shula specifically drafted him to play nose in the 3-4 defense.

"At first I hated it," admitted Baumhower. "But a lot of that was because the center and two guards I was practicing against were Jim Langer, Bob Kuechenberg and Larry Little, three All Pros, maybe the best trio ever. They bounced me around like a pinball. But I learned a lot, and that made playing other teams easier.

"There are some things that make the job hard. All the offensive linemen tailoring their jerseys real tight so you can't grab them, for instance. And hanging plates from the backs of their shoulder pads, so you can't get a grip on them either. And tight ends coming in motion to get you. And the chop block, which is still legal on running plays.

"But my adrenaline gets pumping so hard in games that I barely feel blows that normally would cause pain. I look at the center, but I don't even see him. It's a sacrificial position, and I know that. But we play a team defense, and we don't let our egos get in the way. I take pride in that."

Bob Baumhower: **"Every nose tackle knows he's going to be banged on in every game."**

Can Baumhower make it back? This past spring he had arthroscopic surgery on his troubled left knee to remove some lesions. His doctors gave him a clean bill of health and Baumhower is confident he can perform as good as he did two years ago.

"I'll say this," said Baumhower. "If I come back healthy, I'll be better than ever. No doubt in my mind. I've certainly had enough rest."

The 1985 absence of Baumhower enabled Mike Charles to shift from one end spot to the middle. At 6-4, 287 pounds, Charles was big enough, and strong enough, too. The third year veteran led the Dolphins in sacks with seven. Betters helped light a fire under Charles.

"I told Mike we needed his enthusiasm on the field," revealed Betters. "I told him it was his job to administer the enthusiasm. Later on it became "Minister of Enthusiasm." It was kind of a joke but he took it pretty seriously."

So much so that Charles feels comfortable at nose tackle although he was introduced to the position in earnest only last year. He had an opportunity to become a force on defense and produced.

"It always comes down to the battle in the middle," said Charles. "No one else on defense can be successful if the linemen in the middle are not successful. I feel I've helped the defense quite a bit and I'm getting better and more confident at the position all the time.

"It'll be interesting to see how they distribute the personnel on the line after Bob comes back. I don't think they would be very interested in moving me back to end after the way I've developed at nose tackle. I would hope I have a shot at the job. Maybe Bob might even move back to end. That's where he played at Alabama."

It'll be up to Chuck Studley, the Dolphins' defensive coordinator. He liked what he saw of Charles at nose tackle, however.

"Putting him on the nose was something that happened more or less by accident, but it's one of the best things that has happened," remarked Studley. "Of course I keep telling him, 'You've still got a long way to go, baby.' "

One thing is certain. Charles will be playing somewhere. Besides a valuable full year of experience, at age 24 he has youth on his side.

"I feel like I've arrived as a force on defense," exclaimed Charles. "I always knew I could play. I finally just found a spot where I can really do things for the team. The more I worked against Dwight Stephenson, the better I got."

Stephenson noticed the improvement in Charles' play with every passing week.

"He became sure of himself," said

Stephenson. "I used to mix him up once in awhile before and it got to where I couldn't do it. He became more aggressive and just comes at you. Before I could step one way and take him out of the play. Now he attacks instead of waiting for me to attack him."

Last year Betters missed two games. It was like a whole season for him. During his eight-year career, Betters has been one of the Dolphins' standards for durability. He had missed only two games and at one span had 30 sacks in 32 games. In 1984, he led the team in that category with 14, a year before he was named the AFC's Defensive Player of the Year when he registered 16 sacks.

"I'm in on every play," pointed out Betters. "In 1984 I was in on 97 percent of the plays, the year before that 98. You are talking about being out of 15 plays in 1,500. Win, lose or draw I'm out on the field.

"I think I was bearing some of the heat for our lack of performance as a defensive unit. In 1984 I got a lot of attention because of our good performance as a unit. You live and die with the way the defense plays."

Although 1985 was not one of his more productive years, Betters played steady football in the wake of the team's defensive woes, leading the linemen in solo tackles with 53 in the 14 games in which he appeared.

> Doug Betters: **"Defensively, I want to see us get back to where we were."**

"Defensively, I want to see us get back to where we were," said Betters. "This is my ninth year and I'm getting to be one of the old men out there. I want to provide a leadership role for the younger players. The only way you can lead is by example. All the yelling and talking doesn't do anything. You need to play inspirational football like A.J. used to play. We need to make the big plays and we need to get tighter as a unit on and off the field.

"It was nice to be the defensive player of the year. That's something I can hold onto for life. But that doesn't win games for you. Actually, I considered 1984 a better season because we went to the Super Bowl. Coach Shula always says that team honors are more important and he's right."

Things have to get better for Kim Bokamper. In 1984, he missed almost half the season with a broken leg. Last year he felt the tinge of pain every week from a bursitis condition in his shoulder, the one he hits a ball carrier with, and one which grew more painful as the game progressed. The condition was so painful that all Bokamper could do at practice every week was

Doug Betters

Mike Charles

run to keep in shape.

"I know I didn't play as well as I could," admitted Bokamper. "Sometimes I made the play, other times I didn't. I know I have some improving to do. I guess you could say that I was not overly satisfied with the season I had."

Yet, Studley knew what Bokamper was going through week after week.

"The guy was courageous just to be out on the field," said Studley. "He showed a lot of guts to stay in there every week. He rarely had been able to put on a pad in practice."

Bokamper never complained about the pain. He could live with that. What bothers him, however, is the criticism of his run defense.

"Sure the criticism bothers you, but what can you do?" asks Bokamper. "At times I fall short, but everyone in the league has a knock on him. I've had the tag put on me that I can't play against the run."

Studley is quick to come to Bokamper's defense.

"To say he's what's wrong with our run defense is not accurate," pointed out Studley. "It's unfair to him."

At times last year, Mark Moore demonstrated pass rushing skills in his first season with the Dolphins. He wasn't one of your ordinary rookies either. Instead, Moore, who was drafted by the Dolphins in 1981, had played in the Canadian League all these years, and led the league in quarterback sacks with 16 in 1983.

"Up there in Canada they have two guys in motion and they always would be turning up and cutting you at your legs when you rushed," revealed Moore. "Here you have only the tackle to beat and maybe the guard too if he steps back. I have to be aggressive and take advantage of every opportunity."

Rookie George Little had a busy season, alternating between end and nose tackle. He'll be used strictly at end in 1986.

"Little was moved back and forth from nose tackle to defensive end," said Shula. "I think this hurt him, but he should be more aware in his second season. We are thinking about using him more at end. He's an excellent athlete that just needs experience and confidence."

The versatility demanded at playing

Mack Moore

Kim Bokamper

Glenn Blackwood

two positions, end and nose tackle, will rest with Bill Barnett. Beginning his seventh year, Barnett is more suitable for the challenge.

"The reason he's here is because he's a dependable player who can play anywhere on the line and can also help you on special teams," said Shula.

Barnett has no illusions about his role.

"I'm not going to go out there and try to be an All-Pro in one game or anything like that," remarked Barnett. "You've just got to play your game."

With Hugh Green on one side and Bob Brudzinski on the other, the Dolphins are fortified at outside linebacker. The two sentinels protect the flanks

making it difficult for opponents to get outside on the Dolphins. Having Green work from the beginning with Brudzinski this year should make the performance of both even more efficient. An indication of their effectiveness occurred during the AFC championship game against New England. In a valiant performance, Brudzinski set a championship record of 19 solo tackle and one assist. Still, he couldn't find any solace in the wake of the 31-14 defeat.

"I could have had 50 tackles and 20 sacks," lamented Brudzinski. "It doesn't mean a thing if you don't win. Not a thing. If you feel good after a loss, there's something wrong with you. Even if you do play halfway de-

cent it doesn't matter if you don't win. It just doesn't matter.

"We had some bad moments last year, but we also had some good ones. People wrote us off when we were 5-4 and then we won eight or nine games in a row and played some good football doing it. But they'll forget all the good things, they'll forget the winning streak. All they'll remember is that we lost this game, lost the championship."

Brudzinski said it all. That put the entire 1985 season in focus. It's also about as vocal as Brudzinski can get. Once his battle armor is removed, he is in fact quiet and soft spoken.

"You are two different people when you're off the field and when you're on the field," explained Brudzinski. "Once you start playing, it's the time of day to get your frustrations out."

Brudzinski's quiet style is not lost. Shula looks upon him as a steady player. Linebacker Jay Brophy is more explicit.

"He's not one of those jump-up-and-down guys," said Brophy. "He's just a quiet guy. That's his style. He's been here so many years you don't realize he's been around here that long. He looks the same every time you see him."

Brudzinski has been a starter since the fourth game of the 1981 season when he joined the Dolphins in a trade with the Los Angeles Rams. He considers the move the turning point of his career, yet quietly he goes about trying to improve.

"Earlier during last season I was making some dumb mistakes," admitted Brudzinski. "My reads weren't that sharp. I could be better. I'm not satisfied. Each week I concentrate on what I have to do. I watch a lot of film, studying the guys I'll be playing and their tendencies. It's like any job. The more you know about someone or something, the better you'll perform."

The inside linebacker play needs improvement. Injuries hampered the position throughout most of the 1985 campaign. Mark Brown led the team in tackles for the second straight year, but Shula is looking for more. Still, Brown has done well after being drafted ninth in the 1983 draft. He is learning.

"A rookie year is always a tough year," revealed Brown. "You have to get used to a new city and a new coach. I had a lot to learn and the transition from college to pros was difficult because the game became so complex."

Brown is a hitter who excels on stopping the run. In his final year at Purdue, he established a school record of 161 solo tackles. He just loves contact. He started all 15 games he appeared in last year.

"I've always been a big hitter, no matter what my size was," exclaimed Brown. But I worked really hard on the weights, and I am stronger now. Before I was just playing on the ability God gave me. Now I'm working hard to perfect every tool he's given me. I don't think I've come anywhere close to what my potential could be. I'm young and I'm learning. I don't think I've played the best I can play yet."

Miami expected a great deal of help from Jackie Shipp, a number one draft choice from Oklahoma in 1984. He not only has speed but is strong as indicated by the fact that he can bench press 415 pounds. Shipp improved his play on 1985 but the coaches feel he has to be more consistent. Even though he started only 11 games, Shipp finished third in total tackles with 83. It's just that Shipp has carried a monkey on his back since his rookie season that he can't seem to shake.

"It's just that there was so much expected of me," exclaimed Shipp. "Fans and the media feel I'm supposed to be like Lawrence Taylor. But I'm an inside linebacker, not an outside linebacker. The impact isn't the same. I've been cautious to the point that I'm concerned about making a mistake.

"I may be wrong but I don't think any Dolphin ever got the negative publicity I got. I'm going to keep having good games until I can get all those people off my back. I'm not satisfied with being a good player. I want to be a great player. Hopefully, I'm on my way."

What Jay Brophy lacks is strength and speed he compensates with an intense desire to play football. He's made it happen through hard work.

"I'm probably the slowest linebacker we have," offered Brophy. "It wouldn't surprise me if the other linebackers we have are stronger than I am. If it were up to talent, up to the computer, you wouldn't find me on this team. But there's more to football than size and speed.

"Football isn't played in the weight room or on the track. It's a mental game, a game of leverage. And it's aggressiveness. I don't care who you are, I'll hit you. There are a lot of guys who are fast and big as hell but don't make it in pro football. There are a lot of things the computer can't measure.

A deep thigh injury that sidelined him for two months severely hampered rookie Alex Moyer's development last year. He appeared in only 10 games, played well at times and at others showed how inexperience hurt him.

"The thing I have to learn is that everything takes time," said Moyer. "It will take time to be the player I have to be here."

Yet winning was a new experience alone for Moyer. In the four years he played at Northwestern, the Wildcats were 7-36. Nevertheless, he found something positive about it.

"It was discouraging, but you have to look at the plus side," reasoned Moyer. "Like the opportunity to play in the Big Ten and against Big Ten com-

Don McNeal

Bob Brudzinski

Bud Brown

William Judson

Lyle Blackwood

petition. You see a lot of good players."

The injuries that thinned the line-backing unit brought Robin Sendlein to Miami from Minnesota in a trade just before the 1985 season opened. He had to work extra hard to learn the Dolphins' defensive philosophy.

"At first, I felt uncertain out there," admitted Sendlein. "I had to learn new techniques, new terminology a new alignment. It's been totally a new learning situation. It's just a matter of time, as I get the repetition, that I get it cleared up."

The loss of Charles Bowser practically the entire 1985 campaign was a severe blow. It was also a deeply personal one for the four year veteran outside linebacker. His wife was tragically killed in a car crash in October and his injured ankle never came around to enable him to play a single down after the second week of the season.

"There has to be some reason why all of this happened," analyzed Bowser. "For a time all I could think was why?"

Bowser credits linebacker coach Bob Matheson with his development. Matheson, who played at Duke, coached there in Bowser's final season in 1981.

"I wish he would've gotten there two years earlier," claimed Bowser. "Before he came, I had a pretty good idea of how to play. But he taught me all the new techniques and really changed my game for the better. He made me into a much better player."

The injury bugaboo made its presence felt in the secondary, also. First cornerback Don McNeal went down and then safety Mike Kozlowski and cornerback Robert Sowell finished the year on injured reserve.

McNeal's injury gave Paul Lankford a chance to start and he made the most of it after alternating between cornerback and safety. He intercepted four passes and was credited with defensing 14 of them, most on the squad. Before the season, Shula had planned on using him both on the corner and at safety.

"Paul is a very good athlete who hadn't been able to show that he's a number one, so we've made him responsible for both positions," declared Shula. "He has good range as a safety and maybe a little too streamlined for a cornerback. He's built like Mike Haynes of the Raiders."

Lankford was ready to do both.

"I've got to do whatever is needed," was the way he looked at it. "If they want me to play corner, I'll play corner. If they want me to play safety, I'll play safety. And if they tell me they are going to keep me at one position, I won't complain."

Defensive backfield coach Mel Phillips helped Lankford settle in at cornerback.

"He helped me anticipate receivers' moves," disclosed Lankford. "That's been the biggest improvement in my game."

William Judson also came up with four interceptions at the other corner.

Judson, who started every game in 1985, had perhaps his most consistent season, although Shula feels his best years are still ahead. The fact that Judson started every game for the past three years indicates he is a fixture on the left side.

"I had better consistency last year than I did in the past," claimed Judson. "But I admit that at times my concentration has drifted. If you're not getting the pressure and you're not getting tested, you can get a little lax. You have to be extra strong in concentration. If the ball hasn't been thrown your way in several weeks, it throws your timing off."

McNeal's injury was just another in a series of mishaps that has punctuated his career. A number one pick out of Alabama in 1980, McNeal has been hurt in every season except 1982, and was on injured reserve the entire 1983 campaign. McNeal is a walking testimonial for blue Cross with a list of injuries that include: ruptured Achilles tendon; torn knee ligaments; torn hamstring; broken wrist; torn thumb ligaments; fractured forearm and a sprained knee.

"I'm tired of injuries," cried McNeal. "I really am. But all I can do is just keep working. I don't believe in a jinx. I just go out and play hard, that's all I can do. Being out the whole year in 1983, not being able to contribute at all, that was tough. It builds patience. You've got to be patient to wait for your injuries to heal before you can go back.

"Coaches seem to treat you different. The players don't treat you different but you feel distant from the team. It's frustrating. But it's not their fault. When you're hurt, what can you do for them?"

Shula is waiting to see. In fact, Shula, a former defensive back, has a high regard for McNeal.

"Injuries have plagued Don's career and have kept him from being re-graded as one of the outstanding cornerbacks in the NFL," believes Shula. "If he stays healthy, Don McNeal can be one of the best cornerbacks in the league."

Sowell also suffered the injury hex that McNeal did. He had an opportunity to crack the starting lineup after McNeal went down but he got hurt himself.

"I hated to see Mac get hurt," said Sowell, "but I wanted to prove that I can play. It was my chance. All people know about me is that I can play special teams. I wanted to prove that I could play cornerback, too."

All the injuries in the secondary opened up a roster spot for Mike Smith near the end of the season when Sowell was placed on injuried reserve. Smith saw action in seven games.

There is no denying how hard Glenn and Lyle Blackwood play in the secondary. They are the only brother combination playing on the same team in the NFL and they are known as the Bruise Brothers. That's how hard they play. Glenn, at 29, is six years younger than Lyle. The brothers are close.

"He's always intimidated me," joked Glenn.

"I just used to beat him up in the backyard," explained Lyle.

"I think he has always looked up to me," continued Lyle. "Six years at an early age makes a big difference. When he got to high school, I would relate what I was learning in college. When he got to college, I gave him tips on what I was learning in the pros. The quality of coaching improves at every level and I passed it on to him along with all other other things he should know about the game."

One of Glenn's best years was in 1984 when he had six interceptions, and led the NFL for a while.

"I was just lucky," smiled Glenn.

Studley just looked at him. Blackwood is too much of a player for just that.

"He's not just lucky," offered Studley. "In my experience, players make their own luck. Glenn is prepared for what's going to happen on the field. That combination of mental quickness and physical ability is very, very unusual. I've never had a player like him. He not only has great instincts, but he has constructive knowledge of the game. The term 'coach on the field' is over-used and unjustified most of the time, but in his case, it's no exaggeration."

Lyle has reached an age where his football days are numbered. There aren't many 35 year old safeties around the league, and a good reason why he didn't get to start a game last season.

"I played well enough in 1984 to come back for another season," said Lyle. "But football is an emotional game. It's a confidence game. You have to know the people have confidence that you can do the job when you get older. I've had a lot of ups and downs in my career. But there are so many positive things."

Still, both Blackwoods are Shula's type of players, smart and aggressive.

"They line up and play every play," praised Shula. "They give you everything they have. They're the type of players who play self-destruct. They

Paul Lankford

put so much into it that they can't help but come up with a bruised shoulder or knee every once in a while."

In training camp Kozlowski had a shot to move into the starting lineup. After a promising start, the hard-hitting Kozlowski got injured and missed practically the entire season.

"Mike has been sitting in the wings for several years vying for the strong safety job," pointed out Studley. "The job is his. He knows it and he has the bit in his mouth and is running with it. I don't think we have one guy on defense who does as much. He's involved in all our coverages, special teams, goal line defenses, you name it."

Kozlowski had plugged away for six years. His toughness and 38" vertical leap had attracted attention.

"I'm not going to call myself a starter until I've played all 16 games," claimed Kozlowski. "If I'm the starter after the last game of the season, then I'll be happy. Until then, I won't be satisfied."

Bud Brown will never forget his second year on the Dolphins. The feisty 11th round draft choice from Southern Mississippi established himself for the future by leading the club in unassisted tackles with 79 and finished second to Mark Brown in total tackles with 94. Throw in two interceptions, nine defensed passes and five forced fumbles and young Mr. Brown had quite a year indeed in his first season as a starter.

"We had a lot of people out of training camp and Bud was very impressive in his attitude and his hustle and his knowledge of the game," observed Phillips. "He really improved since his rookie season. He's a very astute player and very aggressive."

Phillips calls Brown a natural hitter who plays the game with a lot of emotion. Such emotion sometimes erupts into altercations.

"Sometimes I have a temper," admitted Brown. "It's an emotional game. Somebody pops you, you pop him back. That's one thing I like about football, if they hit you, you can get them back. I really don't care if I get the wrong reputation. I'm not a trouble maker although some people might look at it like that. It's like my father told me: 'Don't start a fight, but don't take nothing from anybody.' "

He sounds just like a Killer Bee...

REGGIE ROBY AND FUAD REVEIZ

Physically they are opposites. One is big with powerful, muscular thighs while the other is shorter with a strange sounding name that sounds like something out of the Arabian Nights. That's where the physical comparisons end. Few around the league will argue that in punter Reggie Roby and kicker Fuad Reveiz the Dolphins possess the strongest kicking unit that anyone can remember.

Roby is so good in fact that the Dolphins have never drafted a kicker since he joined the squad as a sixth round pick from Iowa in 1983. They wouldn't even waste a last round draft choice if only for the purpose of bringing another punter to training camp just to push Roby. It's a situation that has been productive to both Roby and the Dolphins, one in which the punter thoroughly enjoys.

"It makes me motivated when there is no one else in camp to challenge me," revealed Roby. "It just makes me work harder because I like to keep it that way. There are players coming in thinking they have to work hard to get a job. I have to work hard but I already have a job. If I can keep it that way, the better for me."

He indeed has kept it that way, only more so. In his rookie year with Miami, Roby averaged 43.1 yards a punt. The following year he was even better, averaging 44.7 yards a punt. In 1985, Roby continued to boom. His punts averaged 43.7 yards.

What more can he do? While just about any punter in the league would be satisfied with such a consistent performance, Roby is not. Ever mindful of maintaining his consistency, he wants even a better performance over what he has accomplished in three years with his two step, high leg action style which is unlike any other punter. Still, Roby is seeking the ultimate, a punt that will soar so high that its hang time will be clocked at six seconds. It's mind-boggling.

"I think every punter wants to be tops," said Roby. "You want a certain average, a certain net average. Personally, I'd like to set a goal of a net average of 40 yards, which I don't think has ever been done. If I can get a net average of 40 yards, then I don't have to worry about anything else. When I came to Miami three years ago, I worked hard on placements. The

coaches want the ball high, the higher the better. I feel more in control of my kicks than ever before."

"I think I get more power now. I used to pattern my form after Ray Guy, but I decided to alter it. No one else kicks like I do, especially with the two steps. I am harder to block now because I get the ball away faster."

And higher. He works hard in practice by punting 150 balls, running and pumping his legs up even more with weights, a training habit that is shunned by other kickers.

"The size doesn't matter, it's the conditioning," explained Roby. "I'm big on lifting weights. A lot of punters and kickers will not lift weights. If a lineman can bench press 150 pounds do you think he can handle a guy who bench presses 500 pounds? I feel the same way with kicking. You have to be strong to be good."

Roby is unlike any other punter in size. The average size of an NFL punter is about six feet and 193 pounds. At 6-4, 242 pounds, he is by far the biggest in the NFL and could easily be mistaken for a tight end if he didn't walk around at practice with a football under his arms stopping to kick his punts high into the air. His thighs are massive and he gets such tremendous power behind his kicks.

"I'm still young and learning, so who knows how far I can eventually kick?" said Roby. "I'm confident in my ability and if I keep practicing, I think a 49 or 50-yard average might be possible. Some days I wake up and think I must be dreaming. I have the best position in the game and I'm never sore. The biggest injury I've had is probably a sinus headache. It's all a little unreal.

"Maybe it's not a glamour position. It's not like quarterback where the whole offense rises or falls on your performance. But kicking has its own stresses. If I don't punt the ball well past midfield, then my defense is going to have to work harder. If I give the other team good field position, then the heat's on me."

Few will disagree that Roby has certainly made the art of punting a glamour position now.

In fact, Reveiz brought a tinge of glamour with him in his rookie season with the Dolphin last year when he became only the third field goal kicker in Don Shula's 16 years as head coach. Reveiz, a seventh round draft choice from Tennessee, won the field goal kicking job from Eddie Garcia in training camp to take his place along former kickers Garo Yepremian and Uwe von Schamann. The way he performed in his first season, he could outlast both of them combined.

At 5-10, 220 pounds, Reveiz is heavier than most field goal kickers. He also has a powerful and accurate leg that impressed Shula during the hot days of August. Although Reveiz was Tennessee's all-time leading scorer with 314 points, and kicked 71 field goals in four years, including nine from 50 yards or more for an NCAA record, he had an adjustment to make when he put on a Dolphin uniform for the first time. In college he did all of his kicking off a tee. Now he had to quickly adjust to kicking off the ground while at the same time enduring the pressures of competing with von Schamann and Garcia. It didn't seem to bother him at all.

"I knew I had the potential and it was just a matter of working hard at it and letting it come out," disclosed Raviez. "The more you think, the more trouble you get into. The first few days I was out there, I was thinking too much. I was trying to be too perfect, trying too hard to make a quick impression. When I would miss a kick, I would start to panic. I was paying attention to what the other guys were doing. I was even thinking about whether the hold was going to be good. I just didn't want to let anybody down."

As the season progressed, he didn't. Reveiz approached Yepremian's Dolphin record of 118 points by producing 116 chiefly by converting 23 of 26 field goal attempts. Three of his four misses were from 50 yards or more. His biggest field goal perhaps was a 47-yarder in the wind and rain with 4:27 remaining against New England that gave the Dolphins a 30-27 victory and first place in the Eastern Conference the next to final weekend of the regular season.

"I never thought about the score or the conditions," claimed Reveiz. "I just thought of it as just another kick." My high school coach told me something that has stayed with me. He said, 'you're only as good as your next kick.' You have to take them one at a time. Whether you make it or miss it, you can't think about it. The next one won't go in just because the last one did."

As a youngster growing up in Miami, where he once kicked a 60-yard field goal for Miami Sunset High School, Reveiz dreamed about playing for the Dolphins. He couldn't be happier.

"This is something I thought about when I was younger and then when I was in college waiting on the draft," recalled Reveiz. "I'd think how great it would be to stand on the sidelines and wear the aqua and orange. But when I got here I couldn't think like that. It was a whole different situation. I had to go out and do my job and to control my feelings a lot.

"It's a lot like when I was in college and I needed 10 points to set a school record for total points. When I made it there it didn't seem like a big deal. But after the season was over, I was so happy and proud. That's the way I felt after the first year in Miami."

Born in Bogota, Colombia, Reveiz has a strong appeal to Latin fans. He already has a number of television commercials designed for the large Spanish speaking market, including a radio show. That's something he never dreamt about.

June Taylor's Girls

THE MIAMI DOLPHIN CHEERLEADERS

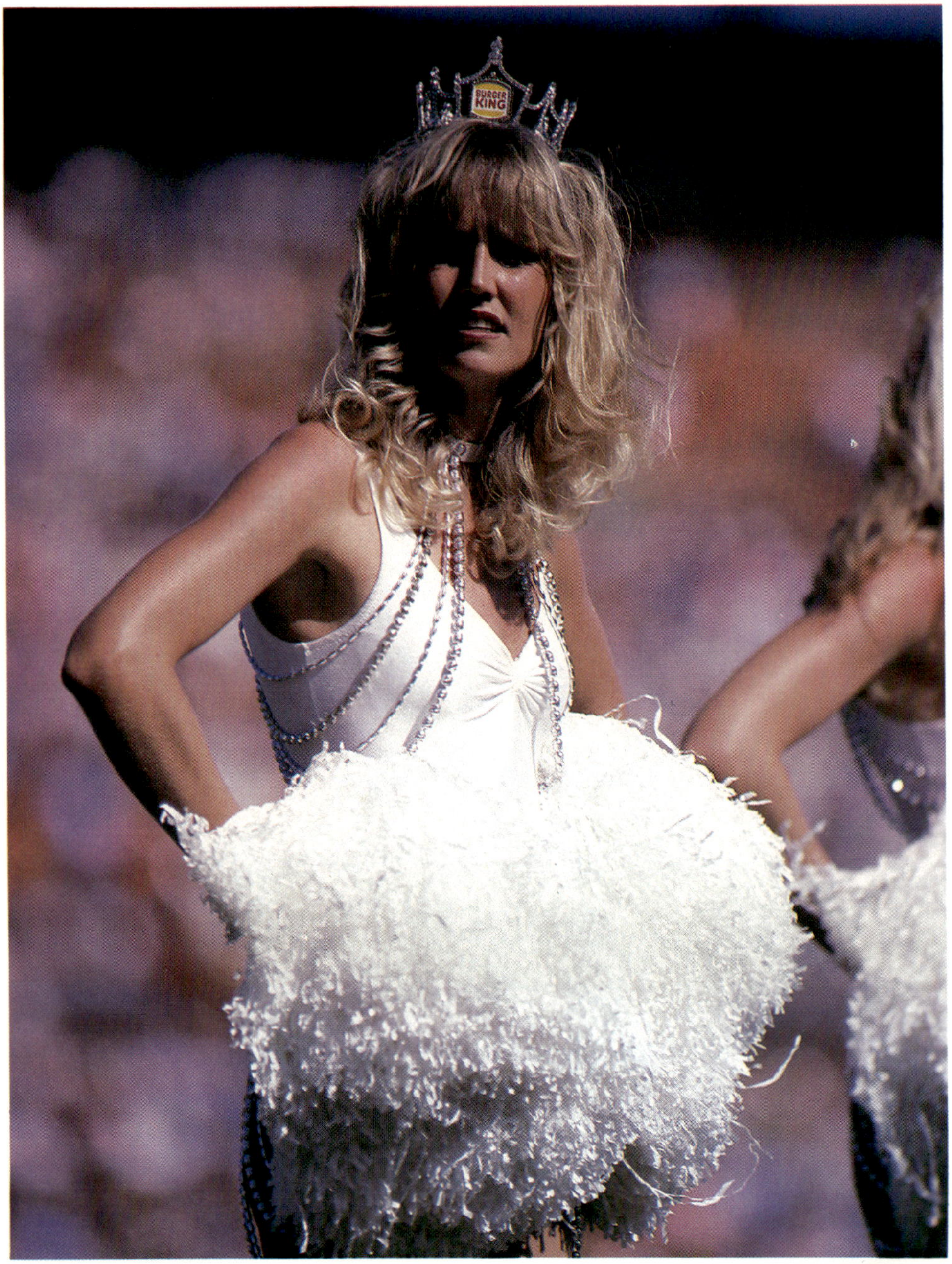

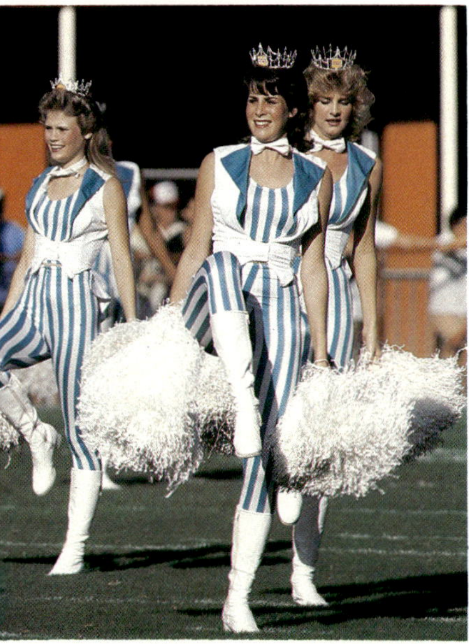

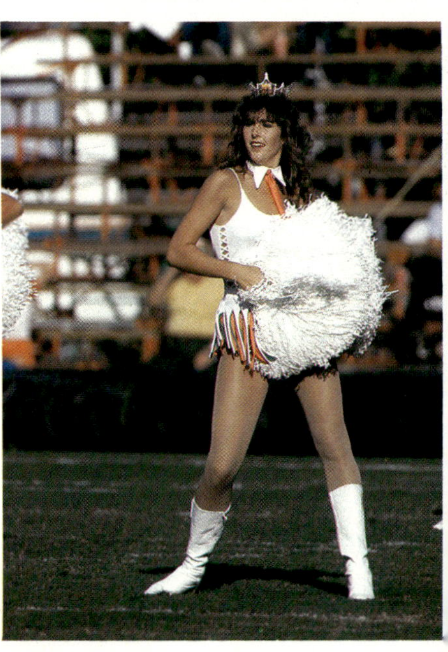

Some of the moves being made on the sidelines during the Dolphin home games can be paralleled to some degree to the ones being made on the field by padded warriors in cleats. There is a certain artistry to a Dan Marino pass, a Mark Duper catch or a Tony Nathan move with the precision movements of the Miami Dolphin Cheerleaders. Both are a sense of art form and both have achieved their goals through a common denominator—hard work.

Many Dolphin fans may dismiss the sight of 32 lovelies as nothing more than window dressing. Don't ever mention anything along those lines to June Taylor, a highly skilled professional, who begins directing her cheerleader contingent as early as June when everyone else is on the golf course far removed from football. Talk about training camp. Look what Taylor has to do. In the course of one weekend she has to look over a group of 400 candidates trying to claim one of the 32 spots on the sideline. Only someone like Taylor, who achieved national acclaim with the June Taylor Dancers on the Jackie Gleason Show of the 1950's, could administer such an undertaking. It's all the more remarkable when realizing that none of the girls are professional dancers and only have been under Taylor's direction since 1980.

"They're down to earth, girl next door types," explains Taylor. "We don't have party girls. The idea of a party is to go to Burger King and have a Coke. We have a very clean, good image. They are pretty, fresh-looking and attractive. I like to please the men but also their wives. We may be cheerleaders for a professional football team but our girls aren't professional cheerleaders. They all have other occupations."

The work is hard and the monetary returns little. The girls have to sacrifice their weekends from summer through the entire length of the football season. The work load consists of eight-hour rehearsals most Saturdays and Sundays in some un-airconditioned gymnasium with little time for a Gatorade break. Even on game day the cheerleaders have to sharpen their act for two hours before the kickoff. All this for $15 a game and an additional $15 for some of the 20 or so charity affairs they appear at each year.

Why should someone give up so much for so little after working a full week in their other occupations? After all, any serious romance has to take a back seat, too. Taylor puts it all into perspective by pointing out that the girls themselves become minor celebrities in their own right and attract autograph seekers in much the same manner as the players in being part of the excitement that is Football Sunday.

June Taylor:

❝They're down to earth, girl next door types.**❞**

"I don't expect to be a movie star or to be discovered or anything like that," exclaims Cheryl Haley, an animal health technologist in Miami. "The first time you step on the field as a Dolphin cheerleader you see the crowd and get tense. You're scared to death. I didn't know what to expect when I started in 1983. You get so worried about being in step. The one thing you have to remember is to keep smiling no matter what."

Sue Paglino, who has been a member of the squad since 1982, can smile now.

"It isn't easy being Dolphin cheerleader," she admits. "It means giving up your social life on weekends during the football season. Miss Taylor is very demanding. She's very professional but demands hard work."

Kerry Wicks, a schoolteacher in Miami agrees.

"Miss Taylor is in total control during our workouts," she says. "Every weekend the cheerleaders have two days of exhausting workouts to look forward to."

Taylor can be charming when the occasion calls for it or intimidating when she has to be. She draws on her vast theatrical experience in not only selecting certain types for the squad but working with them on their poise and mannerisms off the field.

"If they are tall and willowy, they present a far better picture on the field," claims Taylor. "The average height of our squad is around 5-foot-9. It's very difficult to get some of these girls to cut their hair. They'll say, 'Oh my father will die if I cut my hair.' I watch their weight, too. If a cheerleader looks too heavy, I put her on a scale. If she is, and doesn't lose the extra five or so pounds, she's cut from the squad.

"I don't compare the Dolphin cheerleaders with the Cowboy cheerleaders. We are dancers, not clones."

Andy Sidaris, director of Monday Night Football, likes the Dolphin approach.

"I rate them right up there with the best," remarked Sidaris. "I don't know what their bench strength is, but their first line looks damn tough. Sensational in fact. They do a lot of change of outfits which I like. They keep coming out with something that is dazzling every time you look up. I think they're a tribute to the number one sport in America, which is girl-watching. Football is number two and baseball is number three.

"Tall, great figures, great moves. They are choreographed beautifully. I have nothing but praise for those ladies. Put it this way. Anybody can put on a pair of cleats and jam a ball in for a touchdown. But can you make all those moves? Can you attract some attention on the sidelines? I think that's what we're all looking for in America."

Sidaris saves his best for last.

"You might say they're the NFL's class act," he added.

June Taylor likes that.

DOLPHIN STADIUM

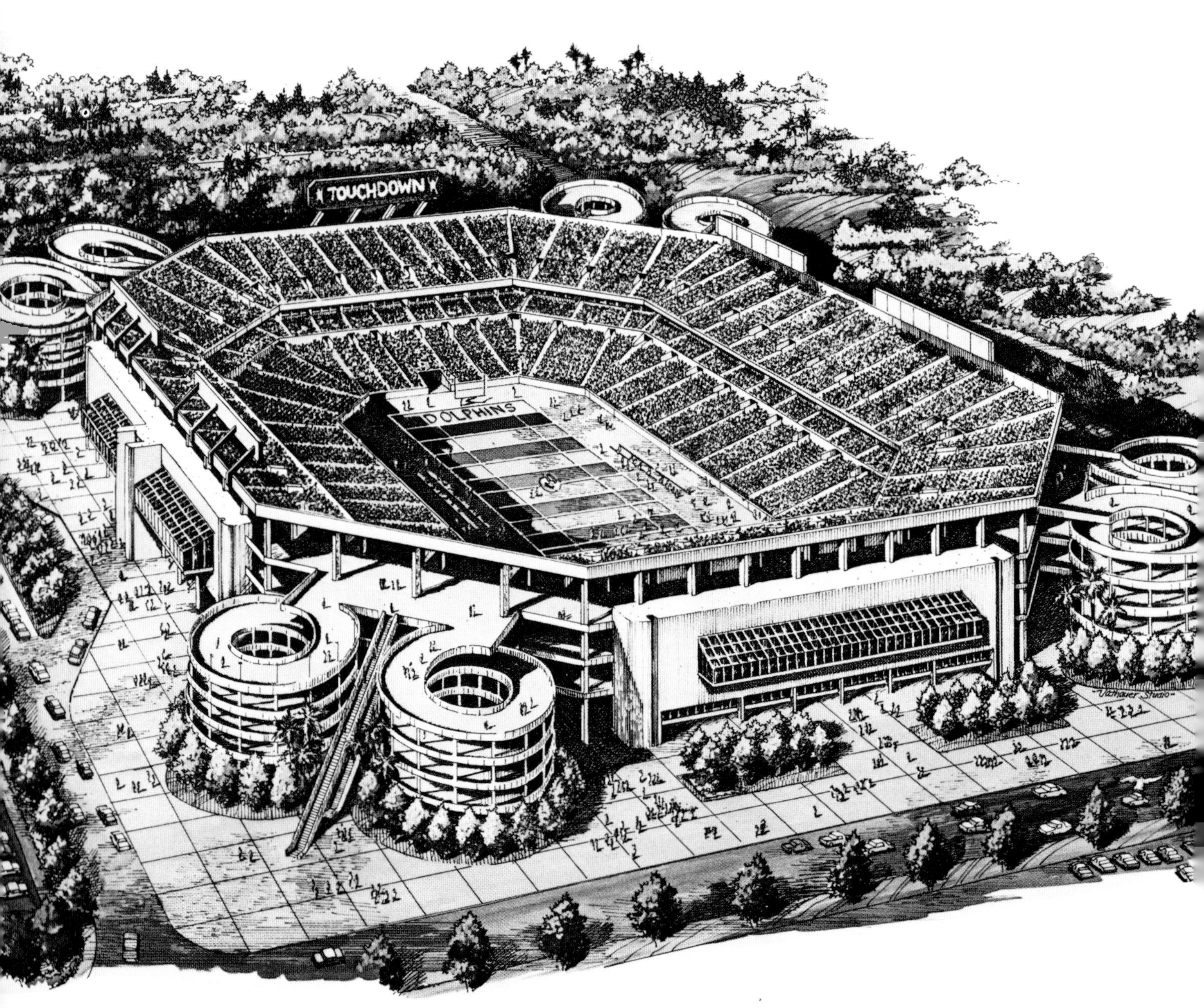

Never one to sit still, Joe Robbie made a dramatic announcement at the Dolphins Award Banquet in 1984 about plans for the erection of a new Dolphin Stadium. The impact was further pronounced when Robbie disclosed that the stadium will be constructed strictly through private funding. Once again the cynics appeared. And once again Robbie proved them wrong. The handsome 73,000 seat stadium will be opened in August of 1987 on a 160 acre tract of land at Lake Lucerne near the Dade-Broward County line. What has made the undertaking even more ambitious is the fact that it is the first privately built and operated stadium in the country in 15 years.

The concept perhaps is more unique in another area—revenue, an area in which Robbie excels, so much so, that he has revolutionized the economics of professional football. Income will come from the sale of 10-year leases of 234 executive suite skyboxes and 10,000 exclusive club seats. If all the leases and seats are sold, and there is no reason why they won't be, the Dolphins will generate $16.5 million in annual payments which is some $500,000 more than the television revenue earned by each of the National Football League's 28 teams, which represents 60% of a club's earnings.

The skyboxes are designed to comfortably seat 10 to 16 people. The cost of the ten-year lease ranges from $290,000 to $650,000. The carpeted suites will contain a wet bar, two television sets and catered food services in an atmosphere conducive to the den in a private home. Climate control will add to the comfort, yet the window can be opened to let in the crowd noise. Skybox tenants will be entitled to valet parking and use of a private elevator to take them to their respective boxes. Besides Dolphin games, boxholders will also have use of their spots for other occasions such as a Bruce Springsteen concert or the possibility of major league baseball games. All they have to do is pay the ticket price for the event scheduled.

The cost of a seat in the Club Level section will go from $6,000 to $14,000 for the ten-year period. The section is located on a level between the skyboxes and the regular stadium seats.

Fans in the club section will have an opportunity to frequent any one of a dozen lounges that circle the stadium. Broken down, the costs aren't that big at all. Membership in most stadium clubs around the league cost $1,000 alone and that doesn't include a single ticket for the game.

"I think the club seat is the best buy in professional sports," pointed out Robbie. "For just more than double the price of a season ticket, you have contoured chairback, arm-rest seats that are wider and more comfortable than those in the stands. These people have food and beverage service in their seating areas and a stadium club with both traditional and closed-circuit television available. They also have preferred parking, and the right of refusal on those seats for concerts or baseball if it becomes available."

Joe Robbie:

> **"I think the club seat is the best buy in professional sports."**

The new stadium has already attracted fans from neighboring cities. Surprisingly, Dolphin fans from Ft.

Lauderdale and the Palm Beach areas have purchased as many season seats for the 1987 inaugural as those from Miami. It didn't surprise Robbie.

"I see the tri-county region as being one big metropolitan area in the next decade," claimed Robbie. "Within the first few years after the stadium is built, Fort Lauderdale will be the hub of that metropolis, and it stands to prosper from the support and enthusiasm it has lent toward the completion of this project."

At first, Robbie had to overcome protests from home owners in Lake Lucerne. He'd been down the road before and wasn't deterred in his efforts toward erecting the stadium.

"We didn't displace anybody but we are beautifying an area that to this point had been used as a refuse dump," explained Robbie. "On top of that, the stadium will stimulate the economy by creating a lot of new jobs. It's beyond me how anybody can find negative aspects about its development."

The success of the Dolphins in recent years have made them an attractive ticket as well as a television vehicle. Over the last 15 years, the Dolphins have gone from the second cheapest seat in the NFL to the third highest.

"Fifteen years ago, we were coming off five years with losing records," pointed out Robbie. "We were trying to break professional sports into the South Florida market. We had to make some sacrifices.

"The price of pro football has gone up considerably. Our overhead has increased dramatically during that time period. We've had a year in which most of the value of our television contract was destroyed by the NFL strike in 1982 which caused an additional financial crunch.

"Tickets haven't gone up nearly as fast as player salaries. Overhead has gone up. Our salaries have increased from $800,000 in 1968 to something in the $10 million area in 1985. What is gratifying is that the season-ticket holders are not paying for the new stadium. The sale of skyboxes and club seats are. Plus, we were using our own money to keep on construction schedule until we obtained permanent financing."

Wonder what Joe Robbie will do next?

THE PLAYERS

BILL BARNETT 70

Defensive End/Tackle ★ Nebraska
7th Year ★ D3, 1980

Played in all 16 regular season games a year ago, but started only one—first game of '85 versus Houston (two tackles)...Used sparingly during the year in place of Mike Charles at nose tackle...Had two tackles against both Houston and Detroit... Forced a fumble against Chicago...Had eight tackles and one assist on the year with one fumble recovered and forced...Reserve specialist, ready to help coming off the bench...Top-notch special teams performer...Appeared in 16 games at nose tackle in '84 with one start.

Ht: 6-4 Wt: 260
Born: 5/10/56

BOB BAUMHOWER 73

Defensive Tackle ★ Alabama
9th Year ★ D2, 1977

Spent entire 1985 season on injured reserve list after knee surgery...Though, intense competitor looks to battle back to regain All-Pro form of seasons past...Courageously endured injury-filled 1984 season, starting 18 or 19 regular season and playoff games...Still managed to earn fifth straight Pro Bowl berth (was unable to play due to injuries) ...Also was chosen Second Team All-Pro by AP and Second Team All-AFC by UPI...Finished '84 season with 56 total tackles (44,12) and two QB sacks for -20 yards...Also had pair of fumble recoveries and one pass defensed...Remains the only Dolphin defensive tackle ever named to the Pro Bowl (1979, 1981-84)...Won most honors ever in 1983 including NFL Defensive Player of the Year (Pro Football Weekly), First Team All-Pro (AP), First Team All-AFC (UPI) and Pro Bowl starter.

Ht: 6-5 Wt: 265
Born: 8/4/55

WOODY BENNETT 34

Fullback ★ Miami (Fla.)
8th year ★ FA, 1980

Played in all 16 games a year ago, starting 13... Dolphins' starting fullback, was used more as a blocker in '85 than previous season when led team in rushing...Considered by many to be team's best blocker among the backs...Played a little at tight end a year ago in two tight end situations and when injuries depleted the TE corps... Team's fourth-leading rusher with 256 yards on 54 carries...Had four receptions for 63 yards versus Kansas City...Top ground effort came at Buffalo when he scampered for 59 yards on 10 carries... Became the starting fullback in game three of 1984 due to knee injury to Andra Franklin... Responded by leading Dolphins in rushing with 606 yards on 144 carries plus seven touchdowns.

Ht: 6-2 Wt: 225
Born: 3/24/56

DOUG BETTERS 75

Defensive End ★ Nevada-Reno
9th year ★ D6, 1978

Started 14 games a year ago...Coming off an off-year, hopes to rebound with fine '86 campaign... Blocked a PAT versus Houston in season's first game last fall...Second on team with 6.5 sacks... Very consistent performer despite injuries...Had five tackles on seven occasions, including AFC title game with New England...had sack and forced fumble versus Jets (11/10)...Finished season in seventh place on team tackle list with 56 (53-3)...was named Dolphins' Defensive Lineman of the Year by South Florida media...Started all 16

Ht: 6-7 Wt: 265
Born: 6/11/56

regular season games plus the three post-season contests...Led all Miami defensive linemen in tackles with 67 on 54 solos and 13 assists...Also had team-leading 14 QB sacks plus three passes defensed and a fumble recovery.

GLENN BLACKWOOD 47

Safety ★ Texas
8th Year ★ D8, 1979

Stands third on all-time Dolphin interception chart with 24, behind Jake Scott (35) and Dick Anderson (34)...Also fourth on Dolphin career interception yards list with 371...Has led Miami in interceptions each of the past two seasons and three of the last five...Started 14 games last year and paced team with six interceptions...Tied for eighth in the AFC in interceptions...Calls Miami defensive signals...Recognized as one of the smartest players in the league...Enjoyed an eight-tackle, three-assist day versus the Jets (10/14)...Had four tackles, two interceptions and one fumble recovery versus Indianapolis (11/17)...Two interceptions, four tackles and an assist versus New England (12/16) ...Ninth on the team in tackles with 56 (44-12)... Prior to 1985 he started every Dolphin regular-season contest for four years.

Ht: 6-0 Wt: 190
Born: 2/23/57

LYLE BLACKWOOD 42

Safety ★ Texas Christian
14th Year ★ FA, 1981

Played in all 16 games a year ago but did not start any...Good special teams performer...Lost starting job early in the year but came on late in season ...Played in place of brother Glenn when needed ...Had three tackles each versus Bears and Cleveland...Dependable off the bench...Tied for 10th with Willie West on all-time Dolphin interception chart with 13 career pilfers...Ended season with 19 tackles (15-4)...Had interception against New England (1)...Along with Glenn, continues as the only pair of brothers playing on the same team in the NFL...Prior to 1985 he started all but two games since his Miami arrival during the 1981 season.

Ht: 6-1 Wt: 190
Born: 5/24/51

KIM BOKAMPER 58

Defensive End ★ San Jose State
10th Year ★ D1b, 1976

Played in all 16 games a year ago, starting 12, despite being bothered by shoulder and neck injuries...Blocked a PAT versus Indianapolis (9/15)... Pass rush specialist...Had three tackles each against Pittsburgh and Buffalo (2)...Had three tackles and two assists in AFC title game with New England...Finished season with 22 tackles (19-3) ...Saw action in 11 games in 1984 with 10 starts at right defensive end...Contributed 29 total tackles (24,5), four quarterback sacks (-35 yards) and two passes defensed...Former linebacker whose outstanding mobility allows for excellent pass rushing ability.

Ht: 6-6 Wt: 255
Born: 9/25/54

"

CHARLES BOWSER 56

Linebacker ★ Duke
5th Year ★ D4, 1982

Played in only two regular-season games (started both) a year ago for the Dolphins...Suffered severe ankle sprain in second game of season (Indianapolis)...Registered four tackles and one sack in season's first contest at Houston...Began to emerge as one of the top pass-rushing linebackers in AFC in 1984...Started 15 games in regular season and finished second on squad in total tackles with 76 on 59 solos and 17 assists...Other stats included nine quarterback sacks (second on club), one fumble recovery, three forced fumbles and three passes defensed...Started all 16 games for the Dolphins at right outside LB in 1983.

Ht: 6-3 Wt: 235
Born: 10/2/59

JAY BROPHY 53

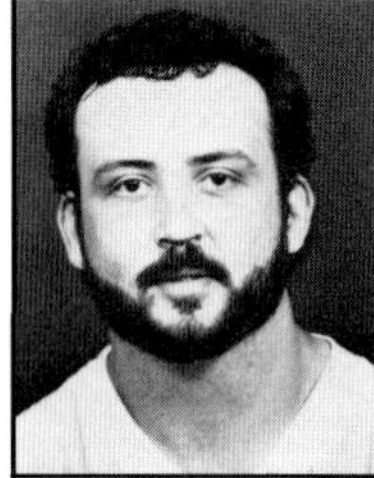

Linebacker ★ Miami (Fla)
3rd Year ★ D2, 1984

Played in 16 games a year ago, starting six...A street-fighter, very competitive...Three tackles, one sack and an interception versus Kansas City ...Had five tackles each against New England in 12/16 game and AFC title matchup...Four tackles versus Cleveland in post season...Finished regular season with 40 tackles (35-5) and added 10 more during the playoffs...Has never been totally healthy for an extended period of time in a Dolphin uniform...Played in 11 games with five starts as a rookie in 1984...Honored as Dolphins' Rookie of the Year in voting by South Florida media.

Ht: 6-3 Wt: 233
Born: 7/27/60

BUD BROWN 43

Safety ★ Southern Miss.
3rd Year ★ D11, 1984

Started all 16 games a year ago...Finished second on the team in tackles with 94 stops (79-15)...Led Dolphins with five fumble recoveries...Second on the team with nine passes defensed...Also added two interceptions...Has reputation as hard hitter, hard worker...Had 12 tackles and interception versus Denver...Added nine tackles against the Jets (2) and Bills (2)...Made eight first hits, two assists, an interception and recovered a fumble in second game versus the Patriots... Came back to record five tackles and recover a fumble in AFC title game against the Pats.

Ht: 6-0 Wt: 194
Born: 4/19/61

MARK BROWN 51

Linebacker ★ Purdue
4th Year ★ D9, 1983

Started 15 games last season and led Dolphins in tackles for second straight year with 96 (78-18)... Suffered ankle injury late in the year...Small, but quick...Also picked up a sack, an interception and two fumble recoveries...Had nine tackles in wins over Indianapolis (1) and the Bears... Recorded eight stops and one interception versus New England (1)...Five tackles, a sack and recovered fumble against the Jets (2).

Ht: 6-2 Wt: 230
Born: 7/18/61

BOB BRUDZINSKI 59

Linebacker ★ Ohio State
10th Year ★ Trade, 1981

Started 13 games a year ago...Finished fourth on the team with 71 tackles (56-15)...Added three sacks, an interception, two fumble recoveries and five passes defensed...Enjoyed banner post season as he led Dolphins with 24 tackles, including 19 versus New England in the AFC title matchup ...Steady work, consistent play are his trademarks ...Compliments High Green, giving Dolphins potent one-two punch at linebacker...Had 14 tackles (seven first hits, seven assists) against Green Bay ...Recorded 10 tackles in first game versus the Jets...Made seven stops, two assists, a sack and an interception versus Detroit...In 1984 started all 16 regular season games, having not missed a start since 1981 Miami arrival (73 games).

Ht: 6-4 Wt: 233
Born: 1/1/55

JOE CARTER 23

Running Back ★ Alabama
3rd Year ★ D4, 1984

Played in 10 games a year ago...Had up-and-down season...Has quickest first step of any back on the team...Suffered a pulled thigh muscle which forced him to miss some action...Finished 1985 with 76 yards rushing on 14 carries...Also had two receptions for seven yards...Had four kickoff returns for 82 yards...Was team's leading rusher in the two playoff games, gaining 62 yards in eight carries (for an impressive 7.8 yards per rush average)...Top game of '85 came in the AFC title matchup with New England when he ran for 56 yards on just six carries...Best regular-season performance also came against the Pats when he rushed for 50 yards on eight carries in the second contest between the two teams.

Ht: 5-11 Wt: 198
Born: 6/23/62

MIKE CHARLES 71

Defensive End ★ Syracuse
4th Year ★ D2, 1983

Started all 16 games a year ago and was named team's Outstanding Defensive Lineman...Led team with seven sacks...Looking for more consistency this fall...Finished fifth on team with 61 tackles (52-9)...Very talented performer...Had eight tackles (seven-one) and a sack in second game versus New England...Recorded six tackles and a sack against the Bills (1) and Bears...Enjoyed a five-tackle performance against New England in the AFC title game.

Ht: 6-4 Wt: 287
Born: 9/23/62

STEVE CLARK 76

Guard ★ Utah
5th Year ★ D9a, 1982

Played in all 16 games in 1985...Very valuable with his keen ability to play both the offensive and defensive lines...After injury to Jeff Toews, he became number one...Finished season as a starter ...Smart, steady performer...Had a tackle versus Denver, Chicago and in playoffs versus Cleveland ...Performed in 12 regular season games in 1984 plus all three playoff games for Miami...Backs up Roy Foster at the Dolphins' guard spots...Had been moved to offensive line in '83 after previously playing on the defensive line...is a valuable special teams player.

Ht: 6-4 Wt: 260
Born: 8/2/60

MARK CLAYTON   83

Ht: 5-9 Wt: 185
Born: 4/8/61

Wide Receiver ★ Louisville
4th Year ★ D8b, 1983

Recognized as one of the finest receivers in all of professional football…Ninth all-time leading Dolphin receiver with 149 catches, 2,499 yards (16.8 average) and 23 touchdowns…Also 10th on the all-time Miami scoring chart with 24 TDS for 144 points…Holds Dolphin single-season records for most receptions (73), reception yards (1389) and touchdown catches (18)…18 TD receptions, which came in 1984, is also an NFL record, breaking former mark of 17 held by Don Hutson (Green Bay, 1942), Elroy Hirsch (L.A. Rams, 1951) and Bill Groman (Houston, 1961)…Those 18 scores tied Marcus Allen of the Raiders for most TDs by any NFL player in '84…His 177 yards on nine catches (two TDs) vs. the Raiders (12/2/84) is the sixth-best single-game performance in Dolphin history…Started all 16 regular-season games for Miami in '85…Finished second on the team in receptions (70), only two behind leader Tony Nathan…1985 stats included 70 catches, 996 yards (14.2 per catch) and four TDs…Had four receptions for 56 yards in postseason action…Named team's outstanding receiver for second straight campaign…First on the team in pass reception yardage…Eighth in the AFC in receptions, seventh in the AFC in reception yardage…Fell short of personal goal of 1,000 yards receiving (four yards).

JOHN CORKER   93

Ht: 6-6 Wt: 245
Born: 12/29/58

Linebacker ★ Oklahoma State
4th Year ★ FA, 1986

Has the potential to step in and contribute immediately…Signed by Dolphins as a free agent 5/19/86…Enjoyed outstanding career in the United States Football League the last three seasons…Named that league's first-ever Defensive Player of the Year in 1983 as a member of the Michigan Panthers…Registered 116 tackles (86, 30) in '83…Also led USFL in both sacks (28) and yards lost (199)…Had five fumble recoveries (second in USFL), two interceptions and six passes defensed to go with other stats in '83 season…In one three-game span, recorded 15 sacks, including six sacks in a game against the New Jersey Generals…Had at least one quarterback sack in 12 of Michigan's 18 regular-season games in 1983…Was a consensus first-team All-USFL selection in both 1983 and '84.

RON DAVENPORT   30

Ht: 6-2 Wt: 230
Born: 12/22/62

Fullback ★ Louisville
2nd Year ★ D6b, 1985

Enjoyed impressive rookie season for the Dolphins in 1985…Played in all 16 regular-season contests, starting once…Was team's second-leading rusher with 370 yards on 98 carries (3.8 average)…Led team with 11 TDs rushing and 13 overall…13 scores was good for third place in AFC and was second highest single-season total in Dolphin history (behind 18 by Mark Clayton in 1984)…Tied Marcus Allen for most rushing TDs (11) in NFL…Was 27th in the AFC in rushing… Fifth in the NFL in scoring (non-kickers)…Had longest run from scrimmage (33 yards) for the Dolphins in 1985…Will challenge Woody Bennett for starting job…Strong, powerful runner…Very good when close to goal line…Bruising back… Second on the team in scoring (78 points) behind Fuad Reveiz (116 points)…Caught 13 passes this

---

past season for 74 yards (5.7 per catch) and two scores.

JEFF DELLENBACH   65

Ht: 6-6 Wt: 280
Born: 2/14/63

Tackle ★ Wisconsin
2nd Year ★ D4b, 1985

Played in 11 games a year ago, starting only against the Bills in Buffalo on November 24…Raw talent who aided the Dolphins last year when injuries arose…Stepped in and did admirable job… *COLLEGE*: Enjoyed standout career at University of Wisconsin…As a senior, was selected Third Team All-America and UPI Honorable Mention All-America…Was also chosen First Team All-Big Ten by AP and UPI and was tabbed as Big Ten's Offensive Lineman of the Year by conference broadcasters.

MARK DENNARD   63

Ht: 6-1 Wt: 260
Born: 11/2/55

Center ★ Texas A&M
8th Year ★ FA, 1986

Re-signed in the off-season after being waived by the Eagles in April when Buddy Ryan took over… Played for Miami for first five seasons in the NFL… Traded to Philadelphia on March 7, 1984, for a third-round draft choice in 1985…Possesses good quickness and strength…Known for his 100 percent effort…Takes pride in his physical and mental toughness…Called a brawler by Dolphin head coach Don Shula…Started all 16 games for Philadelphia and did not miss a single offensive play in 1985…Also got starting call in all 16 games in '84…Spent his first NFL season on injured reserve after suffering broken and dislocated fingers in a preseason game with Philadelphia… Assumed starting role in 1979 when longtime standout Jim Langer was injured in ninth game, ending a streak of 117 consecutive starts.

MARK DUPER   85

Wide Receiver ★ NW State (La.)
5th Year ★ D2, 1982

Early-season injury sidelined one of professional football's most exciting performers…Showed his keen ability to come back, when in his first game against the Jets on Nov. 10, he set a Dolphin record with 217 yards on eight receptions…In his first half back, he caught a 60-yard TD toss from Dan Marino to give the Dolphins their first lead… Then, with :49 left to play he hauled in a one-handed 50-yard TD pass from Marino to lead the Dolphins to a 21-17 victory…Including the Jets game, Duper compiled 555 yards on 31 receptions over the next six games as the Dolphins closed the regular season without a loss…Started eight of nine contests in '85 (came off the bench against the Jets)…Suffered his injury against Houston in the season's first game, but left the lineup the next week versus Indianapolis…His 217 yards versus New York was third best in AFC in '85…Had four catches for 95 yards and a TD against Houston…Was ranked 43rd in the AFC in receiving at season's end…Finished 1985 as the team's fifth-leading receiver with numbers of 35-650-18.6-three TDs…Had three catches for 45 yards in the playoffs…One of the fastest receivers in the NFL, has run a 4.3 40-yard dash in Dolphin camp…Started all 16 games and had 71 catches for 1,306 yards (18.4 average) and eight touchdowns in 1984.

Ht: 5-9 Wt: 192
Born: 1/25/59

ROY FOSTER   61

Guard ★ Southern Cal.
5th Year ★ D1, 1982

Earned first Pro Bowl honor last season…Was alternate the year before…Durable, started all 16 regular-season games for the Dolphins…Big reason why Miami allowed the fewest quarterback sacks in the NFL for the third straight season (19) …Very consistent performer…Replaced Miami legend Bob Kuechenberg…Has potential to become a great one before career is over…UPI first-team All-AFC selection…Just beginning to come into his own and gain just recognition…Mixture of speed and strength has been responsible for emergence as solid offensive lineman… Amazingly, is the first alumnus of USC to ever play for Dolphins…Started all 16 regular season games for Dolphins in 1984 at left guard position …Also started Miami's three post-season contests …After shuttling between tackle and guard positions, remained at guard beginning in '83.

Ht: 6-4 Wt: 275
Born: 5/24/60

JON GIESLER   79

Tackle ★ Michigan
8th Year ★ D1. 1979

Started 13 games a year ago…Played with pain, showed guts and many times left lockerroom after games on crutches…For his efforts was named NFL's "Macho-Man" of the year by Sports Illustrated following '85 campaign…Was a key reason why Miami allowed the fewest quarterback sacks in the NFL for the third straight season (19)…Real battler, blue-collar performer…Very strong player, is equally adept at run or pass blocking…Started all regular season games in 1984…Was selected as an AFC Pro Bowl alternate and was chosen by UPI as Second Team All-AFC…Personally, allowed only one sack and had just two holding penalties in '84.

Ht: 6-5 Wt: 265
Born: 12/23/56

CLEVELAND GREEN   74

Tackle ★ Southern
8th Year ★ FA, 1979

Started all 11 games a year ago…Reliability, consistency are his trademarks…Doesn't make many mistakes…Ankle injury slowed him a bit in 1985… Prior to 1984 was Dolphins' top reserve on the offensive line since beating the odds to make club as free agent in 1979…Saw action in all 16 games in 1984 for Dolphins and had 12 starts (also started all three playoff contests)…Also has been utilized extensively on special teams…Has continued to improve while learning blocking techniques of offensive linemen.

Ht: 6-3 Wt: 262
Born: 9/11/57

HUGH GREEN   55

Linebacker ★ Pittsburgh
6th Year ★ Trade, 1985

Joined the Dolphins in October and immediately added spark and intensity to the Miami defensive attack…Started right away…Acquired from Tampa Bay on October 9 for first- and second-round draft picks in '86…Started 11 games…Had his only interception of 1985 against his old team (Tampa Bay)…Former Pittsburgh standout glad to be back with another former Panther, Dan Marino …Named Dolphin outstanding linebacker for 1985…Looking to regain All-Pro form of years past…Should be potent power after being in camp for full year…Can play every down in every situation…Considered by many to have the best tools of any Dolphin LB ever…Sixth on the team with 58 tackles (46-12) in 1985…Added five sacks, an interception, two forced fumbles and four passes defensed…Combining Tampa Bay stats, he had 95 tackles (76-19), 7 1/2 sacks, one interception, three forced fumbles and four passes defensed…Had nine tackles versus New England (1) and picked up seven with two sacks against Buffalo (1)…Enjoyed fine post season with 17 stops (nine versus Cleveland, eight against New England in AFC title tilt)…Earned six tackles at Detroit, and against the Jets (2) and Indianapolis (2)…Considered one of pro football's premier defensive players…While with Tampa Bay, missed opportunity for a third consecutive Pro Bowl start in '84 after sustaining multiple injuries in an October, 1984 auto accident.

Ht: 6-2 Wt: 225
Born: 7/27/59

LORENZO HAMPTON   27

Running Back ★ Florida
2nd Year ★ D1, 1985

Played in all 16 games, starting once, during rookie year of 1985 with Dolphins…Named Miami's Tommy Fitzgerald Award winner for most outstanding rookie in 1985 training camp… Explosive runner, possesses equally impressive pass-catching ability…Tied Tony Nathan's single-season team kickoff return mark of 45…His 1,020 yards on kickoff returns was second best in Dolphin history behind the 1,136 yards by Mercury Morris in 1969…Averaged 22.7 yards per return a year ago…Was seventh in the AFC in KO returns and 28th in the AFC in rushing…Along with Joe Carter will challenge Tony Nathan for starting berth…Was Miami's third-leading rusher with 369 yards on 105 carries (3.5) average and three scores…Also hauled in eight passes for 56 yards …Had nine kickoff returns for 161 yards (17.9 average) in the two 1985 playoff games.

Ht: 6-0 Wt: 212
Born: 3/12/62

1986 VETERAN ROSTER

NO.	NAME	POS.	HT.	WT.	BIRTH-DATE	NFL EXP.	COLLEGE	HOMETOWN	HOW ACQUIRED
70	Barnett, Bill	DE/DT	6-4	260	5/10/56	7	Nebraska	Stillwater, Minn.	D3-'80
73	Baumhower, Bob	DT	6-5	265	8/4/55	9	Alabama	Palm Beach Gardens, Fla.	D2-'77
34	Bennett, Woody	FB	6-2	225	3/24/56	8	Miami (Fla.)	York, Pa.	FA-80
75	Betters, Doug	DE	6-7	265	6/11/56	9	Nevada-Reno	Arlington Heights, Ill.	D6-'78
47	Blackwood, Glenn	S	6-0	190	2/23/57	8	Texas	San Antonio, Texas	D8b-79
42	Blackwood, Lyle	S	6-1	190	5/24/51	14	Texas Christian	San Antonio, Texas	FA-'81
58	Bokamper, Kim	DE	6-6	255	9/25/54	10	San Jose State	Milpitas, Calif.	D1b-'76
56	Bowser, Charles	LB	6-3	235	10/2/59	5	Duke	Plymouth, N.C.	D4-'82
53	Brophy, Jay	LB	6-3	233	7/27/60	3	Miami (Fla.)	Akron, Ohio	D2-'84
43	Brown, Bud	S	6-0	194	4/19/61	3	Southern Miss.	DeKalb, Miss.	D11-'84
51	Brown, Mark	LB	6-2	230	7/18/61	4	Purdue	Inglewood, Calif.	D9-'83
59	Brudzinski, Bob	LB	6-4	233	1/1/55	10	Ohio State	Fremont, Ohio	Trade-'81
23	Carter, Joe	RB	5-11	198	6/23/62	3	Alabama	Starkville, Miss.	D4-'84
71	Charles, Mike	DE	6-4	287	9/23/62	4	Syracuse	Newark, N.J.	D2-'83
98	Chickillo, Tony	NT	6-4	270	7/8/60	2	Miami (Fla.)	Miami, Fla.	FA-'86
76	Clark, Steve	G	6-4	260	8/2/60	5	Utah	Salt Lake City, Utah	D9a-'82
83	Clayton, Mark	WR	5-9	175	4/8/61	4	Louisville	Indianapolis, Ind.	D8b-'83
57A	Corker, John	LB	6-6	245	12/29/58	4	Oklahoma State	Miami, Fla.	FA-'86
30	Davenport, Ron	FB	6-2	230	12/22/62	2	Louisville	Atlanta, Ga.	D6b-'85
65	Dellenbach, Jeff	T	6-6	280	2/14/63	2	Wisconsin	Wausau, Wis.	D4b-'85
63	Dennard, Mark	C	6-1	260	11/2/55	8	Texas A&M	Bay City, Texas	FA-'86
85	Duper, Mark	WR	5-9	187	1/25/59	5	NW State (La.)	Moreauville, La.	D2-'82
81	Farmer, George	WR	5-10	175	12/5/58	4	Southern	Garden, Calif.	FA-'86
78	Foster, Jerome	DE	6-3	275	7/25/60	3	Ohio State	Detroit, Mich.	FA-'86
61	Foster, Roy	G	6-4	275	5/24/60	5	Southern Cal	Los Angeles, Calif.	D1-'82
79	Giesler, Jon	T	6-5	265	12/23/56	8	Michigan	Woodville, Ohio	D1-'79
74	Green, Cleveland	T	6-3	262	9/11/57	8	Southern	Bolton, Miss.	FA-'79
55	Green, Hugh	LB	6-2	225	7/27/59	6	Pittsburgh	Natchez, Miss.	Trade-'85
27	Hampton, Lorenzo	RB	6-0	212	3/12/62	2	Florida	Lake Wales, Fla.	D1-'85
84	Hardy, Bruce	TE	6-5	232	6/1/56	9	Arizona State	Bingham, Utah	D9-'78
88	Heflin, Vince	WR	6-0	185	7/7/59	5	Central State (Ohio)	Dayton, Ohio	FA-'82
29	Hobley, Liffort	S	6-1	200	5/12/62	2	Louisiana State	Shreveport, La.	FA-'86
11	Jensen, Jim	WR/QB	6-4	215	11/14/58	6	Boston University	Doylestown, Pa.	D11-'81
87	Johnson, Dan	TE	6-3	240	5/17/60	4	Iowa State	New Hope, Minn.	D7a-'82
49	Judson, William	CB	6-2	190	3/26/59	5	South Carolina St.	Atlanta, Ga.	D8-'81
40	Kozlowski, Mike	S	6-1	198	2/24/56	7	Colorado	Encinitas, Calif.	D10b-'79
44	Lankford, Paul	CB	6-2	187	6/15/58	5	Penn State	Farmingdale, N.Y.	D3-'82
66	Lee, Larry	G/C	6-2	263	9/10/59	6	UCLA	Dayton, Ohio	FA-'85
72	Lee, Ronnie	G	6-4	265	12/24/56	8	Baylor	Tyler, Texas	Trade-'84
99	Little, George	DT	6-4	278	6/27/63	2	Iowa	Duquesne, Pa.	D3a-'85
13	Marino, Dan	QB	6-4	214	9/15/61	4	Pittsburgh	Pittsburgh, Pa.	D1-'83
28	McNeal, Don	CB	5-11	192	5/6/58	6	Alabama	Atmore, Ala.	D1-'80
91	Moore, Mack	DE	6-4	258	3/4/59	2	Texas A&M	Monroe, La.	D6a-'81
89	Moore, Nat	WR	5-9	188	9/19/51	13	Florida	Miami, Fla.	D3-'74
54	Moyer, Alex	LB	6-1	221	10/25/63	2	Northwestern	Detroit, Mich.	D3b-'85
22	Nathan, Tony	RB	6-0	206	12/14/56	8	Alabama	Birmingham, Ala.	D3a-'79
39	Neal, Speedy	FB	6-2	254	8/26/62	2	Miami	Key West, Fla.	FA-'86
82	Oatis, Victor	WR	5-11	185	1/6/59	2	NW State (La.)	Winnsboro, La.	FA-'86
96	Pegues, Jeff	LB	6-2	241	11/19/62	1	East Carolina	Laurinburg, N.C.	FA-'86
7	Reveiz, Fuad	PK	5-11	222	2/24/63	2	Tennessee	Bogota, Colombia	D7-'85
4	Roby, Reggie	P	6-2	243	7/30/61	4	Iowa	Waterloo, Iowa	D6-'83
26	Rose, Donovan	CB	6-1	190	3/9/57	2	Hampton Institute	Norfolk, Va.	FA-'86
80	Rose, Joe	TE	6-3	230	6/24/57	7	California	Marysville, Calif.	D7-'80
86	Sampleton, Lawrence	TE	6-6	238	9/25/59	4	Texas	Sequin, Texas	FA-'86
52	Sendlein, Robin	LB	6-3	225	12/1/58	6	Texas	Las Vegas, Nev.	Trade-'85
50	Shipp, Jackie	LB	6-2	236	3/19/62	3	Oklahoma	Stillwater, Okla.	D1-'84
18	Smith, Mike	CB	6-0	171	10/24/62	2	Texas-El Paso	Houston, Texas	D4a-'85
21	Smith, Ricky	CB/S	6-0	190	7/20/60	4	Alabama State	Pensacola, Fla.	FA-'86
45	Sowell, Robert	CB	5-11	175	6/23/61	4	Howard	Columbus, Ohio	FA-'83
57	Stephenson, Dwight	C	6-2	255	11/20/57	7	Alabama	Hampton, Va.	D2-'80
10	Strock, Don	QB	6-5	225	11/27/50	13	Virginia Tech	Pottstown, Pa.	D5-'73
68	Thomas, Kelly	T	6-6	270	9/9/60	3	Southern Cal	La Mirada, Calif.	FA-'86
60	Toews, Jeff	G-C	6-3	255	11/4/57	8	Washington	San Jose, Calif.	D2-'79
32	Vigorito, Tom	WR/RB	5-10	190	10/23/59	4	Virginia	Wayne, N.J.	D5b-'81

BRUCE HARDY   84

Ht: 6-5 Wt: 232
Born: 6/1/56

Tight End ★ Arizona State
9th Year ★ D9, 1978

Enjoyed finest season in Dolphin uniform a year ago...Named WIOD's Special Teams Player of the Year...Started all 16 regular season games for Miami...Took advantage of TE injuries in pre-season and became starter...Finished fourth on team with 39 receptions for 409 yards and four TDs...Now sixth on the all-time Dolphin reception chart with 169-1685 and 18 TDs...Very dependable...Blocks, runs and catches equally well...Had career-high seven catches (for 84 yards) against Pittsburgh...Made key 22-yard grab in last-second drive to set up winning points to defeat Steelers...Also had five catches for 52 yards and two scores against Buffalo (2)...Aided Dolphins against Cleveland in playoffs with five receptions for 51 yards.

VINCE HEFLIN   88

Ht: 6-0 Wt: 185
Born: 7/7/59

Wide Receiver ★ Central State (Ohio)
5th Year ★ FA, 1982

Was released in final cut a year ago but came back when Tom Vigorito was injured...Played in five games for Miami...Enjoyed an excellent outing versus Denver when he grabbed two passes for 57 yards including a 46-yard TD toss from Dan Marino...Also had two receptions for 21 yards against Indianapolis (1)...Finished 1985 with six catches for 98 yards (16.3 average) and one TD...A versatile performer, can play on special teams, at wide receiver or as a return specialist.

JIM JENSEN   11

Ht: 6-4 Wt: 215
Born: 11/14/58

Wide Receiver/
Quarterback ★ Boston University
6th Year ★ D11, 1981

Played in all 16 games in 1985...Held out in pre-season camp a year ago but came back same day as Dan Marino...Can play quarterback, wide receiver or tight end...Excellent special teams performer...Very tough competitor, has "head hunter" reputation...Had only one reception last year, a four-yard TD grab from Marino against Tampa Bay...Had three first hits, one assist for four tackles in '85...Achieved national publicity in '84 by playing quarterback, wide receiver, tight end, punt snapper and on special teams at various times.

DAN JOHNSON   87

Ht: 6-3 Wt: 240
Born: 5/17/60

Tight End ★ Iowa State
4th Year ★ D7a, 1982

Played in 12 games for Dolphins in 1985...Has great potential...Fast, has good hands...Injuries bothered him in 1985...Had season-high three receptions for 19 yards and one TD versus Pittsburgh...Had two catches each against New England (1), Jets (2), Green Bay and Cleveland...Finished the season with 13 receptions for 192 yards (14.8 average) and three scores...Viewed by Dolphin coaches as the complete tight end package, can run, catch and block...In 1984 started all 16 games for Dolphins for second straight season at tight end.

WILLIAM JUDSON 49

Ht: 6-2 Wt: 190
Born: 3/26/59

Cornerback ★ South Carolina
5th Year ★ D8, 1981

Started all 16 regular-season games in 1985 for Miami for second consecutive year…Named team's Outstanding Defensive Back for third straight season…Blocked field goal versus the Jets (1)…Also blocked punt in prime-time win over the Bears…Could be Pro Bowl material…Tied for eighth place on all-time Dolphin interception list with Lloyd Mumphord—both have 14…Finished second on Miami squad with four interceptions (tied with Paul Lankford) for 88 yards, including a 61-yard return for a touchdown against Houston in the season's first encounter…Ended 1985 with 40 first hits and five assists for a total of 45 tackles… Also added two recovered fumbles and four passes defensed…Solid mixture of speed and coverage ability has led to starter's spot in Miami secondary.

MIKE KOZLOWSKI 40

Ht: 6-1 Wt: 198
Born: 2/24/56

Safety ★ Colorado
7th Year ★ D10b, 1979

Played in five games for Dolphins in 1985…Spent much of the year on injured reserve…Excellent nickel back…Also very strong special teams performer…Finished 1985 with 14 first hits, three assists for a total of 17 tackles…Also had one pass defensed…A tough, aggressive player…Used as situational player and special teamer through most of career…Played in all 19 regular season and playoff games for Dolphins in 1984… Seasonal stats included 27 solos, eight assists, one interception, one forced fumble and two passes defensed.

PAUL LANKFORD 44

Ht: 6-2 Wt: 187
Born: 6/15/58

Cornerback ★ Penn State
5th Year ★ D3, 1982

Started 15 regular-season games for the Dolphins in 1985…Led Miami with four fumbles forced and 14 passes defensed…Stepped in when Don McNeal (knee) was injured…Excellent athlete… Runs and jumps very well…Finished eighth on team in tackles with 48-8-56…Also added one sack…Tied with William Judson for second on team with four interceptions…Continues to improve, thanks to world-class speed and athletic ability…Performed in all 16 regular season games for Dolphins in 1984 with six starts.

LARRY LEE 66

Ht: 6-2 Wt: 263
Born: 9/10/59

Guard/Center ★ UCLA
6th Year ★ FA, 1985

Played in five games a year ago for Dolphins… Picked up on waivers from Detroit late in the year to provide help for injured Miami offensive line troops …Very good job on special teams as a snapper… Versatility is one of his key strengths…Part-time starter throughout his NFL career…Started at various times throughout the 1983 season at both right and left guard for Detroit…Even played on the defensive line when injuries mounted during his rookie season of 1981…Started three games at left guard and three games at center for Detroit in 1984…Played in all but one game during four-year Lion career…Drafted in fifth round in 1981 by Detroit.

RONNIE LEE 72

Ht: 6-4 Wt: 265
Born: 12/24/56

Guard ★ Baylor
8th Year ★ Trade, 1984

Played in 15 games for the Dolphins, starting 13… Strong, consistent performer…Has great potential…Best days are ahead…Enters third year of second stint with Miami…Was obtained from Atlanta in August of 1984 along with a draft choice in exchange for cornerback Gerald Small…Saw action in all 16 regular season contests in 1984 as a special teams expert and also as a backup to Cleveland Green at right tackle…A Dolphin tight end from 1979-82, was converted to offensive line by Don Shula in 1983 pre-season training camp… Was released by the Dolphins prior to the '83 regular season, but was picked up by Atlanta prior to third game of the year…Played in 12 games for the Falcons, both on special teams and on the offensive line…Had played in 57 Dolphin games during earlier four-year stay with 35 starts (28 in a row at one point).

GEORGE LITTLE 99

Ht: 6-4 Wt: 278
Born: 6/27/63

Defensive Tackle ★ Iowa
2nd Year ★ D3a, 1985

Played in 14 regular-season games for the Dolphins…Started three…Played very well early at both nose tackle and defensive end…Had season-high four tackles versus the Jets (1) and Tampa Bay…Recorded sacks against Kansas City and Indianapolis (2)…Finished 1985 with 12 first hits, five assists and 17 total tackles…Third-round draft selection, 65th player taken overall in 1985.

DAN MARINO 13

Ht: 6-4 Wt: 215
Born: 9/15/61

Quarterback ★ Pittsburgh
4th Year ★ D1, 1983

Has enjoyed the best first three seasons of any quarterback to ever play in the NFL…Considered by many to be the top attraction in professional football…Strong and adept at avoiding the rush, possesses rifle arm with quickest release in the league…In only three years he has put together these impressive stats: 871 for 1427 (61 percent), 11,341 yards, 98 TDs, 44 INTs…Led NFL in completions (336), yards (4,137) and TDs (30) for second straight season in 1985…Finished fourth in the AFC in passing, fifth in the league…Named team's MVP and outstanding offensive back for third straight year…Started all 16 regular-season games and two playoff contests…Number two on all-time Dolphin passing chart, behind Bob Griese …Street-smart, dedicated to football…Owns 17 of the top 23 300-plus yards passing games in Miami history…Owns NFL mark for yards (5,084), TDs (48) and completions (362) in a season (all came in 1984)…Holds NFL record for most consecutive games with four or more TD passes (four in 1984) …His high for attempts in 1985 was 48 against Indianapolis (1)…High for completions came at Green Bay (30)…Top regular-season yardage game was 390 at Denver…Enjoyed fine '85 performances against Buffalo (2) with 22-31-233 (70.9), Tampa Bay with 27-39-302 (69.2) and Kansas City with 23-35-258 (65.7)…Was 45 for 93 for 486 yards, three TDs, three interceptions in the two playoff games…Highly heralded, he was named to start in the Pro Bowl in '85…Other honors included: NFL Alumni Quarterback of the Year, first-team AP All-Pro, first-team PFWA All-Pro, Sporting News first-team All-Pro, Football Digest first-team All-Pro, and Pro Football Newsweekly first-team All-Pro…First-team All-AFC selection by both UPI and Football News…Had six games over 300 yards passing in 1985…Including playoffs, has thrown at least one TD pass in 38 of Miami's last 41 games…In regular-season contests, has only suffered two sub-50 percent completion games (9/23/84 versus Colts, 11/13/83 versus Patriots)…Career-best single game completion percentage (78.1) came against Houston in 1984 when he connected on 25 of 32 for 321 yards, three TDs and no INTs.

DON McNEAL 28

Ht: 5-11 Wt: 192
Born: 5/6/58

Cornerback ★ Alabama
6th Year ★ D1, 1980

Veteran performer, played in 10 games a year ago for Dolphins, didn't start any…Came back after a knee injury in exhibition game with Buffalo…Saw action as a nickel back…Tremendous athlete, has been plagued by injuries…Has potential to become one of the NFL's top cornerbacks…Made 15 first hits and three assists for 18 total tackles in 1985…Also added two passes defensed…Earned three tackles and a fumble recovery in post-season action…Had season-high three tackles in both Buffalo games…Made two tackles on six occasions, including AFC title matchup versus New England…Recovered a fumble in that game.

MACK MOORE 91

Ht: 6-4 Wt: 258
Born: 3/4/59

Defensive End ★ Texas A&M
2nd Year ★ D6a, 1981

Played in all 16 regular-season games in 1985 for the Dolphins…Started two contests…Picked up from the British Columbia Lions of the Canadian Football League to aid Miami pass rush…Suffered ankle injury late in the year…Registered four tackles and two sacks in prime-time victory over the Bears…Had two tackles and 1 1/2 sacks versus the Jets (2)…Played well in playoffs against Cleveland with two tackles and a sack…Finished 1985 with 15 first hits, two assists and a total of 17 tackles …Added 5 1/2 sacks to Dolphin cause…Signed with the Lions in 1981 after being drafted by Miami …Was a starter at right defensive end for B.C… Possesses great quickness…Drafted in sixth round by Miami in 1981.

NAT MOORE 89

Ht: 5-9 Wt: 188
Born: 9/19/51

Wide Receiver ★ Florida
13th Year ★ D3, 1974

Holds virtually every career receiving record in Dolphin annals…Has had good fortune of not only lengthy career, but to have spent all of it in hometown…Appeared in 15 games a year ago, starting seven…Was sparkplug for Miami when Mark Duper was sidelined with injuries…Finished 22nd in AFC in receiving in 1985…Dolphins' most clutch receiver last season…Had announced his retirement, but came back to enjoy second-best Miami season ever…Great hands and also considered by many to be the finest blocking wide receiver in the game…Consistency and reliability are his calling cards…Versatile, can play running back and return kicks…Was Miami's third-leading receiver in 1985 with 51 receptions for 701 yards (13.7 average) and seven TDs…Those 51 catches were one off his personal high (52) in 1977… Dolphins' third-leading scorer in '85 with seven touchdowns (42 points)…Had seven receptions for 67 yards and a TD versus Indianapolis (1)… Caught six passes for 69 yards and a score at Detroit…Added five catches (66 yards) against New England (2) and picked up five more (109 yards with a TD) at Denver…Led Dolphins in receiving for six years straight (1974-79)…Has tallied more touchdowns than any Dolphin player (68)…#1 all-time Dolphin receiver with 472 catches for 7,116 yards (15.2 average) and 67 TDs…Has one TD rushing…Third all-time scorer for Miami with 408 points (67 receiving TDs, one rushing TD)…10th on all-time Dolphin kickoff return chart (33-858-26.0)…Eighth on all-time Miami punt return list (26-299-11.5)…Tied with Paul Warfield for most 100-yard games (12) in Dolphin history.

ALEX MOYER 54

Ht: 6-1 Wt: 221
Born: 10/25/63

Linebacker ★ Northwestern
2nd Year ★ D3b, 1985

Played in 10 regular-season games for Miami in 1985…Did not start any contests…Was starting OLB in preseason when Bob Brudzinski held out …Blue-collar worker…Very smart…Good special teams performer…Had season-high five tackles and interception versus Green Bay…Registered four tackles each against New England (1) and Indianapolis (2)…Recovered a fumble and added three tackles against the Jets (2)…Finished 1985 with 15 first hits, six assists and 21 total tackles… Also added three passes defensed…Dolphins' second third-round pick, 83rd choice overall in 1985.

TONY NATHAN 22

Running Back ★ Alabama
8th Year ★ D3a, 1979

In 1985 became first Dolphin ever to lead the team in receiving and rushing in the same season… Started 15 regular-season contests…Was seventh in the AFC in receiving, 15th in rushing… Sports Illustrated tabbed him as one of the league's most underrated players in a poll of his peers…Clutch receiver…Durable, dependable performer…Second to Nat Moore (8,521) on the Dolphin all-time all-purpose yardage chart with 7,995…1985 stats included 143 rushes for 667 yards (4.7 average) and five TDs…Also caught 72 passes for 651 yards (9.0 average) and one score …Those 72 receptions were one off the team record of 73 set by Mark Clayton in 1984…In the playoffs, garnered 25 yards on nine carries and caught 15 aerials for 158 yards and one TD…'85 rushing best was 77 yards on 15 carries in prime-time win over Chicago…Tied Dolphin single-game record of 10 receptions (with minimum of 100 yards) with 10 catches for 120 yards at Denver …Shares mark with Duriel Harris who had 10 against Green Bay in 1979…Added 10 catches for 86 yards and a TD versus Green Bay in 1985… Came back in postseason play to grab 10 passes for 101 yards against Cleveland…Pulled in eight receptions for 80 yards in win over Tampa Bay…

Ht: 6-0 Wt: 210
Born: 12/14/56

Fourth on all-time Dolphin rushing chart with 701 carries, 3,320 yards (4.7 average) and 16 TDs… Second on all-time Miami receiving list with 325 catches, 3,058 yards, (9.4 average) and 14 TDs… Tied with Jim Kiick (186 points) for seventh place on all-time Dolphin scoring chart…Fifth on all-time Miami punt return list (51-484-9.5).

FUAD REVEIZ 7

Kicker ★ Tennessee
2nd Year ★ D7, 1985

Enjoyed tremendous first season and was named Dolphin rookie of the year in 1985…Played in all 16 regular-season games and two playoff contests …Led team in scoring with 116 points…Those 116 tallies were one shy of the Dolphin single-season record of 117, set in 1971 by Garo Yepremian…Converted 22 of 27 field goal attempts and 50 of 52 PAT tries…The 50 successful PATs are second-best on the all-time Dolphin single-season chart, falling short of 66, set by Uwe von Schamann in '84…Finished fourth in the AFC in scoring and sixth in the NFL in scoring (kickers only)… Good range, good accuracy are his calling cards …Very cool under pressure…Beat out incumbent von Schamann and veteran Eddie Garcia in '85 camp.

Ht: 5-11 Wt: 222
Born: 2/24/63

REGGIE ROBY   4

Punter ★ Iowa
4th Year ★ D6, 1983

Another consistent year in 1985…Played in all 16 regular-season games along with two playoff contests…Finished second in the league in punting… Named College and Pro Football Newsweekly first-team All-Pro…Also, NEA second-team All-Pro and UPI second-team All AFC…Looks to improve on coffin-corner kicking in 1986…Has picked up more and more hang time with each game…Finished 1985 with 59 punts, 2,576 yards, (43.7 average) and had a long of 63…Was right behind Indianapolis' Rohn Stark in league punting race…Did not have a punt blocked in 1985…His 43.7 average was second-best single-season average in Dolphin history…Roby also owns (44.7 in '84) and third-best (43.1 in '83) Miami single-season averages…Longest punt of '85 came against the Jets (1) with a 63-yarder…Had a 62-yard punt in the playoff game with Cleveland…Is Dolphins' all-time career average leader with 43.7 (ahead of Larry Seiple's 40.0).

Ht: 6-2 Wt: 243
Born: 7/30//61

JOE ROSE   80

Tight End ★ California
7th Year ★ D7, 1980

Played in 16 regular-season games for the Dolphins in 1985…Clutch receiver…Finished 1985 with 19 receptions for 306 yards (16.1 average) and four touchdowns…Enjoyed finest game of '85 at Indianapolis when he grabbed four aerials for 51 yards…Also added three catches (for 49 yards, one TD) against Denver and (for 44 yards, one TD) against Green Bay…Caught two passes for 27 yards in postseason competition… Possessor of sure pair of hands, is Dolphins' top receiving tight end.

Ht: 6-3 Wt: 230
Born: 6/24/57

ROBIN SENDLEIN   52

Linebacker ★ Texas
6th Year ★ Trade, 1985

Played in all 16 regular-season games for the Dolphins in 1985…Started three contests for Miami… Aided special teams corps…Recorded season-high six tackles versus Houston…Registered three tackles against Kansas City…Picked up two stops and a sack at Denver…Finished 1985 with 17 first hits and two assists for a total of 19 tackles …Played against the Dolphins in the pre-season last year, then joined the team from the Minnesota Vikings in a trade for the rights to Anthony Carter …Ranked 10th overall on the Viking defense in '84 with 97 (44-53) tackles.

Ht: 6-3 Wt: 225
Born: 12/1/58

JACKIE SHIPP   50

Linebacker ★ Oklahoma
3rd Year ★ D1, 1984

Played in all 16 regular-season games in 1985 for the Dolphins…Started 11…Great physical athlete …Knows Dolphins system, can be tremendous aid to Miami defensive corps…Finished third on the club with 83 tackles (68-15) a year ago… Worked very hard in off-season program… Recovered two fumbles and broke up three passes last season…Registered double figures in tackles twice in 1985: 11 versus Kansas City and 10 against Detroit…Added eight tackles and a pass defensed at Denver…Picked up seven tackles and recovered a fumble in first game versus New England…Had six tackles and a recovered fumble against Green Bay.

Ht: 6-2 Wt: 236
Born: 3/19/62

MIKE SMITH   18

Cornerback ★ Texas-El Paso
2nd Year ★ D4a, 1985

Let go in final cut a year ago, but was brought back later in the year…Aided Dolphins when injuries sidelined defensive back corps…Played in seven regular-season games for Miami in 1985…Ace special teams performer…Plenty of talent… Finished 1985 with three tackles…Had two versus Denver and one against Buffalo (2)…Drafted in the fourth round, 91st pick overall in 1985.

Ht: 6-0 Wt: 171
Born: 10/24/62

ROBERT SOWELL   45

Cornerback ★ Howard
4th Year ★ FA, 1983

Played in 10 regular-season games for the Dolphins in 1985…Started once…Excellent special teams competitor…Undersized, but awesome hitter…Finished 1985 with 14 tackles, one sack and one pass defensed…Registered four tackles versus the Jets (1) and three against Pittsburgh… Had two tackles and a pass broken up at Denver.

Ht: 5-11 Wt: 175
Born: 6/23/61

DWIGHT STEPHENSON 57

Center ★ Alabama
7th Year ★ D2, 1980

Named 1985's Miller Lite/NFL Man of the Year for his work in charity and community projects (first Dolphin player to win award since its inception in 1970)...Four-time Pro Bowl selection... Considered "best in the business" at his position ...On everybody's All-Pro team...Named team's outstanding offensive lineman for the fourth straight season...Named to the AP, NEA and PFWA All-NFL squads...UPI All-AFC selection... Sporting News All-Pro...Pro Football Weekly All-Pro...Football News All-AFC...Started all games for the Dolphins a year ago despite playing with a broken bone in his leg for most of the season... Very hard worker, hates to lose...Anchor of Miami offensive line that allowed fewest quarterback sacks (19) for third straight season.

Ht: 6-2 Wt: 255
Born: 11/20/57

DON STROCK 10

Quarterback ★ Virginia Tech
13th Year ★ D5, 1973

Despite veteran backup role, is listed fourth on all-time Dolphin passing list (361-645 for 4,347 yards, 37 TDs, 36 INTs)...Played in all 16 games a year ago, mostly as a holder...Was six of seven for 132 yards and a TD at Houston...That score (67 yards to Mark Duper) was longest completion of his career)...Finished 1985 seven of nine for 141 yards, 1 TD, 0 INT...Works sidelines for Dolphins, confers with Shula to offer assistance in play selection ...Knows Shula offense better than anyone... Tremendous help to Dan Marino on sidelines... Best holder Dolphins have ever had...Very valuable asset to the team...Personal touch and friend

Ht: 6-5 Wt: 225
Born: 11/27/50

of Marino, assisted Marino with a clinic in London this past spring...Considered premier back-up quarterback in NFL, could start on several teams.

JEFF TOEWS 60

Guard/Center ★ Washington
8th Year ★ D2, 1979

Played in 11 regular-season games for the Dolphins in 1985...Started five...Injured knee, allowing Jeff Dellenbach to step in...Was career reserve until last season...Reliable, dependable and consistent...Hard-working, strong athlete... Rugged blocker.

Ht: 6-3 Wt: 255
Born: 11/4/57

TOM VIGORITO 32

Wide Receiver/Running Back
Virginia ★ 4th Year ★ D5b, 1981

Played in only nine games for the Dolphins in 1985, but still led Miami in punt returns with 22 for 197 yards (9.0 average)...Finished seventh in the AFC punt returns race...Spent part of last season on injured reserve with hamstring injury...Second on all-time Dolphin punt return yards list with 830 (Jake Scott is first with 1330)...Career punt return stats include: 79 for 830, 10.5 average, 21 fair catches...When healthy, is versatile player who can play wide receiver, running back, and is also return specialist.

Ht: 5-10 Wt: 190
Born: 10/23/59

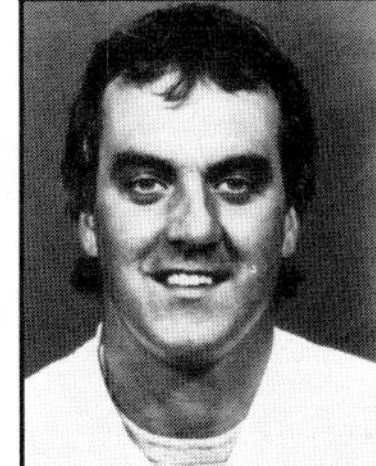

1986 COLLEGE DRAFT

By the time the Dolphins made their first pick in the 1986 college draft, Bobby Monica had already eaten breakfast and lunch and was making plans for dinner. The Dolphins' equipment manager was at draft central in New York monitoring Miami's direct telephone line to the team's training compound at St. Thomas University. It wasn't until 2:39 on draft day that Monica announced Miami's first pick, which actually didn't come until the second round. The Dolphins had given Tampa Bay their first round pick in the trade for Hugh Green last October simply because there wasn't anyone quite resembling him in this year's college crop. Yet, the announcement by Monica of John Offerdahl, linebacker, Western Michigan, brought a look of satisfaction to Don Shula's face. He had spent part of the morning jogging to help break up the anxiety in waiting for the Dolphins' draft turn, all the while hoping he would somehow wind up with Offerdahl.

"Don told us to give up hoping Offerdahl would be available," revealed defensive coordinator Chuck Studley. "When he was still there, it took us about 15 seconds to decide. We went around the table and everyone agreed. We needed somebody who is intelligent enough to make the defensive calls and handle the people up front. We needed an A.J. Duhe type of guy back on our defense. I think Offerdahl can be that guy."

It was not an easy draft for the Dolphins. In 1985 they were looking for running backs in a year that was weak in that commodity. This year it was no secret that they were seeking defensive help, a category that was thin in quality. For three weeks before the April draft, Shula and his staff put in 13-hour days poring over scouting reports, making phone calls and winding and rewinding films, hoping to primarily find defensive help. Chuck Connor, the club's personnel director, knew the difficulty months ahead of time.

"We knew it wasn't going to be easy, but it never is," said Connor. "It's difficult every year after you get by the top 15 players. Look at how many teams picked below 15 last year and got productive players in the first season. Not many. We have to get lucky. Picking as late as we are, it's going to be difficult to find a productive player."

Yet, Shula feels Offerdahl could be that type of player. He was quite impressed with him after watching him in the Senior Bowl game. It took only two tackles by Offerdahl to bring a twinkle to Shula's eye. Both times he stopped Bo Jackson cold in short yardage head-to-head encounters.

"The kid took Jackson on with a vengeance," beamed Shula. "I liked that."

Monica like Offerdahl the first time he met him back at the Dolphins' camp in Miami. The rookie didn't care what jersey number he would get and even liked the first helmet he tried on.

"I like this man," snapped Monica. "He just wants to go out and hit people."

He certainly did a good job of it in college. Offerdahl set a Mid American Conference record for career tackles with 694. It's quite an accomplishment when realizing that he didn't enroll at Western Michigan with a football scholarship tucked underneath his arm. He was only 190 pounds at the time and considered too small to play big time college football. Offerdahl just went out and showed how far desire could go.

"I've been told in the past I was too skinny, too slow, not strong enough," remarked Offerdahl. "Maybe I was, but I set out to do something about it, and I did. Some people don't believe in me now. Great. I like being an underdog. They say I wasn't heavy enough, so I gained 45 pounds since I was a freshman. They say I wasn't strong enough, so I increased my bench press from 225 to 375.

"I can see people wondering. No one knows who I am, but that doesn't bother me. I kind of like it. I guess I even had some doubts that I could play with those guys in the bowl games until I saw they weren't God. There

was no pressure on me. All I could do was good. Besides, when you play with other good players. you don't feel like you have to make the play every time. My job was to prove that I could play with the big guys. I feel I've done that and now I'm ready for the next step."

After his first two weeks or so on campus in Kalamazoo, he impressed Western Michigan head coach John Harbaugh so much with his desire and ability that he was given a four year scholarship. It was just what the doctor ordered for the soft spoken pre-med student. He never missed a game his entire college career and was named a second team All-American by the Associated Press.

"John dedicates himself to something, then it becomes a mission," said Harbaugh. "He seems so shy and naive when you first meet him, but there's a fire inside. We had some pros come in here and say John may be a step too slow, or not big or strong enough. We just chuckled. All you have to do is point him at the field and let him play. There's no doubt in my mind that he's going to be a standout in the NFL. None whatsoever."

Shula certainly hopes so. He doesn't hide the fact that the Dolphins need immediate help on the linebacking brigade, particularly the inside area.

"We haven't been happy with the play of our inside linebackers over the last couple of years," admitted Shula. "We feel like we got the player who can come in and upgrade us right away. He's a hitter and we need more of those. There's no question that we were concerned with improving our defense. And in order to improve your defense, you have to have linebackers like Offerdahl that can hit, fill the holes and do all the things we think he can do."

Several of Shula's assistants, namely linebacker coach Bob Matheson and Studley, rated Offerdahl high, despite his lack of notoriety in coming out of the small Mid American Conference. Yet, it is interesting to note that the Pittsburgh Steelers drafted an unknown line-backer back in 1974 named Jack Lambert from Kent State in the same conference.

"We had Offerdahl rated the second best inside line-backer behind Syracuse's Tim Green," revealed Matheson. "We had him and Thomas Johnson of Ohio State rated neck-and-neck. Offerdahl is a solid player. He's been an achiever all his life, and he should be a very productive, consistent player for us."

"His intelligence was a factor," added Studley. "His counselor told him he'd have trouble playing football and majoring in bio-medicine. He took the two toughest courses the same semester and got A's in both. That's what I like about him. He won't take no for an answer. He's intelligent, he's an intense competitor and he's a winner. You've got to go with people like that."

Five of Miami's first six picks in the draft was on defense. The only exception was James Pruitt, a wide receiver from Fullerton State on the fourth round, in essense, the Dolphins' third pick. By the time Miami got around to selecting Offerdahl, 11 defensive linemen and seven linebackers were already claimed. However, over the years, the Dolphins have fared well in the second round. Since Shula took over in 1970, he has taken such second round players as Jim Mandich, Benny Malone, Freddie Solomon, Bob

Baumhower, Dwight Stephenson, Andra Franklin, Jeff Toews, Mark Duper, Mike Charles and Jay Brophy. Looking further into the draft, Miami has developed nine starters out of picks that were made in rounds six through 12. That's more than any other NFL team can claim.

"I feel pretty good about our picks," claimed Shula. "One of the keys is J.T. Turner. He had some high grades. If we're fortunate enough to make a player out of him, then I think we've got the start of some good things."

Entering his senior year at Houston, Turner, a big 6-4, 282-pound defensive lineman, was projected as a first round choice by the scouting combines. However, he had a totally unexpected disappointing season and his stock rapidly declined. When the Dolphins named him on the third round, in reality their second pick, most looked upon the selection as a gamble.

"We realize there was a certain amount of risk in this pick," disclosed Studley. "Everyone is trying to explain what went wrong his senior year. There are no clear-cut answers. He has shown he has the ability. It's up to us to get it out of him."

How much of a gamble could Turner actually be? He was a bonafide Lombardi and Outland Trophy candidate before his senior campaign. The season before, he led the Cougars in tackles with 105 and produced 11 sacks, a good reason why The Sporting News named him to its All-American team. Turner claimed he was surrounded by too much pressure and too much criticism from the Houston coaches his final year.

"I hated the way it turned out," said Turner. "I'm not a loser. I can play with intensity. I still want to prove that I was the top lineman in college football. I'm not knocking anyone, but the coaches were putting more pressure on me and then criticizing me before the other players rather than taking me off to the side."

Houston's strength coach, Mark Reiman, perhaps had the best perspective on Turner's sub-par year.

"Agents," he snapped. "If he had been drafted at the end of his junior year, he would have gone high in the first round. He had a lot of agents coming after him after that, and he saw dollar signs. In my mind, and it's just

one opinion, he listened to the wrong people, and he paid the price for it. He didn't work out like he should have between seasons and he came back in terrible shape. It was a tough, tough lesson for him."

Yet, Turner is thankful that the Dolphins drafted him. In fact, at times he day dreamed that one day he might be playing in Miami.

"Three years ago when we played the Hurricanes, I told my wife I wanted to live in Miami," revealed Turner. "I told her that the Dolphins would draft me."

Miami's third choice, Pruitt, raised a few eyebrows. After all, the Dolphins seemed secure at wide receiver, what with Mark Duper, Mark Clayton, Nat Moore and Vince Heflin. Actually, the Dolphins are hoping that Pruitt comes somewhat close to being another Clayton, who was drafted on the eighth round in 1983. Like Clayton, Pruitt can jump vertically, and was measured at 35".

"We got a couple of little guys who can jump, now we got a big guy who can," exclaimed Shula.

Pruitt is big, 6-2, and quick. He was clocked at 4.5 in the 40. He's excited about getting a chance with the Dolphins.

"I'm the protype receiver," said Pruitt. "I'm not as fast as the little guys but I can make the tough catch and still run pretty well. You know, if you aren't drafted real high, the next best thing is going to a good team. I'm excited about playing for the Dolphins. Any receiver that's going to play with Dan Marino and the Marks Brothers has to be excited. What else can you say about the Marks Brothers?"

After Pruitt, the Dolphins drafted Kevin Wyatt, a corner-back from Arkansas; Brent Sowell, a defensive tackle from Alabama; Larry Kolnic, a linebacker-nose tackle from Ohio State; John Stuart, an offensive tackle from Texas; Reyna Thompson, a defensive back from Baylor and Jeff Wickersham, a quarterback from LSU. All have dreams of playing with the Dolphins. Not all of them will be fulfilled.

"We wanted to come out of this draft with two or three of four players who can compete for starting jobs, or become special teams players and learn to be starters," Shula summed up.

That about says it all.

1986 DRAFT CHOICES

RND	NO	PLAYER	POS	HT	WT	COLLEGE
2	52	John Offerdahl	LB	6-2	232	Western Michigan
3	81	T.J. Turner	DT	6-4	265	Houston
4	107	James Pruitt	WR	6-2	199	Cal. State-Fullerton
5	136	Kevin Wyatt	CB	5-10	190	Arkansas
6	163	Brent Sowell	DT	6-5	256	Alabama
7	193	Larry Kolic	LB	6-1	242	Ohio State
8	218	John Stuart	T	6-4	280	Texas
9	240	Reyna Thompson	S	5-11	194	Baylor
10	274	Jeff Wickersham	QB	6-2	195	Louisiana State
11	303	Arnold Franklin	TE	6-3	253	North Carolina
12	329	Rickey Isom	RB	6-0	225	N.C. State

JOHN OFFERDAHL   48

Linebacker ★ Western Michigan
D-2, 52

Ht: 6-2 Wt: 232
Born: 8/17/64

First player chosen by Dolphins in draft as they did not have a pick in first round…Started every game for Broncos over four-year career…Named team MVP in '84 and '85 seasons…Won honors as top defensive player in '83…Selected to the All-Mid American Conference first team in 1983, 1984 and 1985 (unanimous)…Also chosen as MAC "defensive player of the year" in '85…Won AP All-America honors three straight seasons—1985 (second team), 1984 (third team), 1983 (honorable mention)…Named the most valuable defensive player of North team in 1986 Senior Bowl after stopping Heisman Trophy winner Bo Jackson twice on fourth-and-one plays…Also participated in 1986 East-West Shrine Game…MAC career leader in tackles with 694…WMU career leader in tackles, forced fumbles (17) and fumbles recovered (eight)…Also WMU season record holder in tackles (192 in 1983), forced fumbles (five in 1984) and fumble recoveries (four in 1985)…Led Broncos in solo, assisted and total tackles all four years …Best game in 1985 was against Central Michigan, when he had 24 tackles (15 solo), forced two fumbles and intercepted one pass…Went to Western Michigan on a half scholarship, but it was elevated to a full scholarship after first week of practice…Majored in bio-medical sciences.

T.J. TURNER   95

Defensive Tackle ★ Houston
D-3, 81

Ht: 6-4 Wt: 265
Born: 5/16/63

Four-year starter for Cougars…Specializes in rushing the passer…Completed Houston career with 58 tackles for 276 yards in losses, including 30 quarterback sacks…Finished with a total of 294 tackles…(185 unassisted)…Had outstanding junior season, Consensus first-team All-Southwest Conference selection…Also named as an honorable mention on the AP and UPI All-America teams…Despite constant double-teaming, put together 23 tackles for loss, including 11 quarterback sacks…Top performance in '81 was vs. Baylor when he was in on 18 tackles (11 unassisted), including three tackles for losses of 14 yards…Amassed 105 total tackles in '84…Numbers fell off slightly as a senior…Had 75 total tackles to go with 13 tackles for 71 yards in losses (eight sacks) …Best effort in '85 came against Texas with six unassisted tackles and eight assisted tackles…A first team All-SWC selection by UPI as a senior… Participated in both Hula Bowl and Blue-Gray game…Had 52 tackles in 1982, the most by a freshman in Houston history…1983 second-team All-SWC pick by AP…Best game in '83 was

against Miami (Fla.) when he was in on eight tackles (five unassisted) and one for loss of yardage…One of most pupular players on Houston squad, a near-unanimous choice of teammates for 1985 co-captain…Bench presses 365 pounds …Only fifth freshman to start at defensive tackle in Bill Yeoman's 23 seasons, and his 260 minutes in '82 was the most played by a freshman in Yeoman's tenure…Majored in therapeutic recreation.

JAMES PRUITT   3

Wide Receiver ★
Cal. State-Fullerton
D-4, 107

Ht: 6-2 Wt: 199
Born: 1/29/64

Four-year letterman for Titans…Has excellent height and speed (4.5 in the 40) for a receiver… Also has a 35-inch vertical jump…Runs precise routes…Finished career as the No. 2 all-time leading receiver at Fullerton in both receptions (74) and yardage gained (1,323)…His nine touchdown catches ranks him fifth in that category… Caught 21 passes for 467 yards and six touchdowns as a senior…Had best games against Wyoming (4-71, 1 TD) and New Mexico State (2-109, 1 TD)…Also returned kickoffs in '85 (first season he had done so in college) and averaged 26.6 yards a return…Named second-team All-Pacific Coast Athletic Association…Served as team captain his senior season…Played in the Blue-Gray Classic, catching two passes…Best game as a junior came vs. Fresno State as he caught five balls for 73 yards…Missed two games that year with a badly sprained ankle…Capped off sophomore season with selection as Fullerton's Player of the Game in the California Bowl, catching six passes for 133 yards…Had caught game-winning touchdown pass versus Fresno State with leaping, fourth-down reception in end zone that put Titans into the Cal Bowl…Member of "The Bomb Corps" at Fullerton, a quartet of receivers who lettered together for four years…Majored in communications.

KEVIN WYATT   41

Cornerback ★ Arkansas
D-5, 136

Ht: 5-10 Wt: 190
Born: 3/14/64

Three-year starter and four-year letterman for Razorbacks…Has great speed and quickness… Named second team All-Southwest Conference in senior season after earning consensus All-SWC honors his junior year…Plays with a lot of confidence…Has a great attitude…Specializes in man-to-man coverage…Picked off three passes in senior season…Also had 26 total tackles, including 16 unassisted…Played in Hula Bowl for West squad…Led Arkansas with five interceptions and nine deflections in 1984…Had 27 tackles (15 unassisted) that year…Outstanding at returning punts and kickoffs…Returned three punts for 47 yards in 1985…Almost switched to quarterback, a position he played in high school, prior to his junior year…Made 51 tackles as a sophomore… Majored in marketing and broadcasting.

BRENT SOWELL 77

Defensive Tackle ★ Alabama
D-6, 163

Two-year letterman for Crimson Tide…Split time at defensive tackle with Larry Roberts (drafted in second round by San Francisco), starting in 10 games and playing in 11…One of Alabama's most consistent players in 1985 on the defensive side of the ball…Registered 41 total tackles, two quarterback sacks and three tackles for loss on season…Will be tried on both the offensive and defensive lines with Dolphins…Best performance of '85 came in 16-14 loss to SEC champ Tennessee, when he had five solo hits and three assists for eight total tackles…Strong and smart player who also has played some nose tackle…Holds B.S. in psychology.

Ht: 6-5 Wt: 256
Born: 3/27/63

LARRY KOLIC 94

Linebacker ★ Ohio State
D-7, 193

Two-year starter and three-year letterman for Buckeyes…Sat out redshirt year in 1983…Logged time as an up linebacker and a nose tackle in 1985…Term "nose backer" coined by him to refer to his stint at middle guard…Started all 12 games in senior season…Racked up 46 total tackles (27 unassisted)…Best game came in Citrus Bowl…Named as game MVP…Intercepted two passes, and returned one 10 yards for the winning touchdown in Ohio State's 10-7 win over BYU…Also had outstanding performance against Wisconsin, making 11 tackles (six unassisted)…Put together 74 total tackles in '84, third highest on team, even though he missed four games…Played strictly at inside linebacker that season…Had a vital 25-yard interception return for a touchdown in '84 Iowa game…Strong, physical player known for his bone-crunching hits…One of strongest players on OSU team, bench presses 420 pounds and lifts 725…Majored in industrial technology.

Ht: 6-1 Wt: 242
Born: 8/31/63

JOHN STUART 93

Tackle ★ Texas
D-8, 218

Moved into a starting role at tackle in his senior season after spending two seasons as a backup…Possesses good speed and agility for a big man (5.1 in the 40)…Missed last year's Oklahoma game because of suspension…Known for his consistency although he got off to a slow start last season…Was a pre-season All-Southwest Conference selection in 1985…Played in the Japan Bowl for Longhorn coach Fred Akers, who coached the West squad…Among the leaders in "pin" blocks—dumping a defender on his back—for Texas last season…Hold B.B.A. in data processing.

Ht: 6-4 Wt: 280
Born: 2/25/63

REYNA THOMPSON 19

Safety ★ Baylor
D-9, 240

Won two letters for Bears after walking on from Baylor track team…Played both safety and cornerback in career…Used extensively as a nickel back…Spent much of 1985 season as a backup at right cornerback, but moved into starting lineup for final four games…In '85, had 23 total tackles (16 unassisted), one interception, two passes broken up and one fumble recovery…Top game of season came vs. Rice, when he had five tackles and an interception…Made 25 tackles (18 unassisted) in '84…Was a top special teams player early in career…Considered a "real sleeper" by Miami Director of Player Personnel Chuck Connor…Has blazing speed, runs a 4.45 40…Broke the Southwest Conference record in the high hurdles last spring, running a 13.3…Member of Baylor's third-place 400-relay at 1985 NCAA championships…Holds a B.A. in communications.

Ht: 5-11 Wt: 194
Born: 8/28/63

JEFF WICKERSHAM 9

Quarterback ★ Louisiana State
D-10, 274

Three-year starter and four-year letterman for Tigers…Figures to provide stiff challenge to veteran Jim Jensen for spot on roster…Also may be tried at wide receiver…Third-leading passer in Southeastern Conference history with 6,921 career yards…Also the third most accurate passer in SEC history with a .584 completion percentage…One of only eight quarterbacks in SEC history to log more than 6,000 career yards in total offense (6,705—good for seventh place on SEC career list)…Holder of 16 LSU passing records…Career records are total offense yards (6,705), passing yards (6,921), pass completions (587) and pass attempts (1,005)…Season records are passing yards (2,542 in 1983), pass completions (209 in 1985) and pass attempts (346 in 1985)…Enjoyed third-best passing day of his career in 1985, when he threw for 294 yards in LSU's 10-7 win over Notre Dame in South Bend…Completed 31 of 42 passes in that game, the most completions ever by one quarterback against a Notre Dame team…Owns eight of the top 10 passing games in LSU history…Only LSU quarterback to pass for 2,000 yards in a season, doing it three times…Florida's John Reaves (1969-71) is only other quarterback in SEC history to pass for 2,000 yards in three successive seasons…Played in Japan Bowl after leading Tigers to Liberty Bowl against Baylor…Captained team his senior season…Earned Academic All-SEC honors in '85 for his 3.20 grade point average…Majored in business.

Ht: 6-2 Wt: 195
Born: 12/5/63

ARNOLD FRANKLIN 92

Tight End ★ North Carolina
D-11, 303

Four-year starter and letterman for Tar Heels…Good blocker and catches the ball well…Has plenty of untapped talent…Finished career at Carolina with 78 receptions for 861 yards and six touchdowns…His 78 catches make him the school's seventh-leading receiver of all-time…Played in all 11 games as a senior, starting 10…Missed other starting assignment because of a sprained ankle…Best game of 1985 came versus LSU, when he caught six passes for 65 yards…Had 16 receptions for 163 yards (10.2 average)

Ht: 6-3 Wt: 242
Born: 12/6/63

and two touchdowns in '85…Had an even better 1984 season with 27 receptions for 315 yards (11.7 average) and two TDs…Excellent performance in '84 followed a great showing in '83 as a sophomore…Had 25 catches for 271 yards (10.8 average) and one touchdown…His 25 receptions were the most ever by a Carolina sophomore… Finished 10th in the ACC in receiving…Had brilliant game at Maryland, catching six passes for 83 yards…Those six catches equalled the most ever by a UNC player against Maryland…Played considerably as a freshman, taking over the starting job midway through the season…Had 10 receptions for 112 yards (11.2 average) in '82…Set a Carolina record for catches in a game by a freshman with five against Virginia…Named ACC Rookie of the Week for that performance… Selected to Football News' Freshman All-America team…Majored in industrial relations.

RICKEY ISOM 25

Running Back ★ N.C. State
D-12, 329

Known primarily for his receiving ability…Had 70 receptions for 597 yards in his career at N.C. State …Plagued by injuries during his senior season… Missed three games in 1985 with a lower leg contusion…Fourth-leading receiver for the Wolfpack in '85 with 20 catches for 165 yards (8.3 average) and one touchdown…Also averaged 7.4 yards per game on the ground, rushing 18 times for 59 yards…Is a good blocker in addition to receiving ability…Picked things up very fast at team mini-camp in May, according to Miami Director of Player Personnel Chuck Connor…Second-leading receiver for N.C. State in his junior season, catching 23 balls for 215 yards (9.4 average)… Rushed 24 times for 86 yards in '84 season…His 70 career catches places him sixth on State's all-time list…Is tied for 12th on all-time list for number of passes caught in one game with six receptions …Majored in broadcast communications and political science.

Ht: 6-0 Wt: 225
Born: 11/30/63

THE COACHES

CHUCK CONNOR

**Director of Player Personnel,
9th NFL Season,
9th with Dolphins
Born: July 7, 1937**

The Dolphins' guru when it comes to scouting college players is Director of Player Personnel Chuck Connor, currently in his ninth season in that capacity. Preparing for the NFL's annual college draft is Connor's primary concern, and he has done that well during his Dolphin tenure, boasting 37 players from his first eight drafts who remain on the team's roster heading into the '86 pre-season.

Since Connor's arrival, the Dolphins have slowly rebuilt several key areas, including the defensive backfield, the offensive line, running back and the kicking game. Connor's astute scouting and drafting has accomplished this without missing a competitive beat. The Dolphins won divisional titles in 1979, '81, '83, '84 and '85, and made it to the Super Bowl in '82 and '84.

The McKees Rocks, Pennsylvania, native joined the Dolphins in February, 1978 after spending the previous three years scouting for BLESTO, an organization that provides college player evaluations to subscribing NFL teams. In his last year with BLESTO, Connor had been promoted from area to regional scout, responsible for a nine-state area in the southeastern United States.

Connor began his career as a coach on the high school level, spending 15 years (1960-74) at Montour High near Pittsburgh. Eight of those seasons were spent as a head coach, with his 1967 squad going undefeated. In '74, he continued as a teacher at Montour while becoming the defensive backfield coach at Carnegie-Mellon University. While at Montour, Connor had begun evaluating players from film for the Pittsburgh Steelers, which eventually led to his BLESTO position.

BOB LUNDY

**Head Trainer
20th NFL Season,
20th with Dolphins
Born: March 28, 1936**

For 19 years, the job of taking care of the Dolphin players' daily assortment of major and minor injuries has belonged to Head Trainer Bob Lundy. One of the most respectful trainers in the NFL, Lundy is responsible for the day-to-day treatment of injured Dolphins in coordination with team physicians. In conjunction with Assistant Coach, Junior Wade, Lundy also oversees the team's off-season conditioning program.

Lundy keeps abreast of the latest advances in training technology through his regular attendance at NATA conventions. Perhaps his highest honor came in 1974 when Dolphin players awarded Lundy the game ball following Miami's fourth consecutive AFC Eastern Division title.

Lundy joined the Dolphins for their inaugural 1966 season under then-Head Coach George Wilson, and has been with the club for all but one of its campaigns (he sold real estate in 1973). When Don Shula took over as head coach in 1970, Lundy was retained and he has been manning the training room ever since.

A native of Wollaston, Massachusetts, Lundy is a 1958 graduate of Boston University. While a graduate student at Indiana University, he served as the Hoosiers' assistant trainer before becoming the head trainer at Detroit University (1960-63). Lundy's first professional job came in 1964 when he served two seasons as the Detroit Lions' assistant trainer.

This past May Lundy was honored by the National Athletic Trainers Association with a "Twenty-Five Year Award," which is the most prestigious award in the training profession.

BILL DAVIS

**Assistant Trainer
4th NFL Season,
4th with Dolphins
Born: April 8, 1954**

In his fourth season as the Dolphins' Assistant Trainer is 32-year-old Bill Davis. Davis assists Head Trainer Bob Lundy with injury treatment and rehabilitation of Dolphin players. He has been a full-time member of the Dolphin staff since May, 1983 after spending five pre-seasons (1975-79) as a summer training camp assistant to Lundy.

Davis initially got involved in athletic training while he was a student at Davidson College. He aided current Dolphin Assistant Coach Junior Wade while Wade was baseball coach and assistant trainer for the Wildcats. Davis received his B.A. degree from Davidson in 1976, and earned his NATA certification the following year.

In 1978, Davis got his master's degree in health and physical education from Tennessee Tech. The following fall, he was named Athletic Trainer for Men at the University of Tennessee-Martin, a position he held until accepting his current post.

BOB MONICA

**Equipment Manager
6th NFL Season,
6th with Dolphins
Born: May 6, 1957**

Bob Monica began his second year as Dolphin equipment manager after four seasons as assistant equipment manager. Monica, a visible figure around the Dolphins' training camp, is responsible for issuing and ordering all playing equipment for the team.

The 29-year-old Monica earned a B.S. in sports administration from Miami's St. Thomas University. He transferred to St. Thomas from Furman University in Greenville, South Carolina, where he had been attending college on a football scholarship. A native of Madison, New Jersey, Monica captained Madison High School's 1976 football state champions. In addition, he was New Jersey state wrestling champion in the 188 lb. division (1976). In 1975, Monica traveled with the USA Junior Olympic Wrestling team to Germany and Bulgaria.

Prior to joining the Dolphins, Monica was a production manager for Electric Factory Concerts in Philadelphia. Single, he resides in Pembroke Pines. One of Bob's personal highlights came when he appeared as a bartender in the January 10, 1986 episode of Miami Vice.

MEL PHILLIPS

Defensive Backfield
7th NFL Season, 2nd with Dolphins

Mel Phillips begins his second season as defensive backfield coach for the Dolphins. Last year, in his initial campaign with Miami, Phillips saw his DBs finish tied for third place in the AFC in interceptions. Before coming to Miami, the 44-year-old Phillips had previously held the same position for five seasons for the Detroit Lions (1980-84).

Known for his outstanding rapport with his players, Phillips coached in Detroit under then-Head Coach (and former Dolphin assistant) Monte Clark. In Miami, Phillips inherited a defensive backfield rich in experience that features quality veterans like Don McNeal, William Judson, Mike Kozlowski, Lyle and Glenn Blackwood, Paul Lankford and Bud Brown.

JOHN SANDUSKY

Offense/Offensive Line
28th NFL Season,
11th with Dolphins

John Sandusky—and his offensive line—just keeps getting better. A veteran of 28 NFL coaching seasons, Sandusky begins his 11th year with the Dolphins looking for continued success. Last season the Dolphin offensive resembled a solid brick wall, allowing the fewest sacks (19) in the league for the third straight season. The next lowest total in the league was 33 by Pittsburgh. Miami was also third in the NFL in scoring with 428 points.

Despite his assistant coaching title, he is also quite knowledgeable about defense, having spent seven of his 26 seasons coaching the other side of the line of scrimmage. In each of the past two campaigns, four Dolphin offensive linemen have been singled out for some type of post-season honors.

The 60-year-old Sandusky joined the Dolphins in 1976 after spending three seasons (1973-75) as an assistant coach for the Philadelphia Eagles. Prior to that, he was a coach for the Baltimore Colts from 1959-72, including the 1963-69 seasons under then-Colt Head Coach Don Shula. When Shula moved to Miami in 1970, he attempted, but was unable, to bring Sandusky with him. Sandusky was on the Colt staff for their two Super Bowl appearances in games III and V.

When Don McCafferty was fired as Baltimore's head coach after winning only one of the first five games in 1972, Sandusky became the Colt boss and led his charges to four victories in their final nine games. Two of Sandusky's losses that season were to Shula's undefeated Dolphin team.

DAN SEKANOVICH

Defensive Line
10th NFL Season,
1st with Dolphins

A nine-year veteran of the NFL coaching ranks, Dan Sekanovich begins his first season with the Dolphins. The 53-year-old Sekanovich most recently spent three seasons (1983-85) as the assistant head coach/defensive line mentor with the Atlanta Falcons. While with Atlanta he helped develop two top young linemen in Rick Bryan and Mike Gann.

Prior to his Atlanta post, Sekanovich developed one of the NFL's most feared defensive units, "The New York Sack Exchange" while defensive line coach for the New York Jets from 1977-82. In 1981, the Sack Exchange led the NFL in sacks with the defensive line getting 59 of 66.

Before joining the Jets, the West Hazelton, Pa., native enjoyed his first professional coaching experience when he served on Marv Levy's staff for the Montreal Alouettes of the Canadian Football League from 1973-76. Montreal captured the Grey Cup title in 1974 as Sekanovich coached both the offensive and defensive lines.

DAVID SHULA

Assistant Head Coach
Receiver and Quarterback
5th NFL Season, 5th with Dolphins

Last February David Shula added the title of assistant head coach to his previous duties as receivers and quarterbacks coach for the Dolphins. With his new responsibility, Shula, one of brightest young minds in pro football, will get more involved in the overall football operation.

After three years as the Dolphins' receivers coach, Shula was given the added duties of working with Miami quarterbacks in 1985. He proved he takes after his famous father in two important characteristics—hard work and dedication.

Last year the Dolphins again enjoyed another successful season through the air as Miami was second in the league in passing as a team and Dan Marino was fourth in the individual rankings. In addition, Tony Nathan (seventh) and Mark Clayton (eighth) were ranked among the league's top-10 receivers.

In 1983 (David's first full season), the results of his endeavors were very apparent. During the '82 post-season, Shula spent considerable time with wide receiver Mark Duper and incoming rookie quarterback Dan Marino. The results were that Duper, a seldom-used player in '82, emerged as the Dolphins' first-ever 1000-yard receiver, and Marino emerged as perhaps the finest rookie QB in NFL history. In the '83 off-season, Shula redirected much of his energies towards another second-year receiver, Mark Clayton, while continuing to work with Duper and Marino. The results were again spectacular as Clayton set club records for receptions and yards with Duper close behind.

CHUCK STUDLEY

Defense
18th NFL Season,
3rd with Dolphins

In 1986, Chuck Studley enters his third season as the man in charge of the Dolphin defense. The '84 campaign was a transition year for Miami's defenders as Studley installed his defensive schemes following the departure of long-time Dolphin defensive coordinator Bill Arnsparger. With two Dolphin seasons under his belt, Studley is looking for improvement from his defensive troops who were overshadowed the past two years by the spectacular exploits of the team's record-setting offense.

Studley, who was named to his current post on December 27, 1983, had begun the '83 season as the defensive coordinator for the Houston Oilers. Following the team's 0-6 start, head coach Ed Biles resigned on October 10, with Studley being tabbed as interim head coach. He took over the undermanned Oilers, guiding them to upsets over Detroit and Cleveland, and nearly one over Miami. Studley's Oilers led Shula's Dolphins in the fourth quarter of their December 4 Astrodome encounter before the visitors finally prevailed, 24-17.

Prior to his service in Houston, Studley spent the 1979-82 seasons as the defensive coordinator for the San Francisco 49ers. The '81 49er squad went all the way, capturing Super Bowl XVI with a victory over the Cincinnati Bengals. Before heading to California, Studley had been a Bengal assistant for ten seasons (1969-78).

CARL TASEFF

Offensive Backs
20th NFL Season,
17th with Dolphins

When Don Shula arrived in Miami in 1970, so too did Carl Taseff. Taseff and Shula's relationship dates back to their college days when they played in the same backfield together for Coach Herb Eisele's John Carroll squad. They were also roommates while both played for Cleveland (1951-52) and Baltimore (1953-56). Taseff has coached the Dolphins' offensive backs since coming to South Florida, and he's done it with great success. In fact, in the eight-year span from 1970-77, Taseff's backs ranked fifth or higher in NFL rushing on seven occasions. More importantly, Taseff has been able to change with the times. During the 1970s, the Dolphins employed a grind-it-out style that featured powerful fullback Larry Csonka. Since Dan Marino's emergence as Miami's air-oriented quarterback, Taseff's charges have become more a part of the passing game (i.e. Tony Nathan led the team in receptions last year).

Taseff came to Miami after spending two years working for the CEPO scouting combine (1968-69). Prior to that, he had coaching stints with the AFL's Boston Patriots (1964) and the NFL's Detroit Lions (1965-66).

JUNIOR WADE

Strength and Conditioning
12th NFL Season,
12th with Dolphins

In his fourth season as the Dolphins' Strength and Conditioning Coach, Junior Wade also administers the team's successful off-season conditioning program and assists with the Miami special teams. Previously, Wade had served eight years as the club's assistant trainer. The promotion to assistant coaching status was a well-deserved reward for the affable Wade. As a trainer, he had long had the respect of the Dolphin players for his knowledge and his willingness to boost player morale by putting himself through the same rigorous rehabilitation as that prescribed for injured Dolphins.

Appointed to his present position on February 15, 1983, Wade first joined the Dolphins as training camp assistant for the 1973-74 pre-seasons. He was hired by the Dolphins on a full-time basis in time for the 1975 campaign. Wade's past job experience includes having worked as an athletic trainer and guidance counselor at Fayetteville State and as the trainer for the St. Louis Cardinals' baseball farm team in Orangeburg, South Carolina.

MIKE WESTHOFF

Special Teams and Tight Ends
4th NFL Season, 1st with Dolphins

One of the newcomers to the Dolphins staff in 1986 is tight ends and special teams coach Mike Westhoff. Westhoff comes to Miami after spending a year in the United States Football League with the Arizona Outlaws, where he was the offensive line coach for Frank Kush.

Before his one-year stint in the USFL, Westhoff spent three seasons under Kush with the Baltimore/Indianapolis Colts (1982-84). While with the Colts his responsibilities included tight ends, special teams and weight training.

The 38-year-old Westhoff began his collegiate playing career at Wyoming in 1965 where he was a starting outside linebacker as a freshman. He then transferred to Wichita State, where he was a three-year starter at linebacker and center.

CHARLEY WINNER

Director of Pro Personnel,
Administrative Asst.
32nd NFL Season,
6th with Dolphins
Born: July 2, 1925

Two years ago, Charley Winner was given the responsibility of negotiating most player contracts. That duty goes along with Winner's other tasks that include scouting upcoming Dolphin opponents, searching for free agent talent and handling waiver and trade transactions. A true veteran of the National Football League, Winner is in his 32nd league season and sixth with the Dolphins.

Winner joined the Dolphins in 1981 after working one year for a cable television company. Prior to that, he enjoyed a distinguished coaching career which began in 1948 as an assistant under future father-in-law Weeb Ewbank at Washington University in St. Louis. He moved to Case Tech in 1950 under Head Coach Lou Saban, remaining there for four seasons. In 1954, Winner began his professional coaching career at Baltimore, again with Ewbank at the helm. From 1954-65, he coached Colt ends, defensive backs, linebackers and served as defensive coordinator. During his Baltimore stint, he coached a defensive back named Don Shula, later serving on Shula's staff when he became the Colt boss.

In 1966, Winner accepted the head coaching position of the St. Louis Cardinals, a post he held for five seasons. His teams had a 35-30-5 record, including an outstanding 9-4-1 mark in 1968. From 1971-72, Winner coached defensive backs for George Allen's Washington Redskins, whose '72 squad lost to the Dolphins in the Super Bowl. He was again reunited in 1973 with Ewbank, this time as an assistant for the New York Jets. Winner took over as Jet head coach the following year, posting a 9-14 slate in two seasons. He then coached Cincinnati's defensive backfield from 1976-79. Under Winner's guidance, Bengal DBs had conference rankings of first (1976) and second (1978) during his tenure.

A native of Somerville, New Jersey, Winner attended Southeast Missouri State College for one year before being drafted into the service in 1942. A radio operator and gunner in the Air Force, he flew 17 missions over Germany, and once spent six weeks in a German POW camp. Following the war, he completed his education at Washington University, earning letters in football and track.

ALL-TIME RECORD SECTION

1985 DOLPHIN STATISTICS

PRE-SEASON (2-2)

DATE	OPPONENT	SCORE		ACTUAL ATTENDANCE
Aug. 10	MINNESOTA	13-16 (OT)	L	41,129
Aug. 17	BUFFALO	27-17	W	37,557
Aug. 24	at L.A. Raiders	23-17	W	45,733
Aug. 30	at Atlanta	17-19	L	32,768

REGULAR SEASON RESULTS (12-4)

DATE	OPPONENT	SCORE		ACTUAL ATTENDANCE
Sept. 8	at Houston	23-26	L	47,656
Sept. 15	INDIANAPOLIS	30-13	W	53,693
Sept. 22	KANSAS CITY	31-0	W	69,791
Sept. 29	at Denver	30-26	W	73,614
Oct. 6	PITTSBURGH	24-20	W	72,820
Oct. 14	at N.Y. Jets	7-23	L	73,807
Oct. 20	TAMPA BAY	41-38	W	62,335
Oct. 27	at Detroit	21-31	L	75,291
Nov. 3	at New England	13-17	L	58,811
Nov. 10	N.Y. JETS	21-17	W	73,965
Nov. 17	at Indianapolis	34-20	W	59,666
Nov. 24	at Buffalo	23-14	W	50,474
Dec. 2	CHICAGO	38-24	W	75,594
Dec. 8	at Green Bay	34-24	W	52,671
Dec. 16	NEW ENGLAND	30-37	W	69,489
Dec. 22	BUFFALO	28-0	W	64,811

TEAM STATISTICS

	Dolphins	Opponent
TOTAL FIRST DOWNS	361	314
By Rushing	116	135
By Passing	218	160
By Penalty	27	19
Third Down: Made/Att	88/193	88/216
Third-Down Efficiency	45.6	40.7
Fourth Down: Made/Att	8/11	8/13
TOTAL NET YARDS	5843	5767
Average Per Game	365.2	360.4
Total Plays	1039	1033
Average Per Play	5.6	5.6
NET YARDS RUSHING	1729	2256
Average Per Game	108.1	141
Total Rushes	444	509
Average Per Rush	3.9	4.4
NET YARDS PASSING	4114	3511
Average Per Game	257.1	219.4
Tackled/Yards Lost	19/164	38/278
Gross Yards	4278	3789
Attempts/Completions	576/343	487/257
Pct. of Completions	59.5	52.8
Had Intercepted	21	23
PUNTS/AVERAGE	59/43.7	73/40.7
NET PUNTING AVERAGE	34.7	34.2
PENALTIES/YARDS	77/637	112/854
FUMBLES/BALLS LOST	31/20	36/18
TOUCHDOWNS	52	38
By Rushing	19	15
By Passing	31	21
By Returns	2	2
TOTAL POINTS	428	320

Score By Quarters	1	2	3	4	OT	TOTAL
DOLPHINS	88	136	95	109	0	428
OPPONENTS	44	96	78	102	0	320

RUSHING

	ATT.	YDS.	AVG.	LG	TD
Nathan	143	667	4.7	22	5
Davenport	98	370	3.8	33	11
Hampton	105	369	3.5	15	3
Bennett	54	256	4.7	17	0
Carter	14	76	5.4	19	0
N. Moore	1	11	11.0	11	0
Clayton	1	10	10.0	10	0
Strock	2	-6	-3.0	-3	0
Marino	26	-24	-.9	2	0
TOTALS	444	1729	3.9	33	19
Opponents	509	2256	4.4	32	15

PASSING

	ATT	COMP	YDS	PCT.	TD	INTC.	PCT./ INTC.	LG	LOST/ ATT	RATING
Marino	567	336	4137	59.3	30	21	3.7	73	157/18	84.1
Strock	9	7	141	77.8	1	0	0.0	67	0/0	154.7
Clayton	0	0	0	0.0	0	0	0.0	0	7/1	–
TOTALS	576	343	4278	59.5	31	21	3.6	73	164/19	85.6
Opponents	487	257	3789	52.8	21	23	4.7	80	278/38	73.3

RECEIVING

	NO.	YDS.	AVG.	LG	TD
Nathan	72	651	9.0	73	1
Clayton	70	996	14.2	45	4
N. Moore	51	701	13.7	69	7
Hardy	39	409	10.5	31	4
Duper	35	650	18.6	67	3
Rose	19	306	16.1	42	4
Johnson	13	192	14.8	61	3
Davenport	13	74	5.7	17	2
Bennett	10	101	10.1	27	1
Hampton	8	56	7.0	15	0
Heflin	6	98	16.3	46	1
Harris	3	24	8.0	11	0
Carter	2	4	4.0	4	0
Vigorito	1	9	9.0	9	0
Jensen	1	4	4.0	4	1
TOTALS	343	4278	12.5	73	31
Opponents	257	3789	14.7	80	21

INTERCEPTIONS

	NO.	YDS.	AVG.	LG	TD
G. Blackwood	6	36	6.0	17	0
Judson	4	88	22.0	61t	1
Lankford	4	10	2.5	6	0
B. Brown	2	40	20.0	26	0
Brophy	1	41	41.0	41	0
H. Green	1	28	28.0	28	0
Shipp	1	7	7.0	7	0
M. Brown	1	5	5.0	5	0
Brudzinski	1	6	6.0	6	0
L. Blackwood	1	0	0.0	0	0
Moyer	1	4	4.0	4	0
TOTALS	23	265	11.5	61	1
Opponents	21	100	4.8	40	0

KICKOFF RETURNS

	NO.	YDS.	AVG.	LG	TD
Hampton	45	1020	22.7	46	0
x- Carter	4	82	20.5	25	0
L. Blackwood	2	32	16.0	17	0
Hardy	1	11	11.0	11	0
y- Kozlowski	0	32	–	–	–
TOTALS	52	1177	22.6	46	0
Opponents	63	1359	21.6	50	0

(x) Includes 8 yards on handoff from Hampton; (y) handoff from Hampton

PUNT RETURNS

	NO.	FC	YDS.	AVG.	LG	TD
Vigorito	22	5	197	9.0	21	0
Kozlowski	7	2	65	9.3	17	0
Lockett	5	0	23	4.6	8	0
G. Blackwood	3	3	20	6.7	18	0

	NO.	YDS.	AVG.		LG	
Clayton	2	0	14	7.0	11	0
L. Blackwood	0	4	0	0.0	0	0
TOTALS	39	14	319	8.2	21	0
Opponents	27	6	371	13.7	70	1

PUNTING

	NO.	YDS.	AVG.	TB	IN20	LG	BLK.
Roby	59	2576	43.7	8	19	63	0
TOTALS	59	2576	43.7	8	19	63	0
Opponents	73	2972	40.7	8	13	67	1

FIELD GOALS

	1-19	20-29	30-39	40-49	50+	TOTAL
Reveiz	0/0	8/9	5/5	9/10	0/3	22/27
TOTALS	0/0	8/9	5/5	9/10	0/3	22/27
Opponents	2/2	5/5	7/9	4/10	1/2	19/28

SCORING

	TDR	TDP	TDRt	PAT	FGs	POINTS
Reveiz				50	22	116
Davenport	11	2				78
N. Moore		7				42
Nathan	5	1				36
Clayton		4				24
Rose		4				24
Hardy		4				24
Duper		3				18
Hampton	3					18
Johnson		3				18
Bennett		1				6
Judson			1			6
Jensen		1				6
Heflin		1				6
Brudzinski			1			6
TOTALS	19	31	2	50/52	22/27	428
Opponents	15	21	2	35/38	19/28	320

THE 1985 SEASON AT A GLANCE

Miami	10	3	3	7	—	23
Houston	0	9	3	14	—	26

Miami—FG Reveiz 33
Miami—Judson 61 int. return (Reveiz kick)
Miami—FG Reveiz 36
Houston—Woolfolk 80 pass from Moon (kick blocked)
Houston—FG Zendejas 35
Miami—FG Reveiz 23
Houston—FG Zendejas 46
Houston—Rozier 3 run (Zendejas kick)
Miami—Duper 67 pass from Strock (Reveiz kick)
Houston—Rozier 1 run (Zendejas kick)
A—47,656 actual, 50,157 paid

	Miami	Houston
First Downs	17	21
Rushes – Yards	24-70	41-165
Passing Yards	290	229
Total Yards	360	394
Had QB Sacked	1-1	3-41
Passes	31-19-2	17-12-1
Punts	2-43.5	2-42.5
Fumbles/Lost	2-1	4-3
Penalties/Yards	5-38	7-57

INDIVIDUAL LEADERS

RUSHING — Miami: Davenport 7-50, Hampton 11-17, Nathan 3-6
Houston: Woolfolk 12-60, Rozier 12-34, Moriarty 9-29, Edwards 3-24
PASSING — Miami: Marino 24-13-2, 159 yards, no TDs; Strock: 7-6-0, 132 yards, 1 TD
Houston: Moon 17-12-1, 270 yards, 1 TD
RECEIVING — Miami: Clayton 5-99, Duper 4-95, N. Moore 4-43, Nathan 4-43
Houston: Woolfolk 3-120, Smith 4-46, Hill 2-70, Williams 2-27

Indianapolis	0	7	0	6	—	13
Miami	3	10	3	14	—	30

Miami—FG Reveiz 22
Miami—FG Reveiz 25
Indianapolis—Beach 2 pass from Pagel (Allegre kick)
Miami—Clayton 6 pass from Marino (Reveiz kick)
Miami—FG Reveiz 40
Miami—Nathan 21 run (Reveiz kick)
Miami—Moore 3 pass from Marino (Reveiz kick)
Indianapolis—Wonsley 1 run (kick blocked)
A—53,693 actual, 57,772 paid

	Indianapolis	Miami
First Downs	17	33
Rushes – Yards	23-96	31-157
Passing Yards	202	329
Total Yards	298	486
Had QB Sacked	2-12	0-0
Passes	32-16-1	48-29-0
Punts	5-43.8	1-62
Fumbles/Lost	1-0	1-1
Penalties/Yards	7-62	3-20

INDIVIDUAL LEADERS

RUSHING — Indianapolis: Wonsley 10-48, McMillan 4-22, Bentley 3-15, Middleton 5-9
Miami: Nathan 6-55, Hampton 13-53, Davenport 12-49
PASSING — Indianapolis: Pagel 32-16-1, 214 yards, 1 TD
Miami: Marino 48-29-0, 329 yards, 2 TDs
RECEIVING — Indianpolis: Butler 3-68, Wonsley 3-38, Beach 3-44
Miami: Clayton 8-106, Moore 7-67, Rose 4-51, Nathan 3-44

Kansas City	0	0	0	0	—	0
Miami	0	0	14	17	—	31

Miami—Hardy 9 pass from Marino (Reveiz kick)
Miami—Bennett 27 pass from Marino (Reveiz kick)
Miami—Davenport 1 run (Reveiz kick)
Miami—Davenport 3 run (Reveiz kick)
Miami—FG Reveiz 37
A—69,791 actual, 72,238 paid

	Kansas City	Miami
First Downs	15	27
Rushes – Yards	25-97	29-133
Passing Yards	187	258
Total Yards	284	391
Had QB Sacked	3-18	0-0
Passes	38-19-2	35-23-1
Punts	6-39.5	3-40.3
Fumbles/Lost	0-0	1-1
Penalties/Yards	4-20	6-44

INDIVIDUAL LEADERS

RUSHING — Kansas City: Heard 12-53, Horton 3-22, Jones 4-10
Miami: Davenport 12-55, Nathan 10-53, Hampton 6-22
PASSING — Kansas City: Kenney 38-19-2, 205 yards, no TDs
Miami: Marino 35-23-1, 258 yards, 2 TDs
RECEIVING — Kansas City: Marshall 4-67, Paige 2-48, Heard 2-12
Miami: Bennett 4-63, Moore 4-55, Hardy 4-32, Clayton 3-27, Rose 1-30

Miami	7	13	7	3	—	30
Denver	7	10	6	3	—	26

Denver—Lang 10 run (Karlis kick)
Miami—Moore 69 pass from Marino (Reveiz kick)
Miami—FG Reveiz 40
Denver—Winder 7 run (Karlis kick)
Miami—FG Reveiz 24
Miami—Rose 24 pass from Marino (Reveiz kick)
Denver—FG Karlis 43
Denver—Winder 1 run (kick failed)
Miami—Heflin 46 pass from Marino (Reveiz kick)
Miami—FG Reveiz 27
Denver—FG Karlis 34
A—73,614 actual, 75,100 paid

	Miami	Denver
First Downs	19	23
Rushes – Yards	22-53	31-169
Passing Yards	365	226
Total Yards	418	395
Had QB Sacked	3-25	3-24
Passes	43-25-0	38-18-1
Punts	7-45.0	8-41.0
Fumbles/Lost	1-1	2-1
Penalties/Yards	4-41	9-93

INDIVIDUAL LEADERS

RUSHING — Miami: Nathan 14-38, Bennett 2-9, Davenport 2-5
Denver: Winder 20-103, Elway 4-32, Lang 6-30
PASSING — Miami: Marino 43-25-0, 390 yards, 3 TDs
Denver: Elway 37-18-1, 250 yards, no TDs
RECEIVING — Miami: Nathan 10-120, Moore 5-109, Rose 3-49, Heflin 2-57
Denver: Watson 4-67, Kay 4-33, B. Johnson 2-58

Pittsburgh	0	17	0	3	—	20
Miami	7	7	3	7	—	24

Miami—Nathan 1 run (Reveiz kick)
Pittsburgh—Abercrombie 1 run (Anderson kick)
Pittsburgh—FG Anderson 48
Miami—Johnson 2 pass from Marino (Reveiz kick)
Pittsburgh—Thompson 1 pass from Malone (Anderson kick)
Miami—FG Reveiz 35
Pittsburgh—FG Anderson 33
Miami—Hampton 2 run (Reveiz kick)
A—72,820 actual, 75,070 paid

	Pittsburgh	Miami
First Downs	15	24
Rushes – Yards	30-137	29-122
Passing Yards	145	277
Total Yards	282	399
Had QB Sacked	0-0	0-0
Passes	33-14-1	45-27-3
Punts	8-39.0	4-44.8
Fumbles/Lost	3-0	1-1
Penalties/Yards	1-10	4-62

INDIVIDUAL LEADERS

RUSHING — Pittsburgh: Abercrombie 14-91, Pollard 14-46
Miami: Nathan 9-51, Bennett 6-30, Hampton 7-29
PASSING — Pittsburgh: Malone 33-14-1, 145 yards, 1 TD
Miami: Marino 45-27-3, 277 yards, 1 TD
RECEIVING — Pittsburgh: Stallworth 4-41, Lipps 3-43, Erenberg 3-33, Pollard 3-27
Miami: Hardy 7-84, Clayton 5-71, Nathan 5-40, N. Moore 3-39

Pittsburgh	0	17	0	3	—	20
Miami	7	7	3	7	—	24

Miami—Nathan 1 run (Reveiz kick)
Pittsburgh—Abercrombie 1 run (Anderson kick)
Pittsburgh—FG Anderson 48
Miami—Johnson 2 pass from Marino (Reveiz kick)
Pittsburgh—Thompson 1 pass from Malone
(Anderson kick)
Miami—FG Reveiz 35
Pittsburgh—FG Anderson 33
Miami—Hampton 2 run (Reveiz kick)
A—72,820 actual, 75,070 paid

	Pittsburgh	Miami
First Downs	15	24
Rushes – Yards	30-137	29-122
Passing Yards	145	277
Total Yards	282	399
Had QB Sacked	0-0	0-0
Passes	33-14-1	45-27-3
Punts	8-39.0	4-44.8
Fumbles/Lost	3-0	1-1
Penalties/Yards	1-10	4-62

INDIVIDUAL LEADERS

RUSHING — Pittsburgh: Abercrombie 14-91, Pollard 14-46
Miami: Nathan 9-51, Bennett 6-30, Hampton 7-29
PASSING — Pittsburgh: Malone 33-14-1, 145 yards, 1 TD
Miami: Marino 45-27-3, 277 yards, 1 TD
RECEIVING — Pittsburgh: Stallworth 4-41, Lipps 3-43, Erenberg 3-33, Pollard 3-27
Miami: Hardy 7-84, Clayton 5-71, Nathan 5-40, N. Moore 3-39

Tampa Bay	0	14	7	17	—	38
Miami	14	10	14	0	—	41

Miami—Moore 16 pass from Marino (Reveiz kick)
Miami—Jensen 4 pass from Marino (Reveiz kick)
Tampa Bay—Wilder 10 run (Igwebuike kick)
Miami—Davenport 1 run (Reveiz kick)
Miami—FG Reveiz 20
Tampa Bay—Giles 15 pass from DeBerg
(Igwebuike kick)
Miami—Nathan 1 run (Reveiz kick)
Tampa Bay—Giles 39 pass from DeBerg
(Igwebuike kick)
Miami—Hardy 3 pass from Marino (Reveiz kick)
Tampa Bay— Giles 7 pass from DeBerg
(Igwebuike kick)
Tampa Bay—Giles 16 pass from DeBerg
(Igwebuike kick)
Tampa Bay—FG Igwebuike 38
Miami—FG Reveiz 43
A—62,335 actual, 62,987 paid

	Tampa Bay	Miami
First Downs	24	30
Rushes – Yards	25-111	31-144
Passing Yards	365	302
Total Yards	476	446
Had QB Sacked	0-0	0-0
Passes	32-19-1	39-27-1
Punts	4-38.0	2-43.0
Fumbles/Lost	1-0	2-1
Penalties/Yards	7-57	6-50

INDIVIDUAL LEADERS

RUSHING — Tampa Bay: Wilder 24-98, DeBerg 1-13
Miami: Hampton 13-78, Nathan 12-62
PASSING — Tampa Bay: DeBerg 32-19-1, 365 yards, 4 TDs
Miami: Marino: 39-27-1, 302 yards, 3 TDs
RECEIVING — Tampa Bay: Giles 7-116, J. Bell 5-89, House 4-111, Carter 2-45
Miami: Nathan 8-80, Clayton 5-50, N. Moore 5-49, Rose 2-66

Miami	0	14	7	0	—	21
Detroit	10	14	0	7	—	31

Detroit—Jones 6 pass from Hipple (Murray kick)
Detroit—FG Murray 50
Miami—Rose 19 pass from Marino (Reveiz kick)
Detroit—L. Thompson 38 pass from Hipple
(Murray kick)
Miami—Moore 5 pass from Marino (Reveiz kick)
Detroit—Nichols 30 pass from Hipple (Murray kick)
Miami—Brudzinski 7 fumble return (Reveiz kick)
Detroit—Jones 1 run (Murray kick)
A—75,291 actual, 80,638 paid

	Miami	Detroit
First Downs	20	21
Rushes – Yards	17-102	49-152
Passing Yards	239	203
Total Yards	341	355
Had QB Sacked	1-8	4-36
Passes	44-23-2	21-14-0
Punts	4-45.5	4-50.3
Fumbles/Lost	1-1	2-1
Penalties/Yards	4-30	4-35

INDIVIDUAL LEADERS

RUSHING — Miami: Nathan 7-53, Bennett 5-32, Hamilton 3-7
Detroit: J. Jones 36-114, Moore 11-40
PASSING — Miami: Marino 44-23-2, 247 yards, 2 TDs
Detroit: Hipple 19-14-0, 239 yards, 3 TDs
RECEIVING — Miami: Clayton 7-72, N. Moore 6-69, Nathan 4-33, Rose 2-40
Detroit: Thompson 6-133, Nichols 4-66, Lewis 2-31

Miami	7	3	3	0	—	13
New England	0	3	0	14	—	17

Miami—Davenport 3 run (Reveiz kick)
Miami—FG Reveiz 26
New England—FG Franklin 38
Miami—FG Reveiz 32
New England—Hawthorne 28 pass from Grogan
(Franklin kick)
New England—Grogan 1 run (Franklin kick)
A—58,811 actual, 61,000 paid

	Miami	New England
First Downs	19	22
Rushes – Yards	29-91	40-203
Passing Yards	145	177
Total Yards	236	380
Had QB Sacked	3-26	2-11
Passes	33-15-2	31-14-3
Punts	5-41.4	5-39.4
Fumbles/Lost	3-2	3-1
Penalties/Yards	1-10	11-86

INDIVIDUAL LEADERS

RUSHING — Miami: Davenport 11-47, Hampton 10-25, Nathan 6-19
New England: James 23-119, Collins 11-49, Tatupu 3-16
PASSING — Miami: Marino 33-15-2, 171 yards, no TDs
New England: Grogan 31-14-3, 188 yards, 1 TD
RECEIVING — Miami: Clayton 7-122, Johnson 2-22, Nathan 2-10
New England: Collins 4-47, Fryar 3-55, James 3-35, Hawthorne 1-28

N.Y. Jets	0	3	7	7	—	17
Miami	0	7	7	7	—	21

New York—FG Leahy 21
Miami—Duper 60 pass from Marino (Reveiz kick)
Miami—Clayton 27 pass from Marino (Reveiz kick)
New York—McNeil 14 pass from O'Brien
(Leahy kick)
New York—Klever 20 pass from O'Brien
(Leahy kick)
Miami—Duper 50 pass from Marino (Reveiz kick)
A—73,965 actual, 75,275 paid

	N.Y. Jets	Miami
First Downs	27	19
Rushes – Yards	30-120	19-53
Passing Yards	371	347
Total Yards	491	400
Had QB Sacked	5-22	3-15
Passes	43-26-0	37-21-3
Punts	4-39.8	5-37.2
Fumbles/Lost	5-2	4-2
Penalties/Yards	13-81	10-76

INDIVIDUAL LEADERS

RUSHING — New York: McNeil 26-107, Hector 3-12
Miami: Nathan 8-38, Hampton 3-8, Bennett 3-7
PASSING — New York: O'Brien 43-26-0, 393 yards, 2 TDs
Miami: Marino 37-21-3, 362 yards, 3 TDs
RECEIVING — New York: Toon 10-156, McNeil 4-56, Walker 4-48, Townsell 2-57
Miami: Duper 8-217, Nathan 5-53, Clayton 3-36, Johnson 2-33

Miami	3	10	14	7	—	34
Indianapolis	10	3	7	0	—	20

Indianapolis—FG Allegre 28
Indianapolis—Martin 70 run (Allegre kick)
Miami—FG Reveiz 45
Miami—Hampton 4 run (Reveiz kick)
Indianapolis—FG Allegre 30
Miami—FG Reveiz 44
Miami—Davenport 1 run (Reveiz kick)
Miami—Hampton 1 run (Reveiz kick)
Indianapolis—Capers 80 pass from Pagel
(Allegre kick)
Miami—Davenport 17 pass from Marino
(Reveiz kick)
A—59,666 actual, 60,656 paid

	Miami	Indianapolis
First Downs	25	17
Rushes — Yards	37-135	25-142
Passing Yards	323	210
Total Yards	458	352
Had QB Sacked	1-7	3-12
Passes	37-22-0	33-14-2
Punts	4-50.5	4-44.8
Fumbles/Lost	2-2	2-2
Penalties/Yards	4-30	3-25

INDIVIDUAL LEADERS

RUSHING — Miami: Hampton 16-58, Bennett 5-31, Davenport 8-21, Nathan 5-20
Indianapolis: McMillan 10-57, Pagel 4-34, Wonsley 4-29, Dickey 6-23
PASSING — Miami: Marino 37-22-0, 330 yards, 1 TD
Indianapolis: Pagel 33-14-2, 222 yards, 1 TD
RECEIVING — Miami: Duper 5-64, Nathan 4-29, Hardy 3-69, Moore 3-65, Clayton 2-48
Indianapolis: Capers 3-94, Dickey 3-30, Williams 1-30, Butler 1-23

Miami	7	7	3	6	—	23
Buffalo	0	7	7	0	—	14

Miami—Davenport 7 pass from Marino (Reveiz kick)
Miami—Johnson 15 pass from Marino (Reveiz kick)
Buffalo—Reed 11 pass from Mathison
(Norwood kick)
Buffalo—Butler 60 pass from Mathison
(Norwood kick)
Miami—FG Reveiz 22
Miami—Nathan 4 run (kick failed)
A—50,474 actual, 53,529 paid

	Miami	Buffalo
First Downs	28	12
Rushes — Yards	41-172	19-94
Passing Yards	216	161
Total Yards	388	255
Had QB Sacked	1-17	3-35
Passes	31-22-2	28-15-0
Punts	3-30.0	7-39.7
Fumbles/Lost	1-0	2-1
Penalties/Yards	5-41	6-30

INDIVIDUAL LEADERS

RUSHING — Miami: Nathan 14-77, Bennett 10-59, Davenport 9-26
Buffalo: Bell 16-52, Mathison 3-42
PASSING — Miami: Marino 31-22-2, 233 yards, 2 TDs
Buffalo: Mathison 28-15-0, 196 yards, 2 TDs
RECEIVING — Miami: Clayton: 5-60, Duper 4-57, Davenport 4-23, Hardy 3-28
Buffalo: Reed 6-68, Butler 3-87, Burkett 2-21

Chicago	7	3	14	0	—	24
Miami	10	21	7	0	—	38

Miami—Moore 33 pass from Marino (Reveiz kick)
Chicago—Fuller 1 run (Butler kick)
Miami—FG Reveiz 47
Miami—Davenport 1 run (Reveiz kick)
Chicago—FG Butler 30
Miami—Davenport 1 run (Reveiz kick)
Miami—Moore 6 pass from Marino (Reveiz kick)

	Chicago	Miami
First Downs	23	17
Rushes — Yards	37-167	24-90
Passing Yards	176	245
Total Yards	343	335
Had QB Sacked	6-35	3-25
Passes	28-14-3	27-14-1
Punts	3-29.0	3-44.7
Fumbles/Lost	1-1	2-1
Penalties/Yards	7-65	6-61

Chicago—Fuller 1 run (Butler kick)
Miami—Clayton 42 pass from Marino (Reveiz kick)
Chicago—Margerum 19 pass from Fuller
 (Butler kick)
A—75,594 actual, 75,594 paid

INDIVIDUAL LEADERS

RUSHING — Chicago: Payton 23-121, Suhey 7-19, Fuller 6-19
 Miami: Nathan 15-74, Bennett 5-12
PASSING — Chicago: Fuller 21-11-2, 169 yards, 1 TD; McMahon 6-3-1, 42 yards, no TDs
 Miami: Marino 27-14-1, 270 yards, 3 TDs
RECEIVING — Chicago: Margerum 4-61, Moorehead 4-33, Gault 2-79, Payton 2-16
 Miami: Duper 5-107, Clayton 5-88, Moore 4-75

							Miami	Green Bay
Miami	6	14	0	14	—	34		
Green Bay	3	0	14	7	—	24		

	Miami	Green Bay
First Downs	24	20
Rushes — Yards	22-63	29-105
Passing Yards	345	241
Total Yards	408	366
Had QB Sacked	0-0	1-6
Passes	44-30-1	35-20-2
Punts	3-40.7	3-30.7
Fumbles/Lost	3-2	2-2
Penalties/Yards	6-47	5-30

Green Bay—FG Del Greco 22
Miami—Nathan 10 pass from Marino (kick failed)
Miami—Clayton 21 pass from Marino (Reveiz kick)
Miami—Moore 16 pass from Marino (Reveiz kick)
Green Bay—Dennard 29 pass from Zorn
 (Del Greco kick)
Green Bay—Lofton 56 pass from Zorn
 (Del Greco kick)
Green Bay—Ivery 1 run (Del Greco kick)
Miami—Rose 2 pass from Marino (Reveiz kick)
Miami—Johnson 61 pass from Marino (Reveiz kick)
A—52,671 actual, 56,860 paid

INDIVIDUAL LEADERS

RUSHING — Miami: Nathan 10-35, Bennett 5-19
 Green Bay: Ellis 5-50, Clark 11-43, Ivery 10-24
PASSING — Miami: Marino 44-30-1, 345 yards, 5 TDs
 Green Bay: Zorn 35-20-2, 247 yards, 2 TDs
RECEIVING — Miami: Nathan 10-86, Clayton 6-70, D. Johnson 2-65, Rose 3-44, Duper 4-35
 Green Bay: Lofton 4-91, Dennard 3-58, Epps 4-35, Clark 3-22

							New England	Miami
New England	7	0	3	17	—	27		
Miami	7	19	3	10	—	30		

	New England	Miami
First Downs	19	22
Rushes — Yards	34-122	32-92
Passing Yards	199	177
Total Yards	321	269
Had QB Sacked	2-18	2-15
Passes	26-14-3	33-17-1
Punts	4-41.3	2-53.0
Fumbles/Lost	3-1	4-3
Penalties/Yards	6-55	2-9

Miami—Rose 6 pass from Marino (Reveiz kick)
New England—Fryar 10 pass from Eason
 (Franklin kick)
Miami—FG Reveiz 44
Miami—Davenport 1 Run (Reveiz kick)
New England—FG Franklin 22
Miami—FG Reveiz 49
New England—FG Franklin 49
Miami—Davenport run (Reveiz kick)
New England—Tatupu 1 run (Franklin kick)
New England—Jones 15 yd. fumble return
 (Franklin kick)
Miami—FG Reveiz 47
A—69,489 actual, 75,825 paid

INDIVIDUAL LEADERS

RUSHING — New England: James 18-58, Collins 11-44
 Miami: Carter: 8-50, Bennett 4-26, Nathan 7-24
PASSING — New England: Eason 26-14-3, 217 yards, 1 TD
 Miami: Marino 33-17-1, 192 yards, 1 TD
RECEIVING — New England: Morgan 3-61, Collins 4-46, Starring 1-40
 Miami: Duper 5-75, Moore 5-66, Clayton 2-20

							Buffalo	Miami
Buffalo	0	0	0	0	—	0		
Miami	7	7	0	14	—	28		

	Buffalo	Miami
First Downs	11	24
Rushes — Yards	26-111	36-179
Passing Yards	188	129
Total Yards	299	308
Had QB Sacked	0-0	1-16
Passes	24-10-3	26-16-1
Punts	4-44.8	5-41.6
Fumbles/Lost	5-3	3-1
Penalties/Yards	19-123	7-47

Miami—Hardy 19 pass from Marino (Reveiz kick)
Miami—Hardy 5 pass from Marino (Reveiz kick)
Miami—Nathan 1 run (Reveiz kick)
Miami—Davenport 13 run (Reveiz kick)
A—64,811 actual, 65,811 paid

INDIVIDUAL LEADERS

RUSHING — Buffalo: Bell 9-50, Cribbs 14-48
 Miami: Davenport 6-57, Nathan 11-54, Bennett 6-31
PASSING — Buffalo: Mathison 24-10-3, 188 yards, no TDs
 Miami: Marino 24-15-1, 136 yards, 2 TDs
RECEIVING — Buffalo: Bell 3-64, Butler, 1-45, Reed 3-44
 Miami: Hardy 5-52, Nathan 6-45, Clayton 1-23

							Miami	Cleveland
Cleveland	7	7	7	0	—	21		
Miami	3	0	14	7	—	24		

	Miami	Cleveland
First Downs	20	17
Rushes — Yards	19-92	37-251
Passing Yards	238	62
Total Yards	330	313
Had QB Sacked	1-4	0-0
Passes	45-25-1	19-10-1
Punts	5-41.6	6-37.2
Fumbles/Lost	1-0	1-0
Penalties/Yards	2-20	6-49

Miami—FG Reveiz 51
Cleveland—Newsome 16 pass from Kosar
 (Bahr kick)
Cleveland—Byner 21 run (Bahr kick)
Cleveland—Byner 66 run (Bahr kick)
Miami—Moore 6 pass from Marino (Reveiz kick)
Miami—Davenport 31 run (Reveiz kick)
Miami—Davenport 1 run (Reveiz kick)
A—75,128 actual, 75,842 paid

INDIVIDUAL LEADERS

RUSHING — Miami: Davenport 6-48, Nathan 7-21, Bennett 4-17, Carter 2-6
 Cleveland: Byner 16-161, Mack 13-56, Dickey 6-28, Kosar 2-6
PASSING — Miami: Marino 45-25-1, 238 yards, 1 TD
 Cleveland: Kosar 19-10-1, 66 yards, 1 TD
RECEIVING — Miami: Nathan 10-101, Hardy 5-51, Moore 4-29, Johnson 2-17, Rose 1-17, Clayton 1-15, Bennett 1-6, Carter 1-2
 Cleveland: Byner 4-25, Newsome 2-22, Holt 2-2, Weathers 1-12, Fontenot 1-5

							New England	Miami
New England	3	14	7	7	—	31		
Miami	0	7	0	7	—	14		

	New England	Miami
First Downs	21	18
Rushes — Yards	59-255	13-68
Passing Yards	71	234
Total Yards	326	302
Had QB Sacked	0-0	1-14
Passes	12-10-0	48-20-2
Punts	5-40.2	4-41.3
Fumbles/Lost	2-2	5-4
Penalties/Yards	2-15	4-35

New England—FG Franklin 23
Miami—Johnson 10 pass from Marino (Reveiz kick)
New England—Collins 4 pass from Eason
 (Franklin kick)
New England—D. Ramsey 1 pass from Eason
 (Franklin kick)
New England—Weathers 2 pass from Eason
 (Franklin kick)
Miami—Nathan 10 pass from Marino (Reveiz kick)
New England—Tatupu 1 run (Franklin kick)
A—74,978 actual, 76,270 paid

INDIVIDUAL LEADERS

RUSHING — New England: C. James 22-105, Weathers 16-87, Collins 12-61
 Miami: Carter 6-56, Davenport 3-6, Nathan 2-4
PASSING — New England: Eason 12-10-0, 71 yards, 3 TDs
 Miami: Marino 48-20-2, 248 yards, 2 TDs
RECEIVING — New England: Morgan 2-30, D. Ramsey, 3-18, Collins 3-15
 Miami: Nathan 5-57, Hardy 3-51, Duper 3-45, Clayton 3-41

1985 GAMES/STARTS

PLAYER	PLAYED	STARTED	DNP*
Barnett, Bill	16	1	0
Bennett, Woody	16	13	0
Betters, Doug	14	14	2
Blackwood, Glenn	14	14	0
Blackwood, Lyle	16	0	0
Bokamper, Kim	16	12	0
Bowser, Charles	2	2	5
Brophy, Jay	16	6	0
Brown, Bud	16	16	0

PLAYER	PLAYED	STARTED	DNP*
Brown, Mark	15	15	1
Brudzinski, Bob	14	13	0
Carter, Joe	10	0	0
Charles, Mike	16	16	0
Clark, Steve	16	5	0
Clayton, Mark	16	16	0
Davenport, Ron	16	1	0
Dellenbach, Jeff	11	1	5
Duper, Mark	9	8	0
Foster, Roy	16	16	0
Giesler, Jon	13	13	3
Green, Cleveland	12	11	4
Green, Hugh	11	11	0
Hampton, Lorenzo	16	1	0
Hardy, Bruce	16	16	0
Heflin, Vince	5	0	0
Jensen, Jim	16	1	0
Johnson, Dan	12	1	0
Judson, William	16	16	0
Kozlowski, Mike	5	2	0
Lankford, Paul	16	15	0
Lee, Larry	5	0	0
Lee, Ronnie	15	13	1
Little, George	14	3	2
Marino, Dan	16	16	0
McNeal, Don	10	0	0
Moore, Mack	16	2	0
Moore, Nat	15	7	1
Moyer, Alex	10	0	0
Nathan, Tony	16	15	0
Reveiz, Fuad	16	0	0
Roby, Reggie	16	0	0
Rose, Joe	16	1	0
Sendlein, Robin	16	3	0
Shipp, Jackie	16	11	0
Smith, Mike	7	0	3
Sowell, Robert	10	1	0
Stephenson, Dwight	16	16	0
Strock, Don	16	0	0
Toews, Jeff	11	5	0
Vigorito, Tom	9	0	1

*Includes games in which a player was on the 45-man active roster, but did not play.

1985 DEFENSIVE STATISTICS

PLAYER	TACKLES	ASSISTS	TOTAL TACKLES
M. Brown	78	18	96
B. Brown	79	15	94
Shipp	68	15	83
Brudzinski	56	15	71
Charles	52	9	61
†Hugh Green	46 (76)	12 (19)	58 (95)

PLAYER	TACKLES	ASSISTS	TOTAL TACKLES
*Betters	53	3	56
Lankford	48	8	56
G. Blackwood	44	12	56
§Judson	40	5	45
Brophy	35	5	40
‡Bokamper	19	3	22
Moyer	15	6	21
Sendlein	17	2	19
#Shiver	17	2	19
L. Blackwood	15	4	19
McNeal	15	3	18
M. Moore	15	2	17
Kozlowski	14	3	17
Little	12	5	17
Sowell	14	0	14
Barnett	8	1	9
Clayton	8	0	8
Davenport	7	0	7
Rose	6	0	6
Hardy	5	0	5
Bowser	4	0	4
Carter	4	0	4
Jensen	3	1	4
#Lockett	3	1	4
Smith	3	0	3
#Swain	3	0	3
Heflin	3	0	3
Clark	2	0	2
Roby	2	0	2
N. Moore	2	0	2
Carter	2	0	2
Reveiz	1	0	1
H. Green	1	0	1
Stephenson	1	0	1
Johnson	1	0	1
#Walker	1	0	1

†Numbers in parenthesis include Tampa Bay totals   *Blocked PAT vs. Houston, 9/8
§Blocked field goal vs. N.Y. Jets, 10/14 and blocked punt vs. Chicago, 12/2   ‡Blocked PAT vs. Indianapolis, 9/15   # No longer with club

QUARTERBACK SACKS

Charles 7, Betters 6½, M. Moore 5½, H. Green 5, Brudzinski 3, Bowser 2½, Bokamper 2½, M. Brown 1, Lankford 1, Brophy 1, Shiver 1, Little 1, Sowell 1

FUMBLES RECOVERED

B. Brown 5, M. Brown 2, Shipp 2, Brudzinski 2, G. Blackwood 1, Brophy 1, Moyer 1, Barnett 1

FUMBLES FORCED

Lankford 4, Charles 2, Green 2, Judson 2, M. Brown 1, B. Brown 1, Brudzinski 1, Betters 1, Bokamper 1, Moyer 1, Sendlein 1, Shiver 1, M. Moore 1, Barnett 1, N. Moore 1

PASSES DEFENSED

Lankford 14, B. Brown 9, G. Blackwood 8, Brudzinski 5, H. Green 4, Judson 4, M. Brown 3, Shipp 3, Brophy 3, Moyer 3, L. Blackwood 3, Bokamper 2, McNeal 2, Swain 2, Charles 1, Betters 1, M. Moore 1, Kozlowski 1, Sowell 1

NFL TOP 20 COACHES

COACH	YEARS	TEAMS	REGULAR SEASON				CAREER			
			W	L	T	PCT.	W	L	T	PCT.
George Halas	40	Bears	320	148	30	.672	325	151	30	.672
Don Shula	23	Colts, Dolphins	239	86	6	.731	255	99	6	.717
Tom Landry	26	Cowboys	233	132	6	.636	253	148	6	.629
Curly Lambeau	33	Packers, Cardinals, Redskins	231	133	23	.627	234	135	23	.626
Paul Brown	21	Browns, Bengals	166	100	6	.621	170	108	6	.609
Bud Grant	18	Vikings	158	96	5	.620	168	108	5	.607
Chuck Noll	17	Steelers	149	97	1	.605	164	104	1	.612
Steve Owen	23	Giants	151	100	17	.595	154	108	17	.582
Hank Stram	17	Chiefs, Saints	131	97	10	.571	136	100	10	.573
Weeb Ewbank	20	Colts, Jets	130	129	7	.502	134	130	7	.507
Chuck Knox	13	Rams, Bills, Seahawks	120	70	1	.631	127	79	1	.616
Sid Gillman	18	Rams, Chargers, Oilers	122	99	7	.550	123	104	7	.541
George Allen	12	Rams, Redskins	116	47	5	.705	118	54	5	.681
Don Coryell	13	Cardinals, Chargers	110	76	1	.591	113	82	1	.579
John Madden	10	Raiders	103	32	7	.750	112	39	7	.731
Buddy Parker	15	Cardinals, Lions, Steelers	104	75	9	.577	107	76	9	.581
Vince Lombardi	10	Packers, Redskins	96	34	6	.728	105	35	6	.740
Lou Saban	16	Patriots, Bills, Broncos	95	99	7	.490	97	100	7	.493
Jimmy Conzelman	16	Independents, Badgers, Panthers, Steam Roller, Cardinals	88	67	17	.561	89	68	17	.560
Bum Phillips	11	Oilers, Saints	82	77	0	.516	86	80	0	.514

MIAMI DOLPHIN DIRECTORY

ADMINISTRATIVE OFFICE
4770 Biscayne Boulevard
Suite 1440
Miami, Florida 33137
(305) 576-1000

TRAINING CAMP
St. Thomas University
16400-D NW 32nd Avenue
Miami, Florida 33054
(305) 625-6491

ADMINISTRATION

President	Joseph Robbie
Executive VP & General Manager	J. Michael Robbie
Vice-President	Elizabeth Robbie
Vice President, Public Affairs	Joseph K. Abrell
General Counsel	Jann M. Iliff
Director of Publicity	Edward J. White
Security Consultant	Stuart B. Weinstein
Traveling Secretary	Bryan J. Wiedmeier
Publications & Promotions Assistant	H.R. (Dick) Horning
Librarian	Ann Laliotes
Secretary to Executive V. President	Joan Buetel
Executive Secretary	Abby Brower
Executive Secretary/Office Manager	Elisabeth Horky
Secretary	Gayle Baden
Controller	Howard F. Rieman, Jr.
Bookkeeper	Doris L. Young
Accounts Payable Clerk	Mary Scharff
Assistant Bookkeeper	Kenneth Killings
Messenger/Mail Clerk	Jose A. Fiel
Assistant Librarian	Sharon F. Katz
Accounts Payable Clerk	Georgia C. Thompson
Receptionist	Lisa Lee Berns
Chauffeur	Mohammad Alikhanzadeh

TRAINING CAMP

Vice-President/Head Coach	Donald F. Shula
Assistant Head Coach/Receivers & Quarterbacks	David Shula
Assistant Coaches:	
Linebackers	Bob Matheson
Defensive Backs	Mel Phillips
Offense, Offensive Line	John Sandusky
Defensive Line	Dan Sekanovich
Defense	Chuck Studley
Offensive Backs	Carl Taseff
Special Teams	Mike Westhoff
Strength & Conditioning	Junior Wade
Dir. of Pro Scouting & Admin. Asst.	Charley Winner
Director of Player Personnel	Charles T. Connor
College Area Scouts	Milt Davis, Mike Cartwright, Kevin Colbert
Trainer	Bob Lundy
Assistant Trainer	Bill Davis
Equipment Manager	Bob Monica
Assistant Equipment Manager	Bill Herman
Video Manager	Dave Hack
Assistant Video Manager	Mike Gleason
Secretary to Head Coach	Anne Rodriguez
Secretaries	Patricia Daley, Denise Sherry
Team Physician	Dr. Charles E. Virgin
Medical Consultant	Dr. Edward W. St. Mary

DOLPHIN STADIUM CORPORATION

Stadium Coordinator	Marlo W. Hanson
Director of Promotions & Sales	Frank C. Buetel
Stadium Sales Representative	Daniel T. Robbie

TICKETS

Ticket Director	Kevin T. Fitzgerald
Ticket Aides	Mabel Brooker, Lorraine Mondich, Patricia Moran

HOW THE DOLPHINS WERE BUILT

YEAR		DRAFT (41)		FREE AGENTS/WAVERS (9)		TRADE (4)
1973 12-2-0 NFL Champions	**QB** **y-G**	Don Strock (No. 5a) Ed Newman (No. 6)				
1974 11-3-0 1st AFC East	**WR**	Nat Moore (No. 3)				
1975 10-4-0 T-1st, AFC East						
1976 6-8-0 3rd, AFC East	**DE**	Kim Bokamper (No. 1b)				
1977 10-4-0 T-1st, AFC East	**y-DT**	Bob Baumhower (No. 2)				
1978 11-5-0 T-1st, AFC East	**DE** **TE** **C**	Doug Betters (No. 6) Bruce Hardy (No. 9) Mark Dennard (No. 10)**				
1979 10-6-0 1st, AFC East	**T** **y-C/G** **RB** **S** **S**	Jon Giesler (No. 1) Jeff Toews (No. 2) Tony Nathan (No. 3a) Glenn Blackwood (No. 8b) Mike Kozlowski (No. 10b)	**T**	Cleveland Green (FA)		
1980 8-8-0 3rd, AFC East	**CB** **C** **DT** **TE**	Don McNeal (No. 1) Dwight Stephenson (No. 2) Bill Barnett (No. 3) Joe Rose (No. 7)	**FB**	Woody Bennett (waive, NY Jets)		
1981 11-4-1 1st, AFC East	**WR** **CB** **WR**	Tom Vigorito (No. 5B) William Judson (No. 8) Jim Jensen (No. 11)	**S**	Lyle Blackwood (FA)	**LB**	Bob Brudzinski (from L.A. Rams)
1982 7-2-0 AFC Champions	**G** **WR** **CB** **y-LB** **TE** **G**	Roy Foster (No. 1) Mark Duper (No. 2) Paul Lankford (No. 3) Charles Bowser (No. 4) Dan Johnson (No. 7a) Steve Clark (No. 9a)	**y-WR**	Vince Heflin (FA)		
1983 12-4-0 1st, AFC East	**QB** **DE** **P** **WR** **LB**	Dan Marino (No. 1) Mike Charles (No. 2) Reggie Roby (No. 6) Mark Clayton (No. 8) Mark Brown (No. 9)	**y-CB**	Robert Sowell (FA)		
1984 14-2-0 1st AFC Champions	**LB** **LB** **RB** **S**	Jackie Shipp (No. 1) Jay Brophy (No. 2) Joe Carter (No. 4) Bud Brown (No. 11)			***T**	Ronnie Lee (from Atlanta)
1985 12-4-0 1st AFC East	**RB** **DT** **LB** **CB** **T** **FB** **PK**	Lorenzo Hampton (No. 1) George Little (No. 3a) Alex Moyer (No. 3b) Mike Smith (No. 4a) Jeff Dellenbach (No. 4B) Ron Davenport (No. 6b) Fuad Reveiz (No. 7)	**G/C** **#DE**	Larry Lee (waive, Detroit) Mack Moore (B.C. Lions, CFL)	**LB** **LB**	Hugh Green (from Tampa Bay) Robin Sendlein (from Minnesota)

*drafted No. 3c by Dolphins in 1979   **(waive, Philadelphia Eagles in 1986)
#drafted No. 6a by Dolphins in 1981

ALL-TIME DRAFT CHOICES

(Bold Face Indicates Made Active Roster)

1966 EXPANSION DRAFT

FROM NEW ENGLAND

Eddie Wilson	QB	Arizona
Billy Neighbors	G	Alabama
Ross O'Hanley	S	Boston College
Jack Rudolph	LB	Georgia Tech

FROM BUFFALO

Billy Joe	FB	Villanova
Bo Roberson	WR	Cornell
x-Jim Davidson	OT	Ohio State
Howard Simpson	DT	Auburn

FROM DENVER

John McGeever	S	Auburn
Ed Cooke	DE	Maryland
Tom Erlandson	LB	Washington St.
Tom Nomina	DT	Miami (Ohio)

FROM HOUSTON

Norm Evans	OT	Texas Christian
Tom Goode	C	Miss. State
Jack Spikes	FB	Texas Christian
Maxie Williams	OT	SE Louisiana

FROM KANSAS CITY

Al Dotson	DT	Grambling
Mel Branch	DE	Louisiana St.
Frank Jackson	WR	SMU
Ron Caveness	LB	Arkansas

FROM NEW YORK JETS

Wahoo McDaniel	LB	Oklahoma
Willie West	S	Oregon
Mike Huddock	C	Miami (Fla.)
LaVerne Torczon	DE	Nebraska

FROM OAKLAND

Rich Zecher	DT	Utah State
Dick Wood	QB	Auburn
Ken Rice	G	Auburn
Gene Mingo	K	No College

FROM SAN DIEGO

Dave Kocourek	TE	Wisconsin
Ernie Park	G	McMurry
Jimmy Warren	CB	Illinois
Dick Westmoreland	CB	N.C. A&T

x-retired

1966

1a	x-Jim Grabowski	RB	Illinois
1b	**Rick Norton**	QB	Kentucky
2	**Frank Emanuel**	LB	Tennessee
3	x-Larry Gagner	G	Florida
4	x-Dick Leftridge	RB	West Virginia
5	Grady Bolton	DT	Miss. St.
6	x-Ed Weisacosky	LB	Miami (Fla.)
7	x-Don Hansen	LB	Illinois
8	**Bob Petrella**	S	Tennessee
9	x-Bill Matan	DE	Kansas St.
10	x-Pat Killorin	C	Syracuse
11	**Sam Price**	RB	Illinois
12	**Howard Twilley**	WR	Tulsa
13	x-Ken Kramer	TE	Minnesota
14	Phil Scoggin	P	Texas A&M
15	Jerry Oliver	OT	SW Texas
16	Don Lorenz	DE	Stephen Austin
17	x-Mike Bender	G	Arkansas
18	x-Rick Kestner	E	Kentucky
19	**Doug Moreau**	TE	Louisiana St.
20	Jon Tooker	CB	Adams State

x-signed with National Football League

1966 REDSHIRT DRAFT

1	**John Roderick**	WR	SMU
2	Harold Fulford	WR	Auburn
3	**Jack Clancy**	WR	Michigan
4	x-Jim Mankins	RB	Florida St.
5	x-Fritz Greenlee	TE	Arizona
6	**Bill Darnall**	DB	North Carolina
7	Don Williams	DE	Wofford
8	Jon Brittenum	QB	Arkansas
9	x-Craig Baynham	WR	Georgia Tech
10	x-Randy Winkler	OT	Tarleton St.
11	Kai Anderson	C	Illinois

x-signed with National Football League

1967

1	**Bob Griese**	QB	Purdue
2	**Jim Riley**	DT	Oklahoma
3	TO DENVER for Cookie Gilchrist		
4	Bob Greenlee	DE	Yale
5a	TO DENVER for Cookie Gilchrist		
5b	x-**Gary Tucker**	RB	Chattanooga
	(from Buffalo for Jack Spikes)		
6	Bud Norris	TE	Washington St.
7	**Larry Seiple**	TE	Kentucky
8	TO OAKLAND for Bill Cronin		
9	**John Richardson**	DT	UCLA
10	**Tom Beier**	S	Miami (Fla.)
11	**Jack Pyburn**	OT	Texas A&M
12a	y-Stan Juk	LB	South Carolina
12b	y-Jim Whitaker	CB	Missouri
	(from Denver for Jerry Oliver)		
13	TO BUFFALO for George Wilson Jr.		
14	Charlie Stikes	CB	Kent State
15	Jake Ferro	LB	Youngstown
16	Maurice Calhoun	RB	Central Ohio
17	Larry Kissam	T	Florida St.

x-taxi squad '67   y-entered medical school

1968

1a	**Larry Csonka**	RB	Syracuse
1b	**Doug Crusan**	OT	Indiana
	(from Cincinnati for John Stofa)		
2a	**Jim Keyes**	LB	Mississippi
2b	**Jim Cox**	TE	Miami (Fla.)
	(from Cincinnati for John Stofa)		
3a	**Jim Urbanek**	DT	Mississippi
3b	**Dick Anderson**	S	Colorado
	(from San Diego for John Brittenum)		
4	TO DENVER for John Bramlett		
5	**Jim Kiick**	RB	Wyoming
6a	**Kim Hammond**	QB	Florida St.
	(from Denver in 7-man deal)		
6b	x-**Jimmy Hines**	WR	Texas Southern
7	x-**John Boynton**	T	Tennessee
	x-taxi squad '68		
8a	TO NEW YORK for Archie Roberts		
8b	**Randall Edmunds**	LB	Georgia Tech
	(From Oakland for Dave Kocourek)		
9a	Sam McDowell	T	SW Missouri
9b	y-Tom Paciorek	CB	Houston
	(from Houston for Billy Anderson)		
10	Joe Mirto	T	Miami (Fla.)
11	Cornelius Cooper	DE	Prairie View
12	Paul Paxton	T	Akron
13	**Bob Joswick**	DE	Tulsa
14	Ray Blunk	TE	Xavier
15	Ken Corbin	LB	Miami (Fla.)
16	Henry Still	DT	Bethune-Cookman
17	Bill Nemeth	C	Arizona

y-pro baseball

1969

1	**Bill Stanfill**	DE	Georgia
2	**Bob Heinz**	DT	Pacific
3	**Mercury Morris**	RB	West-Tex St.
4	**Norm McBride**	LB	Utah
5a	**Willie Pearson**	WR	N.C. A&T
5b	**Karl Kremser**	K	Tennessee
	(from Oakland for John Roderick)		
6	Ed Tuck	G	Notre Dame
7a	John Egan	C	Boston Col.
7b	John Kulka	G	Penn State
	(from San Diego for Tom Erlandson)		
8	Bruce Weinstein	TE	Yale
9	**Jesse Powell**	LB	West Tex St.
10	**Jim Mertens**	TE	Fairmont St.
11	Mike Berdis	DT	N. Dakota St.
12	**Dale McCullers**	LB	Florida St.
13	Amos Ayres	S	Arkansas AM&N
14	Glynn Thompson	DT	Troy State
15	Chick McGeehan	WR	Tennessee
16	**Lloyd Mumphord**	CB	Texas Southern
17	Tom Krallman	DE	Xavier

1970

1	TO CLEVELAND for Paul Warfield		
2	**Jim Mandich**	TE	Michigan
3	**Tim Foley**	CB	Purdue
4	**Curtis Johnson**	CB	Toledo
5	TO NEW ENGLAND in Buoniconti deal		
6	Dave Campbell	DE	Auburn
7	**Jake Scott**	S	Georgia
8	Narvel Chavers	RB	Jackson St.
9	**Hubert Ginn**	RB	Florida A&M
10	Dick Nittinger	G	Tampa
11	Brownie Wheless	DT	Rice
12	**Mike Kolen**	LB	Auburn
13	Dave Buddington	RB	Springfield
14	Gary Brackett	G	Holy Cross
15	Pat Hauser	WR	East Tenn.
16	Charles Williams	G	Tennessee St.
17	George Myles	DT	Morris Brown

1971

1	TO BALTIMORE for Don Shula		
2	**Otto Stowe**	WR	Iowa State
3	**Dale Farley**	LB	West Virginia
4	x-Joe Theismann	QB	Notre Dame
5	TO PITTSBURGH for Willie Richardson		
6	Dennis Coleman	LB	Mississippi
7	Ron Dickerson	CB	Kansas St.
8	TO PITTSBURGH for Bob DeMarco		
9	**Vern Den Herder**	DE	Central, Iowa
10	Ron Maree	DT	Purdue
11	Vic Surma	T	Penn State
12	Leroy Byars	RB	Alcorn A&M
13	Lonnie Hepburn	CB	Texas Southern
14	David Vaughn	TE	Memphis St.
15	Bob Richards	G	California
16	Chris Myers	WR	Kenyon
17	Curt Mark	LB	Mayville, N.D.

x-signed with Canadian Football League

1972

1	x-Mike Kadish	DT	Notre Dame
2	TO CLEVELAND for Bob Matheson		
3	Gary Kosins	RB	Dayton
4a	**Larry Ball**	DE	Louisville
	(from San Diego for Carl Mauck)		
4b	Al Benton	T	Ohio Univ.
5	**Charlie Babb**	S	Memphis St.
6	y-Ray Nettles	LB	Tennessee
7a	Bill Adams	G	Holy Cross
	(from Denver for John Stofa)		
7b	Calvin Harrell	RB	Arkansas St.
8	Craig Curry	QB	Minnesota
9	Greg Johnson	CB	Wisconsin
10	TO HOUSTON for Russell Price		
11	**Ed Jenkins**	WR	Holy Cross
12	Ashley Bell	TE	Purdue
13	Archy Robinson	CB	Hillsdale
14	Willie Jones	LB	Tampa
15	Bill Davis	DT	Wm. & Mary
16	Al Hannah	WR	Wisconsin
17	Vern Brown	S	Western Mich.

x-taxi squad '72   y-signed with Canadian Football League

1973

1	TO BUFFALO for Marlin Briscoe		
2	x-Chuck Bradley	C	Oregon
3	**Leon Gray**	T	Jackson St
4	**Bo Rather**	WR	Michigan
5a	**Don Strock**	QB	Virginia Tech
	(from Buffalo in Frank Cornish deal)		
5b	Dave McCurry	CB	Iowa State
6	**Ed Newman**	G	Duke
7a	Kevin Reilly	LB	Villanova
	(from New England for Wayne Mass)		
7b	Ben Shephard	RB	Arkansas Tech
	(from New England for Bill Griffin)		
7c	Willie Hatter	WR	Northern Ill.
	(from Cleveland for Bob DeMarco)		
7d	**Tom Smith**	RB	Miami (Fla.)
8	Archie Pearmon	DE	NE. Oklahoma
9	Karl Lorch	DE	Southern Cal.
10	Ron Fernandes	DE	Eastern Mich.
11	Chris Kete	G	Boston College
12	Mike Mullen	LB	Tulane
13	Joe Booker	RB	Miami (Ohio)
14	Greg Boyd	RB	Arizona
15	Bill Palmer	TE	St. Thomas
16	James Jackson	DE	Norfolk St.
17	**Charley Wade**	WR	Tennessee St.

x-injured reserve '73

1974

1	**Don Reese**	DE	Jackson St.
2a	y-**Andre Tillman**	TE	Texas Tech
	(from Green Bay for Jim Del Gaizo)		
2b	**Benny Malone**	RB	Arizona St.
	(from Dallas in Otto Stowe deal)		
2c	**Jeris White**	CB	Hawaii
3	**Nat Moore**	WR	Florida
4	x-Bill Stevenson	DT	Drake
5	x-Cleveland Vann	LB	Oklahoma St.
6a	**Randy Crowder**	DT	Penn State
	(from Baltimore in Hubert Ginn deal)		
6b	x-Bob Wolfe	T	Nebraska
7a	Carl Swierc	WR	Rice
	(from New Orleans for Jeff White)		
7b	Joe Sullivan	T	Boston College
8	**Mel Baker**	WR	Texas Southern
9a	**Tom Wickert**	T	Washington St.
	(from Chicago for Dave McCurry)		
9b	x-Bob Lally	LB	Cornell
10	x-Gary Valbuena	QB	Tennessee
11	Gerry Roberts	DE	UCLA
12	Jim Revels	S	Florida
13	x-Clayton Heath	RB	Wake Forest
14	Sam Johnson	LB	Arizona St.
15	Larry Cates	CB	Western Mich.
16	Jesse Wolf	DT	Prairie View
17	Ken Dickerson	CB	Tuskegee

x-signed with World Football League   y-injured reserve '74

1975

1	**Darryl Carlton**	T	Tampa
2a	**Fred Solomon**	WR	Tampa
	(from Green Bay for Jim Del Gaizo)		
2b	**Stan Winfrey**	RB	Arkansas St.
3	Gerald Hill	LB	Houston
4	**Bruce Elia**	LB	Ohio State
5a	**Morris Owens**	WR	Arizona St.
	(from Giants for Henry Stuckey)		
5b	**Barry Hill**	S	Iowa State
6a	**Steve Towle**	LB	Kansas
	(from NY Jets for Larry Woods)		
	TO NY JETS for John Mooring		
7	Phillip Kent	RB	Baylor
8	Barney Crawford	DT	Harding
9	James Wilson	G	Clark
10a	Clyde Russell	RB	Oklahoma
	(from Chicago for Charley Wade)		
10b	Joe Jackson	TE	Penn State
	(from Washington for Howard Kindig)		
10c	Joe Danelo	K	Washington St.
11	John Dilworth	CB	NW St. La.
12	Joe Yancey	T	Henderson
13	Leonard Isabel	WR	Tulsa
14a	James Lewis	CB	Tennessee St.
	(from NY Giants for Ed Jenkins)		
14b	Jack Graham	QB	Colorado St.
15	Skip Johns	RB	Carson-Newman
16	Vernon Smith	C	Georgia
17	Dwaine Copeland	RB	Middle Tenn.

1976

1a	**Larry Gordon**	LB	Arizona St.
	(from Washington for Joe Thiesman)		
1b	x-**Kim Bokamper**	LB	San Jose St.
2	**Loaird McCreary**	TE	Tennessee St.
3	**Duriel Harris**	WR	New Mexico St.
4a	**Melvin Mitchell**	G	Tennessee St.
	(from Detroit for Larry Ball)		
4b	TO PHILADELPHIA for Norm Bulaich		
9	y-Norris Thomas	CB	Southern Miss.
10a	Gary Fencik	S	Yale
	(from Washington for Karl Lorch)		
10b	Dori Testerman	RB	Clemson
11	Dexter Pride	RB	Minnesota
12a	Randy Young	T	Iowa State
12b	Darryl Brandford	DT	Northwestern
	(from St. Louis for Rodrigo Barnes)		

5   TO DETROIT with Larry Ball
6   **Gary Davis** RB Cal Poly/SLO
7a Joe Ingersoll G-T Nevada/Vegas
    (from New Orleans for Mel Baker)
7b Johnny Owens DE Tennessee St.
8   Bob Simpson DT Colorado

13 Bernie Head C Tulsa
14 Bob Gissler LB S. Dakota St.
15 Ron Holmes RB Utah State
16 Mike Green P/WR Ohio Univ.
17 z-Jeff Grantz QB South Carolina

x-injured reserve '76   y-quit camp '76, active roster '77
z-remained at South Carolina as coach

1977

1   **A.J. Duhe** DE Louisiana St.
2   **Bob Baumhower** DT Alabama
3a TO HOUSTON for Ken Ellis
3b Mike Watson T Miami (Ohio)
    (from Chicago for Bo Rather)
4   TO WASHINGTON in Jake Scott deal
5a **Mike Michel** P-K Stanford
    (from Tampa for Ray Nettles' rights)

5b **Leroy Harris** RB Arkansas St.
6   TO NY GIANTS for Andy Selfridge
7   Bruce Herron LB New Mexico
8   Horace Perkins CB Colorado
9   Robert Turner RB Oklahoma St.
10 Mark Carter T Eastern Mich.
11 **John Alexander** DE Rutgers
12 **Terry Anderson** WR Bethune-Cookman

1978

1   TO SAN FRAN in Delvin Williams deal
2   **Guy Benjamin** QB Stanford
3a Lyman Smith DT Duke
    (from NY Giants for Larry Csonka)
3b **Jimmy Cefalo** WR Penn State
4a **Gerald Small** CB San Jose St.
    (from Cleveland for Paul Warfield)
4b **Eric Laakso** T Tulane
5a Ted Burgmeier S Notre Dame
    (from Tampa Bay for Jeris White)
5b TO SAN FRAN in Delvin Williams deal

6   **Doug Betters** DE Nevada/Reno
7a Karl Baldischwiler T Oklahoma
    (from Cleveland for Paul Warfield)
7b Lloyd Henry WR NE Missouri
8   **Sean Clancy** LB Amherst
9   **Bruce Hardy** TE Arizona St.
10 x-**Mark Dennard** C Texas A&M
11 TO SEATTLE for Carl Barisich
12a Mike Moore RB Middle Tenn.
12b Bill Kenney QB Northern Colo.
    (from Denver for Jim Kiick)

x-injured reserve '78

1979

1   **Jon Giesler** T Michigan
2   **Jeff Toews** G Washington
3a **Tony Nathan** RB Alabama
    (from Tampa Bay for Randy Crowder)
3b **Mel Land** LB Michigan St.
    (from NY Giants for Larry Csonka)
3c **Ronnie Lee** TE Baylor
    (from New Orleans for Don Reese)
3d TO ATLANTA for Ralph Ortega
4   **Steve Howell** RB Baylor
5   **Don Bessillieu** S Georgia Tech
6   Steve Lindquist G Nebraska

7   **Uwe von Schamann** K Oklahoma
8a x-Jeff Groth WR Bowling Green
    (from Washington for Jim Mandich)
8b **Glenn Blackwood** S Texas
    (from Denver for Jim Kiick)
8c TO TAMPA BAY for Council Rudolph
9   Jeff Weston DT Notre Dame
10a Jerome Stanton CB Michigan St.
    (from Detroit for Karl Baldischwiler)
10b **Mike Kozlowski** S Colorado
11 Mike Blanton DE Georgia Tech
12 Larry Fortner QB Miami (Ohio)

x-missed final cut but played 4 games

1980

1   **Don McNeal** CB Alabama
2   **Dwight Stephenson** C Alabama
3   **Bill Barnett** DE Nebraska
4   **Elmer Bailey** WR Minnesota
5   TO WASH in Benny Malone deal
6   Eugene Byrd WR Michigan St.
7   **Joe Rose** TE California
8a **Jeff Allen** CB Cal-Davis
8b **David Woodley** QB Louisiana St.
    (from Washington for Jim Mandich)

9   Mark Goodspeed OT Nebraska
10a Doug Lantz C Miami (Ohio)
10b Ben Long LB South Dakota
    (from Philadelphia, past considerations)
11a Phil Driscoll DE Mankato St.
    (from San Francisco for Chas. Cornelius)
11b TO PHILADELPHIA, past considerations
12 Chuck Stone G N. Carolina St.

1981

1   x-**David Overstreet** RB Oklahoma
2a TO L.A. in Bob Brudzinski deal
2b **Andra Franklin** FB Nebraska
    (from L.A. in Bob Brudzinski deal)
4a Sam Greene WR UNLV
    (from N. Orleans for Guy Benjamin)
4b Brad Wright QB New Mexico
5a **Ken Poole** DE NE Louisiana
5b **Tom Vigorito** RB Virginia
    (from Philadelphia for Leroy Harris)

6a x-Mack Moore DE Texas A&M
6b Fulton Walker CB W. Virginia
    (from Minnesota in Jim Langer deal)
8   y-William Judson CB S. Carolina St.
   John Noonan WR Nebraska
10 Steve Folsom TE Utah
11 **Jim Jensen** QB Boston Univ.
12 John Alford DT S. Carolina St.

x-signed with Canadian Football League   y-injured reserve

1982

1   **Roy Foster** G-T Southern Cal
2   **Mark Duper** WR NW St. La.
3   **Paul Lankford** CB Penn State
4   **Charles Bowser** LB Duke
5a Bob Nelson DT Miami
    (from Minnesota in Jim Langer deal)
5b **Rich Diana** FB Yale
6a Thomas Tutson CB S. Carolina St.
    (from San Diego for George Roberts)
6b **Ron Hester** LB Florida St
7a **Dan Johnson** TE Iowa State
    (from New Orleans for Guy Benjamin)

7b Larry Cowan RB Jackson St.
8   Tate Randle S Texas Tech
a   **Steve Clark** DE Utah
    (from Detroit for Steve Towle)
9b Mack Boatner RB SE Louisiana
10a Robin Fisher LB Florida
    (from Philadelphia for Steve Howell)
10b Wayne Jones C-T Utah
11 Gary Crum T Wyoming
12 Mike Rodrigue WR Miami

1983

1   **Dan Marino** QB Pitt
2   **Mike Charles** DT Syracuse
3   **Charles Benson** DE Baylor
4   TO LA RAMS
5   TO HOUSTON
6   **Reggie Roby** P Iowa

7   Keith Woetzel LB Rutgers
8   **Mark Clayton** WR Louisville
9   **Mark Brown** LB Purdue
10 Anthony Reed RB S. Carolina St.
11 Joe Lukens G Ohio State
12 Anthony Carter WR Michigan

1984

1   **Jackie Shipp** LB Oklahoma
    (from Buffalo in draft trade-up)
3   **Jay Brophy** LB Miami (Fla.)
3a TO BUFFALO in trade-up
3b TO BUFFALO in trade-up
    (from Pittsburgh in Woodley deal)
4   **Joe Carter** RB Alabama
5   Dean May QB Louisville
6   Rowland Tatum LB Ohio State
y-injured reserve

7   Bernard Carvalho G-T Hawaii
8   y-Ron Landry FB McNeese St.
9   Jim Boyle G-T Tulane
10 John Chesley TE Oklahoma St.
11 **Bud Brown** S S. Mississippi
12a William Devane DT Clemson
12b Mike Weingrad LB Illinois
    (from San Fran. in Orosz deal)

1985

1   **Lorenzo Hampton** RB Florida
3a **George Little** DT Iowa
3b **Alex Moyer** LB Northwestern
4a **Mike Smith** CB Texas-El Paso
4b **Jeff Dellenbach** T Wisconsin
6a George Shorthose WR Missouri
6b **Ron Davenport** FB Louisville

7   **Fuad Reveiz** PK Tennessee
8   Dan Sharp TE Texas Christian
9   Adam Hinds S Oklahoma State
10 Mike Pendleton CB Indiana
11 Mike Jones RB Tulane
12 Ray Noble CB California

1986

2   John Offerdahl LB West. Michigan
3   T.J. Turner DT Houston
4   James Pruitt WR Cal State-Fullerton
5   Kevin Wyatt CB Arkansas
6   Brent Sowell DT Alabama
7   Larry Kolic LB Ohio State

8   John Stuart T Texas
9   Reyna Thompson S Baylor
10 Jeff Wickersham QB LSU
11 Arnold Franklin TE North Carolina
12 Rickey Isom FB N. C. State

YEAR-BY-YEAR SCORES

● local TV blackout lifted

1966: Won 3, Lost 11 — Head Coach: George Wilson
Fourth (tied) — Eastern Division

Date	Opponent		Score	PAID	ANNOUNCE
9/2	OAKLAND	L	14-23	25,188	26,776
9/9	NEW YORK JETS	L	14-19	33,650	34,402
9/18	at Buffalo	L	24-58	37,176	37,546
10/2	at San Diego	L	10-44	26,451	26,444
10/9	at Oakland	L	10-21	28,863	30,787
10/16	DENVER	W	24-7	22,191	23,393
10/23	at Houston	L	20-13	21,999	23,173
11/6	BUFFALO	L	0-29	36,685	37,177
11/13	at Kansas City	L	16-34	33,733	34,063
11/20	at New York Jets	L	13-20	57,092	58,664
11/27	NEW ENGLAND	L	14-20	22,480	22,754
12/4	at Denver	L	7-17	32,116	32,592
12/11	KANSAS CITY	L	18-19	19,387	17,881
12/18	HOUSTON	W	29-28	19,274	20,045
				416,285	**425,697**

1967: Won 4, Lost 10 — Head Coach: George Wilson
Third (tied) — Eastern Division

Date	Opponent		Score	PAID	ANNOUNCE
9/17	DENVER	W	35-21	29,072	29,381
9/24	KANSAS CITY	L	0-24	33,280	36,272
10/1	at New York Jets	L	7-29	59,433	61,240
10/8	at Kansas City	L	0-41	42,920	45,291
10/15	at New England	L	10-41	17,859	23,955
10/22	NEW YORK JETS	L	14-33	28,392	30,049
11/5	at Buffalo	L	13-35	30,950	31,622
11/12	at San Diego	L	0-24	32,395	34,761
11/19	at Oakland	L	17-31	33,753	37,295
11/26	BUFFALO	W	17-14	24,357	27,050
12/3	at Houston	L	14-17	21,865	20,979
12/10	SAN DIEGO	W	41-24	23,032	23,007
12/17	NEW ENGLAND	W	41-32	22,079	25,969
12/23	HOUSTON	L	10-41	29,628	31,121
				429,015	**457,992**

1968: Won 5, Lost 8, Tied 1 — Head Coach: George Wilson
Third — Eastern Division

Date	Opponent		Score	PAID	ANNOUNCE
9/14	HOUSTON	L	10-24	38,097	40,067
9/21	OAKLAND	L	21-47	28,751	30,021
9/28	KANSAS CITY	L	3-48	27,732	28,501
10/6	at Houston	W	24-7	35,424	36,109
10/12	BUFFALO	T	14-14	28,653	28,559
10/20	at Cincinnati	W	24-22	25,076	25,936
10/27	at Denver	L	14-21	43,411	44,115
11/3	at San Diego	L	28-34	31,686	37,284
11/10	at Buffalo	W	21-17	28,399	28,759
11/17	CINCINNATI	L	21-38	30,304	31,747
11/24	at New England	W	34-10	13,646	18,305
12/1	at New York Jets	L	17-35	60,207	61,766
12/8	NEW ENGLAND	W	38-7	24,902	24,242
12/15	NEW YORK JETS	L	7-31	31,302	32,843
				447,590	**468,271**

1969: Won 3, Lost 10, Tied 1 — Head Coach: George Wilson
Fifth — Eastern Division

Date	Opponent		Score	PAID	ANNOUNCE
9/14	at Cincinnati	L	21-27	24,487	25,335
9/20	at Oakland	L	17-20	48,477	50,277
9/28	at Houston	L	10-22	40,387	41,086
10/4	OAKLAND	T	20-20	32,668	35,614
10/11	SAN DIEGO	L	14-21	33,073	34,585
10/19	at Kansas City	L	10-17	47,038	49,809
10/26	BUFFALO	W	24-6	39,194	39,837
11/2	at New York Jets	L	31-34	60,793	61,761
11/9	at New England	W	17-16	10,665	8,374
11/16	at Buffalo	L	3-28	32,344	32,868
11/23	HOUSTON	L	7-32	27,114	27,218
11/30	New England (at Tampa)	L	23-38	27,179	32,121
12/7	DENVER	W	27-24	24,972	25,332
12/14	NEW YORK JETS	L	9-27	42,148	48,108
				490,539	**512,335**

1970: Won 10, Lost 4 — Head Coach: Don Shula
Second — Eastern Division

Date	Opponent		Score	PAID	ANNOUNCE
9/20	at New England	L	14-27	27,265	32,607
9/27	at Houston	W	20-10	38,779	39,840
10/3	OAKLAND	W	20-13	54,412	57,140
10/10	at New York Jets	W	20-6	61,801	62,712
10/18	at Buffalo	W	33-14	40,820	41,312
10/25	CLEVELAND	L	0-28	70,872	75,313
11/1	at Baltimore	L	0-35	59,305	60,240
11/8	at Philadelphia	L	17-24	53,149	58,171
11/15	NEW ORLEANS	W	21-10	41,557	42,866
11/22	BALTIMORE	W	34-17	63,362	67,699
11/30	at Atlanta	W	20-7	53,303	54,036
12/6	NEW ENGLAND	W	37-20	46,370	51,034
12/13	NEW YORK JETS	W	16-10	71,892	75,099
12/20	BUFFALO	W	45-7	64,957	70,990
				747,844	**789,059**

AMERICAN CONFERENCE PLAYOFF

Date	Opponent		Score	PAID	ANNOUNCE
12/27	at Oakland	L	14-21	52,594	54,401

1971: Won 10, Lost 3, Tied 1 — Head Coach: Don Shula
First — Eastern Division

Date	Opponent		Score	PAID	ANNOUNCE
9/19	at Denver	T	10-10	50,499	51,228
9/26	at Buffalo	W	29-14	44,626	45,139
10/3	NEW YORK JETS	L	10-14	67,161	66,025
10/10	at Cincinnati	W	23-13	59,090	60,099
10/17	NEW ENGLAND	W	41-3	56,222	54,566
10/24	at New York Jets	W	30-14	61,170	62,130
10/31	at Los Angeles	W	20-14	68,386	72,903
11/7	BUFFALO	W	34-0	57,748	52,404
11/14	PITTSBURGH	W	24-21	63,178	61,167
11/21	BALTIMORE	W	17-14	73,063	72,043
11/29	CHICAGO	W	34-3	73,071	75,061
12/5	at New England	L	13-34	60,110	61,457
12/11	at Baltimore	L	3-14	59,293	60,238
12/19	GREEN BAY	W	27-6	74,215	73,122
				867,832	**867,582**

AMERICAN CONFERENCE PLAYOFF

Date	Opponent		Score	PAID	ANNOUNCE
12/25	at Kansas City (2 OT)	W	27-24	50,374	45,822

AMERICAN CONFERENCE CHAMPIONSHIP

Date	Opponent		Score	PAID	ANNOUNCE
1/2	BALTIMORE	W	21-0	78,629	78,939

SUPER BOWL VI AT NEW ORLEANS

Date	Opponent		Score	PAID	ANNOUNCE
1/16	Dallas	L	3-24	81,023	80,591

1972: Won 14, Lost 0 — Head Coach: Don Shula
First — Eastern Division

Date	Opponent		Score	PAID	ANNOUNCE
9/17	at Kansas City	W	20-10	78,736	79,829
9/24	HOUSTON	W	34-13	75,069	71,285
10/1	at Minnesota	W	16-14	45,766	47,900
10/8	at New York Jets	W	27-17	61,720	63,841
10/15	SAN DIEGO	W	24-10	78,212	77,596
10/22	BUFFALO	W	24-23	78,175	75,185
10/29	at Baltimore	W	23-0	59,303	60,000
11/5	at Buffalo	W	30-16	45,659	46,206
11/12	NEW ENGLAND	W	52-0	78,148	75,528
11/19	NEW YORK JETS	W	28-24	78,166	78,914
11/27	ST. LOUIS	W	31-10	78,190	76,801
12/3	at New England	W	37-21	60,144	60,999
12/10	at New York Giants	W	23-13	62,728	62,728
12/16	BALTIMORE	W	16-0	78,202	76,696
				958,218	**953,508**

AMERICAN CONFERENCE PLAYOFF

Date	Opponent		Score	PAID	ANNOUNCE
12/24	CLEVELAND	W	20-14	78,916	78,196

AMERICAN CONFERENCE CHAMPIONSHIP

Date	Opponent		Score	PAID	ANNOUNCE
12/31	at Pittsburgh	W	21-17	50,845	50,350

SUPER BOWL VII AT LOS ANGELES

Date	Opponent		Score	PAID	ANNOUNCE
1/14	Washington	W	14-7	90,182	85,462

1973: Won 12, Lost 2 — Head Coach: Don Shula
First — Eastern Division

Date		Opponent		Score	PAID	ANNOUNCE
9/16	●	SAN FRANCISCO	W	21-13	78,768	68,275
9/23		at Oakland	L	7-12	74,044	74,121
9/30	●	NEW ENGLAND	W	44-23	78,830	62,508
10/7	●	NEW YORK JETS	W	31-3	78,821	63,850
10/15		at Cleveland	W	17-9	78,424	72,070
10/21	●	BUFFALO	W	27-6	78,738	65,241
10/28		at New England	W	30-14	60,268	57,617
11/4		at New York Jets	W	24-14	61,462	57,591
11/11		BALTIMORE	W	44-0	78,584	60,332
11/18		at Buffalo	W	17-0	79,401	77,138
11/22		at Dallas	L	14-7	62,967	58,089
12/3		PITTSBURGH	W	30-26	78,922	68,901
12/9		at Baltimore	L	3-16	57,834	41,005
12/15	●	DETROIT	W	34-7	78,337	53,375
					1,025,400	**822,496**

AMERICAN CONFERENCE PLAYOFF

Date	Opponent		Score	PAID	ANNOUNCE
12/23	CINCINNATI	W	34-16	78,928	75,770

AMERICAN CONFERENCE CHAMPIONSHIP

Date		Opponent		Score	PAID	ANNOUNCE
12/30	●	OAKLAND	W	27-10	79,325	75,105

SUPER BOWL VIII AT HOUSTON

Date	Opponent		Score	PAID	ANNOUNCE
1/13	Minnesota	W	24-7	71,882	68,142

1974: Won 11, Lost 3 — Head Coach: Don Shula
First — Eastern Division

Date		Opponent		Score	PAID	ANNOUNCE
9/15		at New England	L	24-34	54,193	55,006
9/22	•	at Buffalo	W	24-16	79,463	78,990
9/29		at San Diego	W	28-21	44,183	44,706
10/7		NEW YORK JETS	W	21-17	78,219	61,527
10/13	•	at Washington	L	17-20	52,379	54,395
10/20		KANSAS CITY	W	9-3	75,358	67,779
10/27		BALTIMORE	W	17-7	72,849	65,868
11/3		ATLANTA	W	42-7	74,935	64,399
11/10		at New Orleans	W	21-0	73,458	74,289
11/17	•	BUFFALO	L	35-28	78,771	69,313
11/24	•	at New York Jets	L	14-17	60,481	57,162
12/2		CINCINNATI	W	24-3	78,675	71,962
12/8		at Baltimore	W	17-16	40,911	34,420
12/15	•	NEW ENGLAND	W	34-27	78,611	56,920
					942,486	**856,736**

AMERICAN CONFERENCE PLAYOFF
Date		Opponent		Score	PAID	ANNOUNCE
12/21		at Oakland	L	26-28	53,023	52,817

1975: Won 10, Lost 4 — Head Coach: Don Shula
First (Tied) — Eastern Division

Date		Opponent		Score	PAID	ANNOUNCE
9/22		OAKLAND	L	21-31	78,805	78,744
9/28	•	at New England	W	22-14	59,869	59,967
10/5	•	at Green Bay	W	31-7	55,270	55,390
10/12		PHILADELPHIA	W	24-16	62,925	60,127
10/19	•	at New York Jets	W	43-0	60,471	47,191
10/26	•	at Buffalo	W	35-30	79,429	79,080
11/2		at Chicago	W	46-13	56,577	51,298
11/9		NEW YORK JETS	W	27-7	75,631	72,896
11/16	•	at Houston	L	19-20	50,494	48,892
11/23		BALTIMORE	L	17-33	67,029	61,986
12/1		NEW ENGLAND	W	20-7	68,480	61,963
12/7		BUFFALO	W	31-21	78,701	74,573
12/14	•	at Baltimore (OT)	L	7-10	59,808	59,398
12/20		DENVER	W	14-13	56,187	43,064
					909,676	**854,575**

1976: Won 6, Lost 8 — Head Coach: Don Shula
Third — Eastern Division

Date		Opponent		Score	PAID	ANNOUNCE
9/13		at Buffalo	W	30-21	77,800	77,683
9/19		at New England	L	14-30	41,184	41,879
9/26		NEW YORK JETS	W	16-0	53,600	49,754
10/3		LOS ANGELES	L	28-31	65,314	60,753
10/10	•	at Baltimore	L	14-28	59,295	58,832
10/17		KANSAS CITY (OT)	L	17-20	50,471	43,325
10/24		at Tampa Bay	W	23-20	63,016	59,155
10/31		NEW ENGLAND	W	10-3	57,984	52,863
11/7		at New York Jets	W	27-7	58,882	53,344
11/14	•	at Pittsburgh	L	3-14	49,813	48,945
11/22		BALTIMORE	L	16-17	68,372	62,104
11/28		at Cleveland	L	13-17	76,562	74,715
12/5		BUFFALO	W	45-27	51,423	43,475
12/11		MINNESOTA	L	7-29	52,945	46,543
					826,661	**773,370**

1977: Won 10, Lost 4 — Head Coach: Don Shula
First (Tied) — Eastern Division

Date		Opponent		Score	PAID	ANNOUNCE
9/18		at Buffalo	W	13-0	78,048	76,097
9/25		at San Francisco	W	19-15	45,560	40,503
10/2		HOUSTON	W	27-7	50,764	49,619
10/9		at Baltimore	L	28-45	56,829	57,005
10/16		NEW YORK JETS	W	21-17	45,048	43,446
10/23		SEATTLE	W	31-13	38,967	29,858
10/30		SAN DIEGO	L	13-14	47,525	40,670
11/6		at New York Jets	W	14-10	53,698	51,582
11/13		NEW ENGLAND	W	17-5	66,743	67,502
11/20	•	at Cincinnati	L	17-23	58,710	46,733
11/24	•	at St. Louis	W	55-14	50,855	50,269
12/5	•	BALTIMORE	W	17-6	74,216	68,977
12/11	•	at New England	L	10-14	60,329	61,064
12/17		BUFFALO	W	31-14	45,855	39,626
					773,147	**722,951**

1978: Won 11, Lost 5 — Head Coach: Don Shula
First (Tied) — Eastern Division

Date		Opponent		Score	PAID	ANNOUNCE
9/3		at New York Jets	L	20-33	53,941	49,598
9/10		at Baltimore	W	42-0	47,658	46,426
9/17		BUFFALO	W	31-24	51,362	48,373
9/24	•	at Philadelphia	L	3-17	64,328	62,998
10/1		ST. LOUIS	W	24-10	47,650	43,882
10/9		CINCINNATI	W	21-0	57,481	54,729
10/15		at San Diego	W	28-21	51,426	50,637
10/22	•	at New England	L	24-33	60,314	60,424
10/29		BALTIMORE	W	26-8	55,783	53,524
11/5	•	DALLAS	W	23-16	74,058	70,414
11/12		at Buffalo	W	25-24	50,110	48,623
11/20	•	at Houston	L	30-35	51,189	50,290
11/26		NEW YORK JETS	L	13-24	53,900	49,255
12/3	•	at Washington	W	16-0	54,239	52,860
12/10		OAKLAND	W	23-6	73,889	73,003
12/18		NEW ENGLAND	W	23-3	73,945	72,071
					921,273	**887,107**

AFC WILD-CARD PLAYOFF
Date		Opponent		Score	PAID	ANNOUNCE
12/24		HOUSTON	L	9-17	72,445	70,036

1979: Won 10, Lost 6 — Head Coach: Don Shula
First — Eastern Division

Date		Opponent		Score	PAID	ANNOUNCE
9/2		at Buffalo	W	9-7	70,841	69,441
9/9		SEATTLE	W	19-10	60,045	56,233
9/16	•	at Minnesota	W	27-12	47,748	44,187
9/23		CHICAGO	W	31-16	66,598	66,011
9/30		at New York Jets	L	27-33	59,595	51,496
10/8	•	at Oakland	L	3-13	53,419	52,419
10/14		BUFFALO	W	17-7	54,062	45,597
10/21		at New England	L	13-28	60,372	61,096
10/28		GREEN BAY	W	27-7	54,343	47,741
11/5		HOUSTON	L	6-9	73,900	70,273
11/11		BALTIMORE	W	19-0	56,884	50,193
11/18		at Cleveland (OT)	L	24-30	79,819	80,374
11/25		at Baltimore	W	28-24	44,989	38,016
11/29	•	NEW ENGLAND	W	39-24	73,628	69,174
12/9		at Detroit	W	28-10	79,073	78,087
12/15		NEW YORK JETS	L	24-27	58,620	49,915
					993,936	**930,253**

AMERICAN CONFERENCE PLAYOFF
Date		Opponent		Score	PAID	ANNOUNCE
12/30	•	at Pittsburgh	L	14-34	50,320	50,214

1980: Won 8, Lost 8 — Head Coach: Don Shula
Third — Eastern Division

Date		Opponent		Score	PAID	ANNOUNCE
9/7		at Buffalo	L	7-17	79,312	79,598
9/14		CINCINNATI	W	17-16	45,480	38,322
9/21	•	at Atlanta	W	20-17	58,558	55,479
9/28		NEW ORLEANS	W	21-16	46,599	40,946
10/5		BALTIMORE	L	17-30	53,838	50,631
10/12	•	at New England	L	0-34	60,392	60,377
10/19		BUFFALO	W	17-14	49,499	41,636
10/27		at New York Jets	L	14-17	59,677	53,046
11/2		at Oakland	L	10-16	47,274	46,378
11/9	•	at Los Angeles	W	35-14	67,751	62,198
11/16		SAN FRANCISCO	W	17-13	50,219	45,135
11/20		SAN DIEGO (OT)	L	24-27	66,009	63,013
11/30	•	at Pittsburgh	L	10-23	54,082	51,384
12/8		NEW ENGLAND (OT)	W	16-13	62,649	63,292
12/14		at Baltimore	W	24-14	36,136	30,564
12/20		NEW YORK JETS	L	17-24	47,920	41,854
					885,395	**823,853**

1981: Won 11, Lost 4, Tied 1 — Head Coach: Don Shula
First — Eastern Division

Date		Opponent		Score	PAID	ANNOUNCE
9/6		at St. Louis	W	20-7	50,923	50,351
9/10		PITTSBURGH	W	30-10	73,876	74,190
9/20	•	at Houston	W	16-10	51,344	47,379
9/27		at Baltimore	W	31-28	41,630	39,273
10/4		NEW YORK JETS (OT)	T	28-28	68,356	68,723
10/12	•	at Buffalo	L	21-31	79,275	78,576
10/18		WASHINGTON	W	13-10	51,710	47,367
10/25	•	at Dallas	L	27-28	63,695	64,221
11/1		BALTIMORE	W	27-10	50,473	46,061
11/8	•	at New England (OT)	W	30-27	60,334	60,436
11/15		OAKLAND	L	17-33	66,359	61,777
11/22		at New York Jets	L	15-16	59,655	59,962
11/30	•	PHILADELPHIA	W	13-10	73,916	67,797
12/6		NEW ENGLAND	W	24-14	54,326	50,421
12/13		at Kansas City	W	17-7	57,477	57,407
12/19		BUFFALO	W	16-6	73,629	72,956
					976,978	**949,254**

AMERICAN CONFERENCE PLAYOFF
Date		Opponent		Score	PAID	ANNOUNCE
1/2	•	SAN DIEGO (OT)	L	38-41	74,233	73,735

1982: Won 7, Lost 2 — Head Coach: Don Shula
Second (Tied) — American Football Conference

Date		Opponent		Score	PAID	ANNOUNCE
9/12		at New York Jets	W	45-28	54,236	53,360
9/19		BALTIMORE	W	24-20	53,823	51,999
11/21		at Buffalo	W	9-7	54,475	52,945
11/29		at Tampa Bay	L	17-23	70,686	54,854
12/5		MINNESOTA	W	22-14	50,474	45,721
12/12		at New England	L	0-3	33,293	25,716
12/18		NEW YORK JETS	W	20-19	66,056	67,307
12/27		BUFFALO	W	27-10	73,742	73,924
1/2		at Baltimore	W	34-7	22,354	19,073
					479,139	**444,899**

AMERICAN CONFERENCE PLAYOFF (first round)
Date		Opponent		Score	PAID	ANNOUNCE
1/8		NEW ENGLAND	W	28-13	70,881	68,842

Date		Opponent	Result	Score	Paid	Announce
AMERICAN CONFERENCE PLAYOFF (second round)						
1/16	•	SAN DIEGO	W	34-13	73,772	71,383
AMERICAN CONFERENCE CHAMPIONSHIP						
1/23	•	NEW YORK JETS	W	14-0	74,918	67,396
SUPER BOWL XVII AT PASADENA						
1/30		Washington	L	17-27		103,667

1983: Won 12, Lost 4   Head Coach: Don Shula
First — Eastern Division

Date		Opponent	Result	Score	PAID	ANNOUNCE
9/4		at Buffalo	W	12-0	80,020	78,715
9/11		NEW ENGLAND	W	34-24	62,309	59,343
9/19		at L.A. Raiders	L	14-27	60,696	57,796
9/25		KANSAS CITY	W	14-6	55,125	50,785
10/2		at New Orleans	L	7-17	71,081	66,489
10/9		BUFFALO (OT)	L	35-38	62,716	59,948
10/16		at New York Jets	W	32-14	60,370	58,615
10/23		at Baltimore	W	21-7	45,768	32,343
10/30		L.A. RAMS	W	30-14	74,856	72,175
11/6		at San Francisco	W	20-17	61,047	57,832
11/13		at New England	L	6-17	61,150	60,771
11/20		BALTIMORE	W	37-0	59,736	54,482
11/28	•	CINCINNATI	W	38-14	75,007	74,506
12/4		at Houston	W	24-17	50,365	39,434
12/10		ATLANTA	W	31-24	62,552	56,725
12/16		NEW YORK JETS	W	34-14	75,057	59,975
					1,017,855	**939,934**
AMERICAN CONFERENCE PLAYOFF						
12/31		SEATTLE	L	20-27	75,116	71,032

1984: Won 14, Lost 2   Head Coach: Don Shula
First — Eastern Division

Date		Opponent	Result	Score	PAID	ANNOUNCE
9/2	•	at Washington	W	35-17	55,431	52,683
9/9		NEW ENGLAND	W	28-7	67,843	66,083
9/17		at Buffalo	W	21-17	66,317	65,455
9/23		INDIANAPOLIS	W	44-7	57,813	55,415
9/30		at St. Louis	W	36-28	48,605	46,991
10/7	•	at Pittsburgh	W	31-7	59,103	59,103
10/14		HOUSTON	W	28-10	59,106	54,080
10/21		at New England	W	44-24	60,890	60,711
10/28		BUFFALO	W	38-7	61,897	58,824
11/4		at N.Y. Jets	W	31-17	76,891	72,655
11/11		PHILADELPHIA	W	24-23	70,805	70,227
11/18		at San Diego (OT)	L	28-34	60,234	53,041
11/26		N.Y. JETS	W	28-17	75,002	74,884
12/2	•	L.A. RAIDERS	L	34-45	75,151	71,222
12/9	•	at Indianapolis	W	35-17	60,695	60,411
12/17	•	DALLAS	W	28-21	75,105	74,139
					1,030,888	**995,924**
AMERICAN CONFERENCE PLAYOFF						
12/29	•	SEATTLE	W	31-10	74,291	73,469
AMERICAN CONFERENCE CHAMPIONSHIP						
1/6	•	PITTSBURGH	W	45-28	76,029	76,029
SUPER BOWL XIX AT PALO ALTO						
1/20		San Francisco	L	16-38	84,059	84,059

1985: Won 12, Lost 4   Head Coach: Don Shula
First — Eastern Division

Date		Opponent	Result	Score	PAID	ANNOUNCE
9/2		at Houston	L	23-26	50,157	47,656
9/15		INDIANAPOLIS	W	30-13	57,772	53,693
9/22		KANSAS CITY	W	31-0	72,238	69,791
9/29	•	at Denver	W	30-26	75,100	73,614
10/6	•	PITTSBURGH	W	24-20	75,070	72,820
10/14	•	at N.Y. Jets	L	7-23	76,891	73,807
10/20		TAMPA BAY	W	41-38	62,987	62,335
10/27	•	at Detroit	L	21-31	80,638	75,291
11/3	•	at New England	L	13-17	61,000	58,811
11/10	•	N.Y. JETS	W	21-17	75,275	73,695
11/17	•	at Indianapolis	W	34-20	58,924	59,666
11/24		at Buffalo	W	23-14	53,529	50,474
12/2	•	CHICAGO	W	38-24	75,594	75,594
12/8	•	at Green Bay	W	34-24	56,860	52,671
12/16	•	NEW ENGLAND	W	30-27	75,825	69,489
12/22	•	BUFFALO	W	28-0	65,686	64,811
					1,073,546	**1,034,218**
AMERICAN CONFERENCE PLAYOFF						
1/4	•	CLEVELAND	W	24-21	75,842	75,128
AMERICAN CONFERENCE CHAMPIONSHIP						
1/12	•	NEW ENGLAND	L	14-31	76,270	74,978

DOLPHINS VS. THE NFL

MIAMI 4, ATLANTA 0

1970 —Miami 20, at Atlanta 7
1974 —at Miami 42, Atlanta 7
1980 —Miami 20, at Atlanta 17
1983 —at Miami 31, Atlanta 24

MIAMI 32, BUFFALO 7 (1 tie)

1966 —at Buffalo 58, Miami 24
        Buffalo 29, at Miami 0
1967 —at Buffalo 35, Miami 13
        at Miami 17, Buffalo 14
1968 —at Miami 14, Buffalo 14 (tie)
        Miami 21, at Buffalo 17
1969 —at Miami 24, Buffalo 6
        at Buffalo 28, Miami 3
1970 —Miami 33, at Buffalo 14
        at Miami 45, Buffalo 7
1971 —Miami 29, at Buffalo 14
        at Miami 34, Buffalo 0
1972 —at Miami 24, Buffalo 23
        Miami 30, at Buffalo 16
1973 —at Miami 27, Buffalo 6
        Miami 17, at Buffalo 0
1974 —Miami 24, at Buffalo 16
        at Miami 35, Buffalo 28
1975 —Miami 35, at Buffalo 30
        at Miami 31, Buffalo 21
1976 —Miami 30, at Buffalo 21
        at Miami 45, Buffalo 27
1977 —Miami 13, at Buffalo 0
        at Miami 31, Buffalo 14
1978 —at Miami 31, Buffalo 24
        Miami 25, at Buffalo 24
1979 —Miami 9, at Buffalo 7
        at Miami 17, Buffalo 7
1980 —at Buffalo 17, Miami 7
        at Miami 17, Buffalo 14
1981 —at Buffalo 31, Miami 21
        at Miami 16, Buffalo 6
1982 —Miami 9, at Buffalo 6
        at Miami 20, Buffalo 10
1983 —Miami 12, at Buffalo 10
        Buffalo 38, at Miami 35 (OT)
1984 — Miami 21 at Buffalo 17
        at Miami 38, Buffalo 7
1985 — Miami 23, at Buffalo 14
        at Miami 28, Buffalo 0

MIAMI 4, CHICAGO 0

1971 —at Miami 34, Chicago 3
1975 —Miami 46, at Chicago 13
1979 —at Miami 31, Chicago 16
1985 — at Miami 38, Chicago 24

MIAMI 7, CINCINNATI 3

1968 —Miami 24, at Cincinnati 22
        Cincinnati 38, at Miami 21
1969 —at Cincinnati 27, Miami 21
1971 —Miami 23, at Cincinnati 13
1973 —*at Miami 34, Cincinnati 16
1974 —at Miami 24, Cincinnati 3
1977 —at Cincinnati 23, Miami 17
1978 —at Miami 21, Cincinnati 0
1980 —at Miami 17, Cincinnati 16
1983 —at Miami 38, Cincinnati 14

MIAMI 3, CLEVELAND 3

1970 —Cleveland 28, at Miami 0
1972 —*at Miami 20, Cleveland 14
1973 —Miami 17, at Cleveland 9
1976 —at Cleveland 17, Miami 13
1979 —at Cleveland 30, Miami 24 (ot)
1985 — *at Miami 24, Cleveland 21

MIAMI 3, DALLAS 2

1971 —***Dallas 24, Miami 3
1973 —Miami 14, at Dallas 7
1978 —at Miami 23, Dallas 16
1981 —at Dallas 28, Miami 27
1984 – at Miami 28, Dallas 21

MIAMI 5, DENVER 2 (1 tie)

1966 —at Miami 24, Denver 7
        at Denver 17, Miami 7
1967 —at Miami 35, Denver 21
1968 —at Denver 21, Miami 14
1969 —at Miami 27, Denver 24
1971 —Miami 10, at Denver 10 (tie)
1975 —at Miami 14, Denver 13
1985 – Miami 30, at Denver 26

MIAMI 2, DETROIT 1

1973 —at Miami 34, Detroit 7
1979 —Miami 28, at Detroit 10
1985 – a Detroit 31, Miami 21

MIAMI 4, GREEN BAY 0

1971 —at Miami 27, Green Bay 6
1975 —Miami 31, at Green Bay 7
1979 —at Miami 27, Green Bay 7
1985 – Miami 34, at Green Bay 24

HOUSTON 10, MIAMI 9

1966 —Miami 20, at Houston 13
        at Miami 29, Houston 28
1967 —at Houston 17, Miami 14
        Houston 41, at Miami 10
1968 —Houston 24, at Miami 10
        Miami 24, at Houston 7
1969 —at Houston 22, Miami 10
        Houston 32, at Miami 7
1970 —Miami 20, at Houston 10
1972 —at Miami 34, Houston 13
1975 —at Houston 20, Miami 19
1977 —at Miami 27, Houston 7
1978 —at Houston 35, Miami 30
        *Houston 17, at Miami 9
1979 —Houston 9, at Miami 6
1981 —Miami 16, at Houston 10
1983 —Miami 24, at Houston 17
1984 – at Miami 28, Houston 10
1985 – at Houston 26, Miami 23

MIAMI 24, INDIANAPOLIS 9

(formerly Baltimore)

1970 —at Baltimore 35, Miami 0
        at Miami 34, Baltimore 17
1971 —at Miami 17, Baltimore 14
        at Baltimore 14, Miami 3
        **at Miami 21, Baltimore 0
1972 —Miami 23, at Baltimore 0
        at Miami 16, Baltimore 0
1973 —at Miami 44, Baltimore 0
        at Baltimore 16, Miami 3
1974 —at Miami 17, Baltimore 7
        Miami 17, at Baltimore 16
1975 —Baltimore 33, at Miami 17
        at Baltimre 10, Miami 7 (ot)
1976 —at Baltimore 28, Miami 14
        Baltimore 17, at Miami 16
1977 —at Baltimore 45, Miami 28
        at Miami 17, Baltimore 6
1978 —Miami 42, at Baltimore 0
        at Miami 26, Baltimore 8
1979 —at Miami 19, Baltimore 0
        Miami 28, at Baltimore 24
1980 —Baltimore 30, at Miami 17
        Miami 24, at Baltimore 14
1981 —Miami 31, at Baltimore 28
        Miami 27, at Baltimore 10
1982 —at Miami 24, Baltimore 20
        Miami 34, at Baltimore 7
1983 —Miami 21, at Baltimore 7
        at Miami 37, Baltimore 0
1984 – at Miami 44, Indianapolis 7
        Miami 35, at Indianapolis 17
1985 – at Miami 30, Indianapolis 13
        Miami 34, at Indianapolis 20

KANSAS CITY 7, MIAMI 6

1966 —at Kansas City 34, Miami 16
        Kansas City 19, at Miami 18
1967 —Kansas City 24, at Miami 0

at Kansas City 41, Miami 0
1968 —Kansas City 48, at Miami 3
1969 —at Kansas City 17, Miami 10
1971 —*Miami 27, at Kansas City 24
(double overtime)
1972 —Miami 20, at Kansas City 10
1974 —at Miami 9, Kansas City 3
1976 —Kansas City 20, at Miami 17
1981 —Miami 17, at Kansas City 7
1983 —at Miami 14, Kansas City 6
1985 — at Miami 31, Kansas City 0

L.A. RAIDERS 14, MIAMI 3

(1 tie) (formerly Oakland)

1966 —Oakland 23, at Miami 14
at Oakland 21, Miami 10
1967 —at Oakland 31, Miami 17
1968 —Oakland 47, at Miami 21
1969 —at Oakland 20, Miami 17
at Miami 20, Oakland 20 (tie)
1970 —at Miami 20, Oakland 13
*at Oakland 21, Miami 14
1973 —at Oakland 12, Miami 7
**at Miami 27, Oakland 10
1974 —*at Oakland 28, Miami 26
1975 —Oakland 31, at Miami 21
1978 —at Miami 23, Oakland 6
1979 —at Oakland 13, Miami 3
1980 —at Oknld 16, Miami 10
1981 —Oakland 33, at Miami 17
1983 — at L.A. 27, Miami 14
1984 — L.A. 45, at Miami 34

MIAMI 3, L.A. RAMS 1

1971 —Miami 20, at Los Angeles 14
1976 —Los Angeles 31, at Miami 28
1980 —Miami 35, at Los Angeles 14
1983 —at Miami 30, Los Angeles 14

MIAMI 4, MINNESOTA 1

1972 —Miami 16, at Minnesota 14
1973 —***Miami 24, Minnesota 7
1976 —Minnesota 29, at Miami 7
1979 —Miami 27, at Minnesota 12
1982 —at Miami 22, Minnesota 14

MIAMI 25, NEW ENGLAND 15

1966 —New England 20, at Miami 14
1967 —at New England 41, Miami 10
at Miami 41, New England 32
1968 —Miami 34, at New England 10
at Miami 38, New England 7
1969 —Miami 17, at New England 16
New England 38, Miami 23
(Tampa)
1970 —at New England 27, Miami 14
at Miami 37, New England 20
1971 —at Miami 41, New England 3
at New England 34, Miami 13
1972 —at Miami 52, New England 0
Miami 37, at New England 21
1973 —at Miami 44, New England 23
Miami 30, at New England 14
1974 —at New England 34, Miami 24
at Miami 34, New England 27
1975 —Miami 22, at New England 14
at Miami 20, New England 7
1976 —at New England 30, Miami 14
at Miami 10, New England 3
1977 —at Miami 17, New England 5
at New England 14, Miami 10
1978 —at New England 33, Miami 24
at Miami 23, New England 3
1979 —at New England 28, Miami 13
at Miami 39, New England 24
1980 —at New England 34, Miami 0
at Miami 16, New England 13 (ot)
1981 —Miami 30, at New England 27 (ot)
at Miami 24, New England 14
1982 —at New England 3, Miami 0
*at Miami 28, New England 13
1983 —at Miami 34, New England 24
at New England 17, Miami 6
1984 — at Miami 28, New England 7
Miami 44, New England 24
1985 — at New England 17, Miami 13
at Miami 30, New England 27
**New England 31, at Miami 14

MIAMI 3, NEW ORLEANS 1

1970 —at Miami 21, New Orleans 10
1974 —Miami 21, at New Orleans 0
1980 —at Miami 21, New Orleans 16
1983 —at New Orleans 17, Miami 7

MIAMI 1, NY GIANTS 0

1972 —Miami 23, at NY Giants 13

MIAMI 22, NY JETS 18 (1 tie

1966 —NY Jets 19, at Miami 14
at NY Jets 30, Miami 13
1967 —at NY Jets 29, Miami 7
NY Jets 33, at Miami 14
1968 —at NY Jets 35, Miami 17
NY Jets 31, at Miami 7
1969 —at NY Jets 34, Miami 31
NY Jets 27, at Miami 9
1970 —Miami 20, at NY Jets 6
at Miami 16, NY Jets 0
1971 —NY Jets 14, at Miami 10
Miami 30, at NY Jets 14
1972 —Miami 27, at NY Jets 17
at Miami 28, NY Jets 24
1973 —at Miami 31, NY Jets 3
Miami 24, at NY Jets 14
1974 —at Miami 21, NY Jets 17
at NY Jets 17, Miami 14
1975 —Miami 43, at NY Jets 0
at Miami 27, NY Jets 7
1976 —at Miami 16, NY Jets 0
Miami 27, at NY Jets 7
1977 —at Miami 21, NY Jets 17
Miami 14, at NY Jets 10
1978 —at NY Jets 33, Miami 20
NY Jets 24, at Miami 13
1979 —at NY Jets 33, Miami 27
NY Jets 27, at Miami 24
1980 —at NY Jets 17, Miami 14
NY Jets 24, at Miami 17
1981 —at Miami 28, NY Jets 28 (tie)
at NY Jets 16, Miami 15
1982 —Miami 45 at NY Jets 28
at Miami 20, NY Jets 19
**at Miami 14, NY Jets 0
1983 —Miami 32, NY Jets 14
at Miami 34, NY Jets 14
1984 — Miami 31, at NY Jets 17
at Miami 28, N.Y. Jets 17
1985 — at NY Jets 23, Miami 7
at Miami 21, NY Jets 17

MIAMI 3, PHILADELPHIA 2

1970 —at Philadelphia 24, Mirnai 17
1975 —at Miami 24, Philadelphia 16
1978 —at Philadelphia 17, Miami 3
1981 —at Miami 13, Philadelphia 10
1984 — at Miami 24, Philadelphia 23

MIAMI 7, PITTSBURGH 3

1971 —at Miami 24, Pittsburgh 21
1972 —**Miami 21, at Pittsburgh 17
1973 —at Miami 30, Pittsburgh 26
1976 —at Pittsburgh 14, Miami 3
1979 —*at Pittsburgh 34, Miami 14
1980 —at Pittsburgh 23, Miami 10
1981 —at Miami 30, Pittsburgh 10
1984 — Miami 31, at Pittsburgh 7
**at Miami 45, Pittsburgh 28
1985 — at Miami 24, Pittsburgh 20

MIAMI 5, ST.. LOUIS 0

1972 —at Miami 31, St. Louis 10
1977 —Miami 55, at St. Louis 14
1978 — at Miami 24, St. Louis 10
1981 — Miami 20, at St. Louis 7
1984 — Miami 36, at St. Louis 28

SAN DIEGO 8, MIAMI 5

1966 — at San Diego 44, Miami 10
1967 — at San Diego 24, Miami 0
at Miami 41, San Diego, Miami 0
1968 — at San Diego, 34, Miami 28
1969 — San Diego 21, at Miami 14
1972 — at Miami 24, San Diego 10
1974 — Miami 28, at San Diego 21
1977 — San Diego 14, at Miami 13
1978 — Miami 28, at San Diego 21
1980 — San Diego 27, at Miami 24 (ot)
1981 — *San Diego 41, at Miami 38 (ot)
1982 — *at Miami 34, San Diego 13
1984 — at San Diego 34, Miami 28 (ot)

MIAMI 4, SAN FRANCISCO 1

1973 — at Miami 21, San Francisco 13
1977 — Miami 19, at San Francisco 15
1980 — at Miami 17, San Francisco 13
1983 — Miami 20 at San Francisco 17
1984 — ***San Francisco 38, Miami 16

MIAMI 3, SEATTLE 1

1977 – at Miami 31, Seattle 13
1979 – at Miami 19, Seattle 10
1983 – *Seattle 27, at Miami 20
1984 – *at Miami 31, Seattle 10

MIAMI 2, TAMPA BAY 1

1976 – Miami 23, at Tampa Bay 20
1982 – at Tampa Bay 23, Miami 17
1985 – at Miami 41, Tampa Bay 38

MIAMI 4, WASHINGTON 2

1972 – ***Miami 14, Washington 7
1974 – at Washington 20, Miami 17
1978 – Miami 16, at Washington 0
1981 – at Miami 13, Washington 10
1982 ***Washington 27, Miami 17
1984 – Miami 35, at Washington 17

*AFC playoff   **AFC championship

***Super Bowl

DOLPHINS 23-0 VS. 6 CLUBS

The Miami Dolphins have built a perfect 23-0 regular season record against six clubs in the National Football League through the 1986 season.

Those teams which have never beaten Miami are Atlanta (0-4), Chicago (0-4), Green Bay (0-4), New York Giants (0-1), St. Louis (0-5) and San Francisco (0-3).

Miami set an NFL record with 20 consecutive victories over Buffalo from 1970 through 1979.

ALL-TIME PRE-SEASON RESULTS

1966 (0-4)

DATE	SITE	ATT.	SCORE
8/6	at San Diego	25,712	San Diego 38, Miami 10
8/12	at Miami	36,366	Kansas City 33, Miami 0
8/20	at Jacksonville	11,000	N.Y. Jets 31, Miami 14
8/24	at Memphis	18,442	Denver 28, Miami 16

1967 (2-3)

DATE	SITE	ATT.	SCORE
7/29	at Akron	7,000	Miami 19, Denver 2
8/5	at Memphis	21,200	Miami 10, Buffalo 7
8/12	at Miami	35,871	San Diego 20, Miami 19
8/19	at Miami	50,822	Atlanta 27, Miami 17
9/2	at Charleston	11,214	New Orleans 20, Miami 17

1968 (2-2-1)

DATE	SITE	ATT.	SCORE
8/11	at Rochester	12,000	Miami 28, Buffalo 28
8/17	at Miami	41,909	Miami 23, Philadelphia 7
8/23	at Jacksonville	15,003	Boston 19, Miami 17
8/31	at Miami	63,202	Baltimore 22, Miami 13
9/7	at Miami	31,014	Miami 19, Atlanta 13

1969 (1-5)

DATE	SITE	ATT.	SCORE
8/2	at Tampa	32,932	Minnesota 45, Miami 10
8/9	at Miami	49,592	Chicago 16, Miami 10
8/16	at Miami	31,663	Philadelphia 14, Miami 10
8/23	at Cincinnati	24,127	Cincinnati 28, Miami 21
8/30	at Miami	52,680	Baltimore 23, Miami 10
9/6	at Birmingham	10,700	Miami 13, Boston 0

1970 (4-2)

DATE	SITE	ATT.	SCORE
8/8	at Jacksonville	11,800	Miami 16, Pittsburgh 10
8/15	at Miami	56,739	Miami 20, Cincinnati 10
8/22	at Miami	52,812	Miami 17, San Francisco 7
8/29	at Miami	73,533	Miami 20, Baltimore 13
9/5	at Tampa	32,601	Washington 26, Miami 21
9/12	at Miami	43,714	Atlanta 20, Miami 17

1971 (2-3-1)

DATE	SITE	ATT.	SCORE
8/7	at Miami	64,005	Cincinnati 27, Miami 10
8/13	at Miami	57,008	Miami 17, San Francisco 17
8/21	at Milwaukee	46,464	Green Bay 10, Miami 7
8/28	at Miami	59,567	Miami 28, Detroit 24
9/4	at Miami	57,173	Miami 27, Washington 10
9/11	at Minnesota	45,880	Minnesota 24, Miami 0

1972 (3-3)

DATE	SITE	ATT.	SCORE
8/5	at Detroit	53,194	Detroit 31, Miami 23
8/12	at Miami	73,525	Green Bay 14, Miami 13
8/19	at Cincinnati	55,808	Miami 35, Cincinnati 17
8/25	at Miami	73,470	Miami 24, Atlanta 10
8/31	at Washington	52,098	Washington 27, Miami 24
9/10	at Miami	75,826	Miami 21, Minnesota 19

1973 (4-2-1)

DATE	SITE	ATT.	SCORE
7/27	at Chicago	54,103	Miami 14, College All-Stars 3
8/4	at Miami	78,091	Miami 14, Cincinnati 13
8/11	at Miami	78,112	Miami 14, New Orleans 13
8/18	at Miami	78,590	Miami 9, Chicago 9
8/24	at Miami	78,618	Miami 17, Los Angeles 14
8/31	at Minnesota	45,894	Minnesota 20, Miami 17
9/6	at Dallas	58,656	Dallas 26, Miami 23

1974 (4-2)

DATE	SITE	ATT.	SCORE
8/2	at Cincinnati	37,925	Cincinnati 19, Miami 13
8/10	at Miami	55,073	Miami 45, New Orleans 20
8/19	at Miami	67,963	Miami 21, Minnesota 9
8/24	at Los Angeles	64,663	Los Angeles 31, Miami 13
8/30	at Miami	70,406	Miami 21, Green Bay 10
9/7	at Chicago	55,093	Miami 30, Chicago 7

1975 (5-1)

DATE	SITE	ATT.	SCORE
8/9	at Miami	55,567	Miami 7, Cincinnati 3
8/16	at Miami	52,923	Miami 20, Detroit 14
8/23	at New Orleans	59,646	Miami 20, New Orleans 10
9/1	at Minnesota	47,544	Minnesota 20, Miami 7
9/6	at Miami	51,861	Miami 21, Chicago 10
9/13	at Miami	52,835	Miami 31, N.Y. Giants 13

1976 (6-0)

DATE	SITE	ATT.	SCORE
7/31	at Miami	50,469	Miami 16, Minnesota 3
8/8	at Detroit	53,036	Miami 30, Detroit 21
8/14	at Miami	51,869	Miami 24, Philadelphia 16
8/21	at Tampa Bay	67,466	Miami 28, Tampa Bay 21
8/28	at Houston	43,146	Miami 10, Houston 6
9/4	at New Orleans	63,950	Miami 20, New Orleans 7

1977 (4-2)

DATE	SITE	ATT.	SCORE
8/6	at Tampa Bay	62,056	Miami 13, Tampa Bay 7
8/13	at Miami	43,282	Miami 27, Washington 15
8/20	at Dallas	57,482	Miami 20, Dallas 14
8/26	at Minnesota	47,678	Minnesota 33, Miami 7
9/3	at Minnesota	38,235	New Orleans 17, Miami 10
9/11	at N.Y. Giants	51,561	Miami 27, N.Y. Giants 21

1978 (4-1)

DATE	SITE	ATT.	SCORE
7/29	at Canton	18,355	Philadelphia 17, Miami 3
8/5	at Miami	45,068	Miami 28, St. Louis 7
8/12	at New Orleans	53,602	Miami 31, New Orleans 17
8/18	at Miami	52,851	Miami 30, Minnesota 22
8/25	at Tampa Bay	70,321	Miami 24, Tampa Bay 20

1979 (4-0)

DATE	SITE	ATT.	SCORE
8/3	at Miami	46,130	Miami 14, New Orleans 7
8/11	at Tampa Bay	70,631	Miami 13, Tampa Bay 7
8/18	at Minnesota	47,696	Miami 21, Minnesota 10
8/24	at Miami	47,951	Miami 14, Philadelphia 13

1980 (3-1)

DATE	SITE	ATT.	SCORE
8/10	at Miami	41,345	Miami 17, Detroit 7
8/18	at Seattle	63,757	Miami 24, Seattle 7
8/23	at Miami	41,986	Minnesota 17, Miami 10
8/29	at New Orleans	51,473	Miami 20, New Orleans 0

1981 (4-0)

DATE	SITE	ATT.	SCORE
8/8	at Minnesota	47,596	Miami 20, Minnesota 6
8/15	at Miami	41,502	Miami 24, Denver 14
8/22	at Detroit	54,676	Miami 31, Detroit 27
8/28	at Miami	41,290	Miami 31, Kansas City 7

1982 (2-1-1)

DATE	SITE	ATT.	SCORE
8/14	at Miami	45,681	Miami 24, Washington 7
8/21	at Denver	74,465	Denver 17, Miami 14
8/28	at Kansas City	42,403	Miami 17, Kansas City 17
9/3	at Miami	46,257	Miami 16, N.Y. Giants 13

1983 (2-2)

DATE	SITE	ATT.	SCORE
8/6	at Dallas	46,826	Dallas 20, Miami 17
8/13	at Miami	38,735	New Orleans 19, Miami 17
8/19	at Washington	54,750	Miami 38, Washington 7
8/26	at N.Y. Giants	58,732	Miami 24, N.Y. Giants 3

1984 (3-1)

DATE	SITE	ATT.	SCORE
8/4	at Miami	37,559	Miami 24, Indianapolis 3
8/11	at Minneapolis	54,003	Miami 27, Minnesota 7
8/19	at Los Angeles	40,099	Miami 29, L.A. Raiders 23
8/24	at Tampa Bay	53,023	Tampa Bay 14, Miami 13

1985 (2-2)

DATE	SITE	ATT.	SCORE
8/10	at Miami	41,129	Minnesota 16, Miami 13 (OT)
8/17	at Miami	37,557	Miami 27, Buffalo 17
8/24	at Los Angeles	45,733	Miami 23, L.A. Raiders 17
8/30	at Atlanta	32,768	Atlanta 19, Miami 17

INDIVIDUAL RECORDS

1966-77: 14 games   1978-1981: 16 games
1982: 9 games   1983-present: 16 games

*Playoff game

SCORING

TOTAL POINTS
Career
- 830 Garo Yepremian (1970-78), 335XPs, 164 FGs
- 540 Uwe von Schamann (1979-84), 237 XPs, 101 FGs
- 408 Nat Moore (1974-85), 68 TDs
- 342 Larry Csonka (1968-74, 79), 57 TDs
- 198 Mercury Morris (1969-75), 33 TDs
- 198 Paul Warfield (1970-74), 33 TDs

Season
- 117 Garo Yepremian (1971), 33XPs, 28 FGs
- 116 Fuad Reveiz (1985), 50XPs, 22 FGs
- 115 Garo Yepremian (1972), 43XPs, 24 FGs

Game
- 24 Paul Warfield (12/15/73 vs. Detroit), 4 TDs

TOUCHDOWNS
Career
- 68 Nat Moore (1974-85), 67 pass, 1 run
- 57 Larry Csonka (1968-74, 79), 53 run, 4 pass
- 33 Mercury Morris (1969-75), 29 run, 1 pass, 3 return
- 33 Paul Warfield (1970-74), 33 pass

Season
- 18 Mark Clayton (1984), 18 pass
- 13 Ron Davenport (1985), 11 run, 2 pass
- 13 Nat Moore (1977), 12 pass, 1 run
- 13 Larry Csonka (1979), 12 run, 1 pass
- 12 Mercury Morris (1972), 12 run
- 12 Don Nottingham (1975), 12 run

Game
- 4 Paul Warfield (12/15/73 vs. Detroit), 4 TDs

FIELD GOALS MADE
Career
- 165 Garo Yepremian (1970-78), 242 attempts
- 101 Uwe von Schamann (1979-84), 149 attempts

Season
- 28 Garo Yepremian (1971), 40 attempts
- 25 Garo Yepremian (1973), 37 attempts

Game
- 5 Garo Yepremian (9/26/71 vs. Buffalo), 6 attempts
- 4 Garo Yepremian (10/18/70 at Buffalo), 4 attempts
- 4 Garo Yepremian (9/16/73 vs. San Francisco), 4 attempts
- 4 Uwe von Schamann (9/4/83 at Buffalo), 4 attempts

Per Cent
- 82.6 Garo Yepremian (1978), 19 of 23
- 81.3 Garo Yepremian (1975), 13 of 16

Longest
- 54 Garo Yepremian (10/22/72 vs. Buffalo)
- 53 Garo Yepremian (9/16/73 vs. San Francisco)
- 53 Garo Yepremian (12/5/76 vs. Buffalo)
- 53 Uwe von Schamann (10/21/79 at New England)

FIELD GOAL YARDAGE
Career
- 5,224 Garo Yepremian (1970-78), 165 of 242
- 3,256 Uwe von Schamann (1979-84), 101 of 149

Season
- 802 Garo Yepremian (1971), 28 of 40
- 768 Uwe von Schamann (1981), 24 of 31

Game
- 165 Garo Yepremian (10/18/70 at Buffalo) 46, 42, 47, 30
- 151 Garo Yepremian (9/16/73 vs. San Fran.) 31, 53, 45, 22

EXTRA POINTS MADE
Career
- 335 Garo Yepremian (1970-78), 351 attempts
- 237 Uwe von Schamann (1979-84), 250 attempts

Season
- 66 Uwe von Schamann (1984), 70 attempts
- 50 Fuad Reveiz (1985), 52 attempts
- 45 Uwe von Schamann (1983), 48 attempts

Game
- 7 Garo Yepremian (11/12/72 vs. New England), 7 attempts
- 7 Garo Yepremian (11/24/77 at St. Louis), 8 attempts

RUSHING

TOTAL YARDS
Career
- 6,737 Larry Csonka (1968-74, 79), 1506 attempts
- 3,877 Mercury Morris (1969-75), 754 attempts
- 3,644 Jim Kiick (1968-74), 997 attempts
- 3,320 Tony Nathan (1979-85), 701 attempts
- 2,632 Delvin Williams (1978-80), 643 attempts

Season
- 1,258 Delvin Williams (1978), 4.6 per carry
- 1,117 Larry Csonka (1972), 5.2 per carry
- 1,051 Larry Csonka (1971), 5.4 per carry
- 1,003 Larry Csonka (1973), 4.6 per carry
- 1,000 Mercury Morris (1972), 5.3 per carry

Game
- 197 Mercury Morris (9/30/73 vs. New England), 15 attempts
- 172 Gary Davis (12/17/77 vs. Buffalo), 26 attempts
- 151 Abner Haynes (9/17/67 vs. Denver), 12 attempts
- 151 Delvin Williams (11/9/80 at Los Angeles), 12 attempts
- *145 Larry Csonka (1/13/74 vs. Minnesota), 33 attempts
- 144 Mercury Morris (11/11/73 vs. Baltimore), 12 attempts
- 144 Delvin Williams (11/12/78 at Buffalo), 26 attempts
- 140 Leroy Harris (12/5/77 vs. Baltimore), 17 attempts

RUSHING ATTEMPTS
Career
- 1,506 Larry Csonka (1968-74, 79)
- 996 Jim Kiick (1968-74)
- 754 Mercury Morris (1969-75)
- 701 Tony Nathan (1979-85)
- 643 Delvin Williams (1978-80)

Season
- 272 Delvin Williams (1978)
- 224 Andra Franklin (1983)
- 220 Larry Csonka (1979)
- 219 Larry Csonka (1973)
- 219 Mercury Morris (1975)

Game
- *33 Larry Csonka (1/13/74 vs. Minnesota), 145 yards
- 31 Mercury Morris (10/5/75 at Green Bay), 125 yards
- *29 Larry Csonka (12/30/73 vs. Oakland), 117 yards
- 28 Andra Franklin (12/5/82 vs. Minnesota), 129 yards

TOUCHDOWNS RUSHING
Career
- 53 Larry Csonka (1968-74, 79)
- 29 Mercury Morris (1969-75)
- 28 Jim Kiick (1968-74)
- 25 Don Nottingham (1973-77)
- 22 Andra Franklin (1981-84)

Season
- 12 Mercury Morris (1972)
- 12 Don Nottingham (1975)
- 12 Larry Csonka (1979)
- 11 Ron Davenport (1985)
- 10 Mercury Morris (1973)

Game

    3   Jim Kiick (12/20/70 vs. Buffalo), 4, 2, 2
    3   Mercury Morris (11/12/72 vs. New England), 4, 4, 6
    3   Mercury Morris (9/30/73 vs. New England), 24, 70, 35
    3   Larry Csonka (12/30/73 vs. Oakland), 11, 2, 2
    3   Don Nottingham (11/3/74 vs. Atlanta), 1, 2, 1
    3   Don Nottingham (10/5/75 at Green Bay), 11, 1, 11
    3   Don Nottingham (10/26/75 at Buffalo), 1, 1, 1
    3   Larry Csonka (9/23/79 vs. Chicago), 12, 9, 1
    3   Larry Csonka (11/29/79 vs. New England), 1, 1, 1

RUSHING AVERAGE
Career

    5.1   Mercury Morris (1966-75), 754 attempts
    4.7   Tony Nathan (1979-85), 701 attempts
    4.5   Larry Csonka (1968-74, 79), 1,506 attempts
    4.4   Norm Bulaich (1975-79), 340 attempts
    4.4   Gary Davis (1976-79), 318 attempts

Season

    6.4   Mercury Morris (1973), 149/954 yards
    5.4   Larry Csonka (1971), 195/1,051 yards
    5.3   Mercury Morris (1972), 190/1,000 yards
    5.3   Tony Nathan (1981), 147/782 yards
    5.2   Larry Csonka (1972), 213/1,117 yards

Game (10 or more attempts)

    13.1   Mercury Morris (9/30/73 vs. New Eng.), 15/197
    12.6   Abner Haynes (9/17/67 vs. Denver), 12/151
    12.6   Delvin Williams (11/9/80 at Los Angeles), 12/151

LONGEST RUNS

    77t   Leroy Harris (12/5/77 vs. Baltimore)
    70t   Mercury Morris (9/30/73 vs. New England)
    70   Mercury Morris (10/15/73 at Cleveland)
    66t   Benny Malone (10/9/77 at Baltimore)
    65t   Abner Haynes (9/17/67 vs. Denver)
    65t   Gary Davis (9/17/78 vs. Buffalo)
    65   Delvin Williams (11/9/80 at L.A. Rams)
    63   Norm Bulaich (9/10/78 at Baltimore)
    60t   Gary Davis (12/17/77 vs. Buffalo)
    58t   Delvin Williams (9/3/78 at NY Jets)

PASSING

TOTAL YARDS
Career

    25,092   Bob Griese (1967-80)
    11,431   Dan Marino (1983-85)
     5,928   David Woodley (1980-83)
     4,347   Don Strock (1974-85)
     2,335   Earl Morrall (1972-76)

Season

    5,084   Dan Marino (1984)
    4,137   Dan Marino (1985)
    2,473   Bob Griese (1968)
    2,470   David Woodley (1981)
    2,252   Bob Griese (1977)

Game

    470   Dan Marino (12/2/84) vs. L.A. Raiders), 35 of 57
    429   Dan Marino (9/30/84 at St. Louis), 24 of 36
    422   Dan Marino (11/4/84 at N.Y. Jets), 23 of 42
    *421   Dan Marino (1/6/85 vs. Pittsburgh), 21 of 32
    408   David Woodley (10/25/81 at Dallas), 21 of 37

PASS ATTEMPTS
Career

    3,429   Bob Griese (1967-80)
    1,427   Dan Marino (1983-85)
      961   David Woodley (1980-83)
      645   Don Strock (1974-85)
      337   Rick Norton (1966-69)

Season

    567   Dan Marino (1985), 336 completions
    564   Dan Marino (1984), 362 completions
    366   David Woodley (1981), 191 completions
    355   Bob Griese (1968), 186 completions
    331   Bob Griese (1967), 166 completions

Game

    57   Dan Marino (12/2/84 vs. L.A. Raiders), 35 completions
    52   Dick Wood (11/27/66 vs. New England), 17 completions
    *50   Dan Marino (1/20/85 vs. San Francisco), 29 completions
    48   Dan Marino (9/15/85 vs. Indianapolis), 29 completions
    46   Rick Norton (10/15/67 at New England), 19 completions

PASS COMPLETIONS
Career

    1,926   Bob Griese (1967-80)
      871   Dan Marino (1983-85)
      508   David Woodley (1980-83)
      361   Don Strock (1974-85)

Season

    362   Dan Marino (1984), 564 attempts
    336   Dan Marino (1985), 567 attempts
    191   David Woodley (1981), 366 attempts
    186   Bob Griese (1968), 355 attempts
    180   Bob Griese (1977), 307 attempts

Game

    35   Dan Marino (12/2/84 vs. L.A. Raiders), 57 attempts
    30   Dan Marino (12/8/85 at Green Bay), 44 attempts
    *29   Don Strock (1/2/82 vs. San Diego), 43 attempts
    29   Dan Marino (12/9/84 at Indianapolis), 41 attempts
    *29   Dan Marino (1/20/85 vs. San Francisco), 50 attempts
    29   Dan Marino (9/15/85 vs. Indianapolis), 48 attempts

TOUCHDOWN PASSES
Career

    192   Bob Griese (1967-80)
     98   Dan Marino (1983-85)
     37   Don Strock (1974-85)
     34   David Woodley (1980-83)

Season

    48   Dan Marino (1984) of 362 completions
    30   Dan Marino (1985) of 336 completions
    22   Bob Griese (1977) of 180 completions
    21   Bob Griese (1968) of 186 completions
    20   Dan Marino (1983) of 173 completions

Game

    6   Bob Griese (11/24/77 at St. Louis) 4, 7, 9, 28, 17, 37
    5   Dan Marino (9/2/84 at Washington) 26, 74, 6, 9, 11
    5   Dan Marino (12/8/85 at Green Bay) 10, 16, 21, 2, 61
    4   John Stofa (12/18/66 vs. Houston) 27, 48, 4, 14
    4   Bob Griese (11/2/69 at NY Jets) 5, 29, 11, 9
    4   Bob Griese (10/17/71 vs. New Eng.) 22, 32, 14, 14
    4   Bob Griese (12/15/73 vs. Detroit) 21, 7, 16, 4
    *4   Don Strock (1/2/82 vs. San Diego) 1, 40, 15, 50
    4   Dan Marino (10/21/84 at New England) 19, 5, 15, 15
    4   Dan Marino (11/26/84 vs. N.Y. Jets) 15, 1, 7, 12
    4   Dan Marino (12/2/84 vs. L.A. Raiders) 4, 64, 11, 9
    4   Dan Marino (12/9/84 at Indianapolis) 2, 2, 25, 7
    4   Dan Marino (12/17/84 vs. Dallas) 41, 3, 39, 63
    *4   Dan Marino (1/6/85 vs. Pittsburgh) 40, 41, 36, 6

PASSES HAD INTERCEPTED
Career

    172   Bob Griese (1967-80)
     44   Dan Marino (1983-1985)
     42   David Woodley (1980-83)
     36   Don Strock (1974-85)

Season

    21   Dan Marino (1985), 567 attempts
    18   Bob Griese (1967), 331 attempts
    17   Bob Griese (1970), 245 attempts
    17   David Woodley (1980), 327 attempts
    17   Dan Marino (1984), 564 attempts

Game

    5   Bob Griese (12/23/67 vs. Houston), 41 attempts
    5   Rick Norton (11/23/69 vs. Houston), 26 attempts
    5   David Woodley (10/25/81 at Dallas), 37 attempts

LOWEST INTERCEPTION RATE
Season (150 or more attempts)

2.03   Dan Marino (1983), 6 of 296 attempts
3.01   Dan Marino (1984), 17 of 564 attempts
3.42   Bob Griese (1971), 9 of 263 attempts

COMPLETION PERCENT
Career
61.0   Dan Marino (1983-85), 871 of 1,427 attempts
56.3   Bob Griese (1967-80), 1,926 of 3,429 attempts
55.9   Don Strock (1974-85), 361 of 645 attempts
53.9   Earl Morrall (1972-76), 153 of 284 attempts
Season
64.2   Dan Marino (1984), 362 of 564 attempts
63.0   Bob Griese (1978), 148 of 235 attempts
61.8   Bob Griese (1975), 118 of 191 attempts
Game (12 or more completions)
92.3   Bob Griese (12/18/78 vs. New Eng.), 12 of 13 attempts
*84.2 David Woodley (1/8/83 vs. New Eng.), 16 of 19 attempts
82.4   Earl Morrall (12/1/75 vs. New Eng.), 14 of 17 attempts
81.8   Don Strock (12/10/83 vs. Atlanta), 18 of 22 attempts
81.0   Bob Griese (10/22/67 vs. NY Jets), 17 of 21 attempts

LONGEST PASS PLAYS
86t   Bob Griese to Paul Warfield (11/14/71 vs. Pittsburgh)
85t   Dan Marino to Mark Duper (11/20/83 vs. Baltimore)
80t   George Wilson to Bo Roberson (10/23/66 at Houston)
80t   Dan Marino to Mark Duper (9/23/84 vs. Indianapolis)
79t   Bob Griese to Nat Moore (11/2/75 at Chicago)
*76t   David Woodley to Jimmy Cefalo (1/30/83 vs. Washington)
*75t   Bob Griese to Paul Warfield (1/2/72 vs. Baltimore)
74t   Bob Griese to Paul Warfield (10/31/71 at Los Angeles)
74t   Dan Marino to Mark Duper (9/2/84 at Washington)
73t   Bob Griese to Nat Moore (9/25/77 at San Francisco)
73   Dan Marino to Tony Nathan (9/29/85 at Denver)
71   Dick Wood to Bo Roberson (12/4/66 at Denver)

PASS RECEIVING

TOTAL RECEPTIONS
Career
472   Nat Moore (1974-85)
325   Tony Nathan (1979-85)
266   Duriel Harris (1976-83)
221   Jim Kiick (1968-74)
212   Howard Twilley (1966-76)
Season
73   Mark Clayton (1984), 1,389 yards
72   Tony Nathan (1985), 651 yards
71   Mark Duper (1984), 1,306 yards
70   Mark Clayton (1985), 996 yards
67   Jack Clancy (1967), 868 yards
Game (minimum 100 yards)
10   Duriel Harris (10/28/79 vs. Green Bay), 180 yards
10   Tony Nathan (9/29/85 at Denver), 120 yards
9   Marlin Briscoe (9/15/74 at New England), 113 yards
9   Duriel Harris (11/30/81 vs. Philadelphia), 114 yards
*9   Tony Nathan (1/2/82 vs. San Diego), 114 yards
9   Mark Clayton (12/2/84 vs. L.A. Raiders), 177 yards

TOTAL RECEIVING YARDS
Career
7,116 Nat Moore (1974-85), 15.1 per catch
4,510 Duriel Harris (1976-83), 17.0 per catch
3,355 Paul Warfield (1970-74), 21.5 per catch
3,064 Howard Twilley (1966-76), 14.4 per catch
3,058 Tony Nathan (1979-85), 9.4 per catch
Season
1,389 Mark Clayton (1984), 73 receptions
1,306 Mark Duper (1984), 71 receptions
1,003 Mark Duper (1983), 51 receptions
996   Paul Warfield (1971), 43 receptions
996   Mark Clayton (1985), 70 receptions
Game
217   Mark Duper (11/10/85 vs. NY Jets), 8 receptions
210   Nat Moore (10/4/81 vs. NY Jets), 7 receptions
202   Mark Duper (10/9/83 vs. Buffalo), 7 receptions
180   Duriel Harris (10/28/79 vs. Green Bay), 10 receptions

178   Mark Duper (9/2/84 at Washington), 6 receptions
177   Mark Clayton (12/2/84 vs. L.A. Raiders), 9 receptions

TOUCHDOWNS RECEIVING
Career
67   Nat Moore (1974-85), 472 receptions
33   Paul Warfield (1970-74), 156 receptions
23   Howard Twilley (1966-76), 212 receptions
23   Jim Mandich (1970-77), 121 receptions
Season
18   Mark Clayton (1984), 73 receptions
12   Nat Moore (1977), 52 receptions
11   Karl Noonan (1968), 58 receptions
11   Paul Warfield (1971), 43 receptions
11   Paul Warfield (1973), 29 receptions
Game
4   Paul Warfield (12/15/73 vs. Detroit)

RUSHING-RECEIVING

Career
7,425 Larry Csonka (1968-74, 79), 6,737 and 688
7,364 Nat Moore (1974-85), 248 and 7,116
6,378 Tony Nathan (1979-85), 3,320 and 3,058
5,854 Jim Kiick (1968-74), 3,644 and 2,210
4,368 Mercury Morris (1969-75), 3,877 and 491
Season
1,450 Delvin Williams (1978), 1,258 and 192
1,318 Tony Nathan (1985), 667 and 651
1,234 Tony Nathan (1981), 782 and 452
1,168 Mercury Morris (1972), 1,000 and 168
1,165 Larry Csonka (1972), 1,117 and 48
1,164 Larry Csonka (1971), 1,051 and 113
1,155 Jim Kiick (1970), 658 and 497

COMBINED YARDAGE

Career
8,521 Nat Moore (1974-85), 1,157 return yards
7,995 Tony Nathan (1979-85), 1,617 return yards
7,486 Mercury Morris (1969-75), 3,118 return yards
7,425 Larry Csonka (1968-74, 79), no return yards
6,038 Duriel Harris (1976-82), 1,495 return yards
Season
1,603 Tony Nathan (1979), 1,322 return yards
1,502 Mercury Morris (1972), 334 return yards
1,483 Mercury Morris (1969), 1,308 return yards
1,476 Joe Auer (1966), 797 return yards

Game
302   Mercury Morris (11/1/70 at Baltimore)
       8-89 rush, 3-68 pass, 6-145 kickoff returns
254   Freddie Solomon (10/9/77 at Baltimore)
       4-171 kickoff returns, 4-51 pass, 3-32 punt returns
252   Freddie Solomon (12/5/76 vs. Buffalo)
       1-59t rush, 5-114 pass, 1-79t punt return

PUNTING

TOTAL PUNTS
Career
633   Larry Seiple (1967-77), 25, 347 yards
227   George Roberts (1978-80), 9,314 yards

Season
83   Tom Orosz (1981), 40.8 average
81   George Roberts (1978), 40.3 average
80   Larry Seiple (1969), 40.8 average
Game
10   George Wilson, Jr. (9/9/66 vs. NY Jets), 483 yards
10   George Roberts (10/12/80 at New England), 445 yards
9   Larry Seiple (9/18/77 at Buffalo), 325 yards

AVERAGE YARDS
Career
- 43.7 Reggie Roby (1983-85)
- 40.0 Larry Seiple (1967-77)

Season
- 44.7 Reggie Roby (1984), 51 punts
- 43.7 Reggie Roby (1985), 59 punts
- 43.1 Reggie Roby (1983), 74 punts
- 42.6 George Roberts (1980), 77 punts
- 42.3 Larry Seiple (1973), 48 punts

Game (4 or more punts)
- 52.0 Larry Seiple (10/7/73 vs. NY Jets), 4-208 yards
- 50.6 Reggie Roby (11/26/84 vs. NY Jets), 5-253 yards
- 50.5 Reggie Roby (11/17/85 at Indianapolis), 4-202 yards
- 49.6 Reggie Roby (10/30/83 vs. L.A. Rams), 4-248 yards
- 49.0 Reggie Roby (10/2/83 at New Orleans), 4-196 yards

LONGEST PUNTS
- 73 Larry Seiple (11/14/71 vs. Pittsburgh) to end zone
- 71 George Roberts (11/2/80 at Oakland) net 62
- 69 Reggie Roby (11/26/84 vs. NY Jets) to end zone

PUNT RETURNS

TOTAL RETURNS
Career
- 127 Jake Scott (1970-75)
- 79 Tom Vigorito (1981-83,85)
- 71 Freddie Solomon (1975-77)

Season
- 41 Mark Clayton (1983), 9.6 average
- 36 Tom Vigorito (1981), 10.5 average
- 33 Jake Scott (1971), 9.6 average

Game
- 7 Mercury Morris (10/19/69 at Kansas City), 17.6 avg.
- 6 Jake Scott (11/10/74 at New Orleans), 16.5 avg.
- 6 Freddie Solomon (12/5/77 vs. Baltimore), 9.3 avg.
- 6 Tom Vigorito (11/30/81 vs. Philadelphia), 12.2 avg.
- 6 Mark Clayton (11/20/83 vs. Baltimore), 16.2 avg.
- 6 Vince Heflin (9/23/84 vs. Indianapolis), 12.7 avg.

PUNT RETURN YARDAGE
Career
- 1,330 Jake Scott (1970-75)
- 830 Tom Vigorito (1981-83,85)
- 810 Freddie Solomon (1975-77)

Season
- 392 Mark Clayton (1983), 9.6 avg.
- 379 Tom Vigorito (1981), 10.5 avg.
- 346 Jake Scott (1974), 11.2 avg.

Game
- 123 Mercury Morris (10/19/69 at Kansas City), 7 returns
- 99 Jake Scott (11/10/74 at New Orleans), 6 returns
- 97 Mark Clayton (11/20/83 vs. Baltimore), 6 returns

LONGEST PUNT RETURNS
- 87t Tom Vigorito (9/10/81 vs. Pittsburgh)
- 86t Tony Nathan (10/14/79 vs. Buffalo)
- 79t Freddie Solomon (12/5/76 vs. Buffalo)
- 77t Jake Scott (11/22/70 vs. Baltimore)
- 62 Tom Vigorito (9/4/83 at Buffalo)

AVERAGE YARDS
Career
- 11.4 Freddie Solomon (1975-77), 71 returns
- 10.5 Jake Scott (1970-75), 127 returns
- 10.5 Tom Vigorito (1981-83,85), 79 returns

Season (14 or more returns)
- 12.3 Freddie Solomon (1975), 26 returns
- 12.1 Jake Scott (1973), 22 returns

Game
- 18.8 Charlie Babb (11/23/75 vs. Baltimore), 4-75 yards
- 17.6 Mercury Morris (10/19/69 at Kansas City), 7-123 yards

FAIR CATCHES
Career
- 55 Jake Scott (1970-75) of 182 punts
- 29 Dick Anderson (1968-75, 1977) of 74 punts

Season
- 18 Jake Scott (1971) of 51 punts
- 16 Jake Scott (1973) of 38 punts

Game
- 6 Jake Scott (12/20/70 vs. Buffalo) of 8 punts

KICKOFF RETURNS

TOTAL RETURNS
Career
- 123 Fulton Walker (1981-85)
- 111 Mercury Morris (1969-75)
- 56 Duriel Harris (1976-83)

Season
- 45 Lorenzo Hampton (1985), 22.7 avg.
- 45 Tony Nathan (1979), 22.6 avg.
- 43 Mercury Morris (1969), 26.4 avg.
- 40 Don Bessillieu (1980), 22.3 avg.

Game
- 7 Don Bessillieu (10/23/80 at New England), 20.4 avg.
- 7 Fulton Walker (11/8/81 at New England), 23.7 avg.

KICKOFF RETURN YARDAGE
Career
- 2,947 Mercury Morris (1969-75)
- 2,944 Fulton Walker (1981-85)
- 1,416 Duriel Harris (1976-83)

Season
- 1,136 Mercury Morris (1969), 26.4 avg.
- 1,020 Lorenzo Hampton (1985), 22.7 avg.
- 1,016 Tony Nathan (1979) 22.6 avg.
- 962 Fulton Walker (1983) 26.7 avg.
- 932 Fulton Walker (1981), 24.5 avg.

Game
- 204 Gene Milton (9/21/68 vs. Oakland), long 73
- *190 Fulton Walker (1/30/83 vs. Washington), long 98
- 185 Fulton Walker (10/12/81 at Buffalo), long 90t
- 171 Freddie Solomon (10/9/77 at Baltimore), long 90t

LONGEST KICKOFF RETURNS
- 105t Mercury Morris (9/14/69 at Cincinnati)
- *98t Fulton Walker (1/30/83 vs. Washington)
- 96t Mercury Morris (12/6/70 vs. New England)
- 95t Joe Auer (9/2/66 vs. Oakland)
- 95 Bobby Neff (9/14/68 vs. Houston)

AVERAGE YARDS
Career (50 or more returns)
- 26.5 Mercury Morris (1969-75), 111 returns
- 25.3 Duriel Harris (1976-83), 56 returns
- 23.9 Fulton Walker (1981-85), 123 returns

Season
- 32.9 Duriel Harris (1976), 17 returns, 559 yards
- 29.6 Gary Davis (1977), 14 returns, 414 yards
- 29.0 Mercury Morris (1970), 28 returns, 812 yards

Game (4 or more returns)
- *47.5 Fulton Walker (1/30/83 vs. Washington) 4-190
- 42.8 Freddie Solomon (10/9/77 at Baltimore), 4-171
- 34.0 Gene Milton (9/21/68 vs. Oakland), 6-204

INTERCEPTIONS

TOTAL INTERCEPTIONS
Career
- 35 Jake Scott (1970-75)
- 34 Dick Anderson (1968-75, 1977)
- 24 Glenn Blackwood (1979-85)
- 23 Gerald Small (1978-83)
- 22 Tim Foley (1970-1980)
- 22 Curtis Johnson (1970-78)

Season
- 10 Dick Westmoreland (1967), 127 yards
- 8 Willie West (1966), 62 yards
- 8 Dick Anderson (1968, 1970, 1973), 230 yards, 191 yards, 163 yards
- 8 Jake Scott (1974), 75 yards

Game
- 4 Dick Anderson (12/3/73 vs. Pittsburgh), 121 yards
- 3 Willie West (10/23/66 at Houston), 49 yards
- 3 Dick Westmoreland (11/26/67 vs. Buffalo), 43 yards
- 3 Charlie Babb (9/22/75 vs. Oakland), 18 yards
- 3 Curtis Johnson (11/9/75 at NY Jets), 25 yards
- 3 Larry Gordon (12/10/78 vs. Oakland), 35 yards
- 3 William Judson (10/16/83 at NY Jets), 23 yards

INTERCEPTION YARDAGE
Career
- 792 Dick Anderson (1968-75, 1977), 23.3 avg.
- 425 Jake Scott (1970-75), 12.1 avg.
- 378 Gerald Small (1978-83), 16.4 avg.
- 371 Glenn Blackwood (1979-85), 15.5 avg.

Season
230 Dick Anderson (1968), 8 for 28.8 avg.
198 Jimmy Warren (1966), 5 for 39.6 avg.
191 Dick Anderson (1970), 8 for 23.9 avg.

Game
121 Dick Anderson (12/3/73 vs. Pittsburgh), 4 interceptions
109 Dick Anderson (11/24/68 at New England), 2 interceptions

LONGEST INTERCEPTION RETURNS
96t Dick Anderson (11/24/68 at New England), Tom Sherman
86 Dick Anderson (12/20/70 vs. Buffalo), Dennis Shaw
86t William Judson (60t), Mike Kozlowski (26, lateral), (9/9/84 vs. New England), Steve Grogan
70t Jimmy Warren (11/13/66 at Kansas City), Len Dawson
*62t Dick Anderson (1/2/72 vs. Baltimore), John Unitas
61t William Judson (9/8/85 at Houston), Warren Moon
56 Neal Colzie (11/29/79 vs. New England), Steve Grogan

TOUCHDOWN INTERCEPTIONS
3 Dick Anderson (1968-74), 96, 27, 38 yards
2 Dick Westmoreland (1966-69), 39, 19 yards
2 Bill Stanfill (1969-76), 15, 17 yards
2 Lloyd Mumphord (1969-74), 32, 28 yards
2 Mike Kozlowski (1979, 1981-84), 35, 38 yards
2 Don McNeal (1980-82, 84), 19, 11 yards

MISCELLANEOUS RETURNS

BLOCKED FIELD GOAL
51t Lloyd Mumphord (12/6/70 vs. New England), Gino Capelletti
47t Curtis Johnson (12/19/71 vs. Green Bay), Tim Webster

BLOCKED PUNT
8t Tim Foley (11/11/73 vs. Baltimore), David Lee
*5t Charlie Babb (12/24/72 vs. Cleveland), Don Cockroft
5t Tim Foley (11/11/73 vs. Baltimore), David Lee

SHORT FIELD GOAL ATTEMPT
50 Jake Scott (12/6/70 vs. New England), Gino Capelletti

FUMBLE RECOVERY (ALL TDs)
68t A.J. Duhe (10/15/78 at San Diego), Dan Fouts
44t Don Bessillieu (10/19/80 vs. Buffalo), Joe Cribbs
35t Dick Anderson (10/15/72 vs. San Diego), Mike Garrett
25t Mike Kozlowski (12/6/81 vs. New England), Sam Cunningham
21t Bob Baumhower (10/7/84 at Pittsburgh), Mark Malone
13t Nick Buoniconti (9/30/73 vs. New England), John Tarver
13t Bob Baumhower (10/9/78 vs. Cincinnati), Dave Turner
7t Bob Brudzinski (10/27/85 at Detroit), Eric Hipple

DOLPHIN TOP TENS

RUSHING

	PLAYER	YEARS	NO.	YDS.	AVG.	LG	TD
1.	Larry Csonka	1968-74, 1979	1506	6737	4.5	5.4	53
2.	Mercury Morris	1969-75	754	3877	5.1	70	29
3.	Jim Kiick	1968-74	996	3644	3.7	56	28
4.	Tony Nathan	1979-85	701	3320	4.7	46	16
5.	Delvin Williams	1978-80	643	2632	4.1	65	13
6.	Andra Franklin	1981-84	622	2232	3.6	29	22
7.	Benny Malone	1974-78	503	2129	4.2	66	16
8.	Don Nottingham	1973-77	365	1524	4.2	56	25
9.	Norm Bulaich	1975-79	340	1498	4.4	63	17
10.	Gary Davis	1976-79	318	1389	4.4	65	7

PASSING

	PLAYER	YEARS	ATT.	COMP.	YDS.	PCT.	AVG. ATT.	TD	INT.
1.	Bob Griese	1967-80	3429	1926	25092	56.3	7.3	192	172
2.	Dan Marino	1983-85	1427	871	11431	61.0	8.0	98	44
3.	David Woodley	1980-83	961	508	5928	52.9	6.2	34	42
4.	Don Strock	1974-85	645	361	4347	55.9	6.7	37	36
5.	Rick Norton	1966-69	377	156	1751	41.4	4.6	6	30
6.	Earl Morrall	1972-76	284	153	2335	53.9	8.2	17	17
7.	Dick Wood	1966	230	83	989	36.1	4.3	4	14
8.	John Stofa	1966-67, 1969-70	135	61	862	45.2	6.4	7	6
9.	George Wilson, Jr.	1966	112	46	764	41.1	6.8	5	10
10.	George Mira	1971	30	11	159	36.7	5.3	1	1

RECEIVING

	PLAYER	YEARS	NO.	YDS.	AVG.	LG	TD
1.	Nat Moore	1974-85	472	7116	15.2	79	67
2.	Tony Nathan	1979-85	325	3058	9.4	73	14
3.	Duriel Harris	1976-83	266	4510	17.0	64	18
4.	Jim Kiick	1968-74	221	2210	10.0	53	3
5.	Howard Twilley	1966-76	212	3064	14.5	44	23
6.	Bruce Hardy	1978-85	169	1685	9.9	31	18
7.	Mark Duper	1982-85	157	2959	18.8	85	21
8.	Paul Warfield	1970-74	156	3355	21.5	86	33
9.	Mark Clayton	1983-85	149	2499	16.8	65	23
10.	Karl Noonan	1966-71	136	1808	13.3	51	17

SCORING

	PLAYER	YEARS	TD	TDR	TDP	TDRT	FG	PAT	TD
1.	Garo Yepremian	1970-78	0	0	0	0	165	335	830
2.	Uwe von Schamann	1979-84	0	0	0	0	101	237	540
3.	Nat Moore	1974-85	67	1	67	0	0	0	408
4.	Larry Csonka	1968-74, 1979	57	53	4	0	0	0	342
5.	Mercury Morris	1969-75	33	29	1	3	0	0	198
	Paul Warfield	1970-74	33	0	33	0	0	0	198
7.	Jim Kiick	1968-74	31	28	3	0	0	0	186
8.	Tony Nathan	1979-85	31	16	14	1	0	0	186
9.	Don Nottingham	1973-77	25	25	0	0	0	0	150
10.	Mark Clayton	1983-85	24	0	23	1	0	0	144

KICKOFF RETURNS

	PLAYER	YEARS	NO.	YDS.	AVG.	LG	TD
1.	Mercury Morris	1969-75	111	2947	26.5	96	3
2.	Fulton Walker	1981-85	123	2944	23.9	90	1
3.	Duriel Harris	1976-83	45	1416	25.3	69	0
4.	Gary Davis	1976-79	55	1309	23.8	73	0
5.	Joe Auer	1966-67	49	1139	23.2	95	1
6.	Tony Nathan	1979-85	53	1133	21.4	43	0
7.	Don Bessilleu	1979-81	47	1024	21.8	87	0
8.	Lorenzo Hampton	1985	45	1020	22.7	46	0
9.	Bob Neff	1966-68	35	917	26.2	90	0
10.	Nat Moore	1974-85	33	858	26.0	42	0

PUNT RETURNS

	PLAYER	YEARS	NO.	FC	YDS.	AVG.	LG	TD
1.	Jake Scott	1970-75	127	55	1330	10.5	77	1
2.	Tom Vigorito	1981-83,85	79	21	830	10.5	87	2
3.	Freddie Solomon	1975-77	71	4	810	11.4	79	2
4.	Mark Clayton	1983-85	51	13	485	9.6	60	1
5.	Tony Nathan	1979-85	51	26	484	9.5	86	1
6.	Dick Anderson	1968-74, 1976-77	45	29	315	7.0	47	0
7.	Fulton Walker	1981-85	34	15	305	9.0	33	0
8.	Nat Moore	1974-85	26	12	299	11.5	42	0
9.	Charles Leigh	1971-73	31	7	274	8.8	27	0
10.	Jimmy Cefalo	1978-84	30	11	242	8.1	26	0

INTERCEPTIONS

	PLAYER	YEARS	NO.	YDS.	AVG.	LG	TD
1.	Jake Scott	1970-75	35	425	12.1	47	0
2.	Dick Anderson	1968-74, 1976-1977	34	792	23.3	86	2
3.	Glenn Blackwood	1979-85	24	371	15.5	50	1
4.	Gerald Small	1978-83	23	378	16.4	46	1
5.	Curtis Johnson	1970-78	22	150	6.8	34	0
	Tim Foley	1970-80	22	96	4.4	18	0
7.	Dick Westmoreland	1966-69	15	236	15.7	42	1
8.	Lloyd Mumphord	1969-74	14	187	13.4	51	2
	William Judson	1981-85	14	269	19.2	61	1
10.	Willie West	1966-68	13	180	13.8	32	0
	Lyle Blackwood	1981-85	13	161	12.3	45	0

YEAR-BY-YEAR LEADERS

RUSHING

YEAR	PLAYER	G	ATT	YDS	AVG.	LG	TD
1966	Joe Auer	14	121	416	3.4	41	4
1967	Abner Haynes	10	56	274	4.9	65t	2
1968	Jim Kiick	14	165	621	3.8	25	4
1969	Jim Kiick	14	180	575	3.2	27	9
1970	Larry Csonka	14	193	874	4.5	53	6
1971	Larry Csonka	14	195	1051	5.4	28	7
1972	Larry Csonka	14	213	1117	5.2	45	6
1973	Larry Csonka	14	219	1003	4.6	25	5
1974	Larry Csonka	12	197	749	3.8	24	9
1975	Mercury Morris	14	219	875	4.0	49	4
1976	Benny Malone	14	186	797	4.3	31	4
1977	Benny Malone	14	129	615	4.8	66t	5
1978	Delvin Williams	16	272	1258	4.6	58t	8
1979	Larry Csonka	16	220	837	3.8	22	12
1980	Delvin Williams	15	187	671	3.6	65	2
1981	Tony Nathan	13	147	782	5.3	46	5
1982	Andra Franklin	9	177	701	4.0	25t	7
1983	Andra Franklin	15	224	746	3.3	18	8
1984	Woody Bennett	16	144	606	4.2	23	7
1985	Tony Nathan	16	143	667	4.7	22	5

RECEIVING

YEAR	PLAYER	G	NO.	YDS	AVG.	LG	TD
1966	Dave Kocourek	14	27	320	11.9	43	2
1967	Jack Clancy	14	67	868	13.0	44	2
1968	Karl Noonan	14	58	760	13.1	50	11
1969	Larry Seiple	13	41	577	14.1	41t	5
1970	Jim Kiick	14	42	497	11.8	47	0
1971	Paul Warfield	14	43	996	23.2	86t	11
1972	Paul Warfield	12	29	606	20.9	47	3
1973	Marlin Briscoe	14	30	447	14.9	53	2
1974	Nat Moore	13	37	605	16.4	48	2
1975	Nat Moore	14	40	705	17.6	79t	4
1976	Nat Moore	9	33	625	18.9	67t	4
1977	Nat Moore	14	52	765	14.7	73t	12
1978	Nat Moore	16	48	645	13.5	47	10
1979	Nat Moore	16	48	840	17.5	53	6
1980	Tony Nathan	16	57	588	10.3	61	5
1981	Duriel Harris	15	53	911	17.2	55	2
1982	Tom Vigorito	9	24	186	7.8	26	0
1983	Tony Nathan	16	52	461	8.9	25	1
1984	Mark Clayton	15	73	1389	19.0	65	18
1985	Tony Nathan	16	72	651	9.0	73	1

PASSING

YEAR	PLAYER	G	ATT	COM	YDS	PCT.	TD	INT.
1966	Dick Wood	10	230	83	993	36.1	4	14
1967	Bob Griese	12	331	166	2005	50.2	15	18
1968	Bob Griese	13	355	186	2473	52.4	21	16
1969	Bob Griese	9	252	121	1695	48.0	10	16
1970	Bob Griese	14	245	142	2019	58.0	12	17
1971	Bob Griese	14	263	145	2089	55.1	19	9
1972	Earl Morrall	14	150	83	1360	55.3	11	7
1973	Bob Griese	13	218	116	1422	53.2	17	8
1974	Bob Griese	13	253	152	1968	60.1	16	15
1975	Bob Griese	10	191	118	1693	61.8	14	13
1976	Bob Griese	13	272	162	2097	59.6	11	12
1977	Bob Griese	14	307	180	2252	58.6	22	13
1978	Bob Griese	11	235	148	1791	63.0	11	11
1979	Bob Griese	14	310	176	2160	56.8	14	16
1980	D. Woodley	13	327	176	1850	53.8	14	17
1981	D. Woodley	15	366	191	2470	52.2	12	13
1982	D. Woodley	9	179	98	1080	54.7	5	8
1983	Dan Marino	11	296	173	2210	58.4	20	6
1984	Dan Marino	16	564	362	5084	64.2	48	17
1985	Dan Marino	16	567	336	4137	59.3	30	21

PUNT RETURNS

YEAR	PLAYER	NO.	YDS	AVG.	LONG	TD
1966	Joe Auer	5	99	19.8	56	0
1967	Abner Haynes	6	37	6.2	20	0
1968	Bob Neff	8	71	8.9	20	0
1969	Mercury Morris	25	172	6.9	38	0
1970	Jake Scott	27	290	10.7	77t	1
1971	Jake Scott	33	318	9.6	31	0
1972	Charlie Leigh	22	210	9.5	27	0
1973	Jake Scott	22	266	12.1	33	0
1974	Jake Scott	31	346	11.2	30	0
1975	Freddie Solomon	26	320	12.3	50t	1
1976	Freddie Solomon	13	205	15.8	79t	1
1977	Freddie Solomon	32	285	8.9	39	0
1978	Jimmy Cefalo	28	232	8.3	26	0
1979	Tony Nathan	28	306	10.9	86t	1
1980	Tony Nathan	23	178	7.7	30	0
1981	Tom Vigorito	36	379	10.5	87t	1
1982	Tom Vigorito	20	192	9.6	59t	1
1983	Mark Clayton	41	392	9.6	60t	1
1984	Fulton Walker	21	169	8.0	33	0
1985	Tom Vigorito	22	197	9.0	21	0

KICKOFF RETURNS

YEAR	PLAYER	NO.	YDS.	AVG.	LONG	TD
1966	Joe Auer	28	698	24.9	95t	1
1967	Bob Neff	15	351	23.4	69	0
1968	Gene Milton	18	408	22.7	74	0
1969	Mercury Morris	43	1136	26.4	105t	1
1970	Mercury Morris	28	812	29.0	96t	1
1971	Mercury Morris	15	423	28.2	94t	1
1972	Mercury Morris	14	334	23.9	33	0
1973	Charlie Leigh	9	251	27.9	51	0
1974	Nat Moore	22	587	26.7	40	0
1975	Freddie Solomon	17	348	20.5	31	0
1976	Duriel Harris	17	559	32.9	69	0
1977	Gary Davis	14	414	29.6	73	0
1978	Duriel Harris	29	657	22.7	53	0
1979	Tony Nathan	45	1016	22.6	43	0
1980	Don Bessillieu	40	890	22.3	87	0
1981	Fulton Walker	38	932	24.5	90t	1
1982	Fulton Walker	20	433	21.7	32	0
1983	Fulton Walker	36	962	26.7	78	0
1984	Fulton Walker	29	617	21.3	41	0
1985	Lorenzo Hampton	45	1020	22.7	46	0

INTERCEPTIONS

YEAR	PLAYER	NO.	YDS	AVG.	LONG	TD
1966	Willie West	8	62	7.8	27	0
1967	Dick Westmoreland	10	127	12.7	29	1
1968	Dick Anderson	8	230	28.8	96t	1
1969	Lloyd Mumphord	5	102	20.4	51	0
1970	Dick Anderson	8	191	23.9	86	0
1971	Jake Scott	7	34	4.9	21	0
1972	Jake Scott	5	73	14.6	31	0
1973	Dick Anderson	8	163	20.4	38t	2
1974	Jake Scott	8	75	9.4	30	0
1975	Jake Scott	6	60	10.0	38	0
1976	(four players)		(two interceptions)			
1977	Curtis Johnson	4	35	8.8	19	0
1978	Tim Foley	6	12	2.0	8	0
1979	Neal Colzie	5	86	17.2	56	0
	Gerald Small	5	74	14.8	40	0
1980	Gerald Small	7	46	6.6	22	0
1981	Glenn Blackwood	4	124	31.0	39	0
1982	Don McNeal	4	42	10.5	23	1
1983	William Judson	6	60	10.0	29	0
1984	Glenn Blackwood	6	169	28.2	50	0
1985	Glenn Blackwood	6	36	6.0	17	0

SCORING*

YEAR	PLAYER	TDs	RUN	REC	PATs	FGs	TP
1966	Joe Auer	9	5	4	0-0	0-0	54
	Gene Mingo	0	0	0	23-23	10-22	53
1967	Booth Lusteg	0	0	0	18-18	7-12	39
	Jack Harper	4	1	3	0-0	0-0	24
1968	Karl Noonan	11	0	11	0-0	0-0	66
	Jim Keyes	0	0	0	30-30	7-16	51
1969	Karl Kremser	0	0	0	26-27	13-22	65
	Jim Kiick	10	9	1	0-0	0-0	60
1970	Garo Yepremian	0	0	0	31-31	22-29	97
1971	Garo Yepremian	0	0	0	33-33	28-40	117
	Paul Warfield	11	0	11	0-0	0-0	66
1972	Garo Yepremian	0	0	0	43-45	24-37	115
	Mercury Morris	12	12	0	0-0	0-0	72
1973	Garo Yepremian	0	0	0	38-38	25-37	113
	Paul Warfield	11	0	11	0-0	0-0	66
1974	Garo Yepremian	0	0	0	43-43	8-15	67
	Larry Csonka	9	9	0	0-0	0-0	54
1975	Garo Yepremian	0	0	0	40-46	13-16	79

Year	Player						
	Don Nottingham	12	12	0	0-0	0-0	72
1976	Garo Yepremian	0	0	0	29-31	16-23	77
1977	Nat Moore	13	1	12	0-0	0-0	78
	Garo Yepremian	0	0	0	37-41	10-22	67
1978	Garo Yepremian	0	0	0	41-45	19-23	98
	Nat Moore	10	0	10	0-0	0-0	60
1979	Uwe von Schamann	0	0	0	36-40	21-29	99
	Larry Csonka	13	12	1	0-0	0-0	78
1980	Uwe von Schamann	0	0	0	32-32	14-23	74
	Nat Moore	7	0	7	0-0	0-0	42
1981	Uwe von Schamann	0	0	0	37-38	24-31	109
1982	Uwe von Schamann	0	0	0	21-22	15-20	66
	Andra Franklin	7	7	0	0-0	0-0	42
1983	Uwe von Schamann	0	0	0	45-48	18-27	99
	Mark Duper	10	0	10	0-0	0-0	60
1984	Mark Clayton	18	0	18	0-0	0-0	108
	Uwe von Schamann	0	0	0	66-70	9-19	93
1985	Fuad Reveiz	0	0	0	50-52	22-27	116
	Ron Davenport	13	11	2	0-0	0-0	78

*In years where only one player is listed, several players were tied with the same point total.

DOLPHIN TEAM RECORDS

SCORING

MOST POINTS SCORED
Season 513 1984
Game 55 11/24/77 at St. Louis

MOST POINTS ALLOWED
Season 407 1967
Game 58 9/18/66 at Buffalo

FEWEST POINTS SCORED
Season 213 1966
Game 0 seven times, last 1980

FEWEST POINTS ALLOWED
Season 150 1973, 14 games
131 1982, 9 games
Game 0 18 times, last 1985

MOST POINTS, BOTH TEAMS
82 at Buffalo 58, Miami 24 (9/18/66)
79 San Diego 41, at Miami 38 (1/2/82)
79 L.A. Raiders 45, at Miami 34 (12/2/84)
79 at Miami 41, Tampa Bay 38 (10/20/85)
73 at Miami 41, Boston 32 (12/17/67)
73 at Baltimore 45, Miami 28 (10/9/77)
73 Miami 45, at N.Y. Jets 28 (9/12/82)
73 Buffalo 38, at Miami 35 (10/9/83)

FEWEST POINTS, BOTH TEAMS
3 at New England 3, Miami 0 (12/12/82)
12 at Miami 9, Kansas City 3 (10/20/74)
12 Miami 12, at Buffalo 0 (9/4/83)
13 Miami 13, at Buffalo 0 (9/18/77)

MOST DECISIVE WIN
52 52-0 vs. New England (11/12/72)
44 44-0 vs. Baltimore (11/11/73)
43 43-0 at N.Y. Jets (10/19/75)

MOST DECISIVE LOSS
45 48-3 vs. Kansas City (9/28/68)
41 41-0 at Kansas City (10/8/67)
35 35-0 at Baltimore (11/1/70)

MOST TOUCHDOWNS SCORED
Season 70 1984
Game 8 11/24/77 at St. Louis

MOST TOUCHDOWNS ALLOWED
Season 53 1967
Game 8 9/18/66 at Buffalo

FEWEST TOUCHDOWNS SCORED
Season 26 1966

FEWEST TOUCHDOWNS ALLOWED
Season 15 1973
21 1972

MOST TOUCHDOWNS BY
Rushing
Season 26 1972 and 1975
Game 4 five times

Passing
Season 49 1984
Game 6 11/24/77 at St. Louis

Intercept
Season 4 1966
Game 2 12/3/73 vs. Pittsburgh
2 9/12/82 vs. N.Y. Jets
2 12/16/83 vs. N.Y. Jets
KO Return 1 seven times, last 1981
Punt Return 1 six times, last 1983
Fumble Return 1 seven times, last 1985
Block Punt 2 1973

FEWEST TOUCHDOWNS BY
Rushing 5 1966
Passing 12 1969

MOST TDs ALLOWED BY
Rushing
Season 19 1968
Game 4 four times

Passing
Season 31 1967
Game 5 four times, last 1983
Intercept 3 1967, 1969, 1979
KO Return 1 1966, 1970, 1975
Punt Return 1 four times, last 1985

FEWEST TDs ALLOWED BY
Rushing 8 1972
Passing 5 1973

MOST PATs SCORED
Season 66 1984
Game 7 11/12/72 vs. New England
7 11/24/77 at St. Louis

MOST PATs, OPPONENT
Season 47 1967
Game 7 9/18/66 at Buffalo

MOST FGs SCORED
Season 28 1971
Game 5 9/26/71 at Buffalo

SCORE BY QUARTERS, DOLPHINS
1st — 21 12/20/70 vs. Buffalo
21 10/2/77 vs. Houston
2nd — 28 12/17/67 vs. Boston
24 10/23/77 vs. Seattle
24 10/29/78 vs. Baltimore
24 11/20/83 vs. Baltimore
3rd — 21 11/3/74 vs. Atlanta
21 9/12/83 vs N.Y. Jets
21 9/12/84 at Washington
4th — 21 9/30/73 vs. New England
21 9/29/74 at San Diego

SCORE BY QUARTERS, OPPONENTS
1st — 24 9/28/68 vs. Kansas City
24 1/2/82 vs. San Diego
2nd — 27 9/18/66 at Buffalo
3rd — 17 12/23/67 vs. Houston
4th — 28 10/2/66 at San Diego

SCORE BY HALVES, DOLPHINS
1st — 35 12/17/67 vs. Boston
31 12/20/70 vs. Buffalo
31 12/2/85 vs. Chicago
2nd — 31 9/22/85 vs. Kansas City
28 12/10/67 vs. San Diego
28 12/5/76 vs. Buffalo
28 9/23/79 vs. Chicago
28 10/9/83 vs. Buffalo
28 10/21/84 at New England
28 12/9/84 at Indianapolis

SCORE BY HALVES, OPPONENTS
1st — 48 9/18/66 at Buffalo
2nd — 38 10/2/66 at San Diego
31 10/3/76 vs. Los Angeles

SCORE BY QUARTERS, BOTH TEAMS
1st — 27 9/28/68 vs. Kansas City
Kansas City 24, Miami 3
2nd — 34 9/18/66 at Buffalo
Buffalo 27, Miami 7
34 9/30/84 at St. Louis
Miami 20, St. Louis 14
3rd — 28 12/10/67 vs. San Diego
Miami 14, San Diego 14
4th — 35 11/17/74 vs. Buffalo
Buffalo 21, Miami 14

SCORE BY HALVES, BOTH TEAMS
1st — 58 9/18/66 at Buffalo
Buffalo 48, Miami 10
2nd — 52 10/9/83 vs. Buffalo
Miami 28, Buffalo 24

FIRST DOWNS

MOST FIRST DOWNS
Season 387 1984
Game 34 11/24/77 at St. Louis
33 10/21/84 at New England
33 9/15/85 vs. Indianapolis

MOST FIRST DOWNS ALLOWED
Season 314 1984, 1985
Game 34 1/2/82 vs. San Diego
34 11/18/84 at San Diego

MOST FIRST DOWNS, BOTH TEAMS
Season 701 1984
Game 59 1/2/82 vs. San Diego
59 10/9/83 vs. Buffalo

FEWEST FIRST DOWNS
Season 200 1966
Game 7 10/3/70 vs. Oakland
8 9/24/67 vs. Kansas City
8 10/12/80 at New England

FEWEST FIRST DOWNS ALLOWED
Season 186 1972
Game 4 11/11/73 vs. Baltimore

| | 5 | 9/2/79 at Buffalo |
| | 7 | 9/24/72 vs. Houston |

MOST FIRST DOWNS BY

Rushing

Season	170	1972
Game	19	10/29/72 vs. Baltimore
	19	11/24/77 at St. Louis

Passing

Season	243	1984
Game	24	9/15/85 vs. Indianapolis

Penalty

Season	31	1979, 1983
Game	6	12/4/66 at Denver
	6	11/26/67 at Buffalo

FEWEST FIRST DOWNS BY

Rushing

Season	65	1967
Game	0	10/15/67 at Boston

Passing

Season	91	1973
Game	1	9/4/83 at Buffalo

Penalty

13	1973

MOST FIRST DOWNS ALLOWED BY

Rushing

Season	135	1985
Game	17	12/11/76 vs. Minnesota
	16	11/14/76 at Pittsburgh
	16	1/20/85 vs. San Francisco

Passing

Season	172	1984
Game	21	1/2/82 vs. San Diego

Penalty

Season	22	1978
	21	1967
Game	7	10/9/83 vs. Buffalo

FEWEST FIRST DOWNS ALLOWED BY

Rushing

Season	66	1969
Game	0	12/20/70 vs. Buffalo
	0	10/13/74 at Washington

Passing

Season	78	1973

Game	0	12/8/68 vs. Boston
	1	11/5/79 vs. Houston
	1	12/12/82 vs. New England
Penalty	8	1973, 1974

TOTAL YARDS

MOST NET YARDS GAINED
Season	6936	1984
	5322	1981
Game	552	9/30/84 at St. Louis
	552	10/21/84 a New England
	529	10/25/81 at Dallas
	515	10/14/84 vs. Houston
	515	12/2/84 vs. L.A. Raiders
Playoffs	569	1/6/85 vs. Pittsburgh

MOST NET YARDS, BOTH TEAMS
Season	12356	1984
	10685	1981
Game	1036	1/2/82 vs. San Diego
	1024	1/6/85 vs. Pittsburgh
	997	9/30/84 at St. Louis

FEWEST NET YARDS GAINED
Season	3458	1966
Game	88	10/12/80 at New England
	111	9/6/66 vs. N.Y. Jets
	124	9/24/67 vs. Kansas City

MOST NET YARDS ALLOWED
Season	5767	1985
Game	593	10/3/76 vs. Los Angeles
	564	1/2/82 vs. San Diego
	546	10/4/81 vs. N.Y. Jets

FEWEST NET YARDS ALLOWED
Season	3281	1973
Game	76	10/21/73 vs. Buffalo
	118	10/16/66 vs. Denver
	121	9/2/79 at Buffalo
	132	11/11/73 vs. Baltimore

RUSHING

MOST YARDS RUSHING
Season	2960	1972
	2521	1973
Game	315	11/11/73 vs. Baltimore
	304	12/3/72 at New England
	302	11/7/71 vs. Buffalo
	301	9/30/73 vs. New England

MOST YARDS RUSHING, BOTH TEAMS
Season	4627	1978
	4529	1976
Game	487	12/5/76 vs. Buffalo
	444	9/30/73 vs. New England

FEWEST YARDS RUSHING
Season	1323	1967
Game	23	9/24/67 vs. Kansas City
	25	12/11/77 at New England
	25	12/30/79 at Pittsburgh
	25	1/20/85 vs. San Francisco

MOST YARDS RUSHING ALLOWED
Season	2411	1976
	2261	1978
Game	279	12/3/67 at Houston
	278	9/19/76 at New England
	269	12/5/76 vs. Buffalo

FEWEST YARDS RUSHING ALLOWED
Season	1453	1970
Game	16	9/2/66 vs. Oakland
	26	10/13/74 at Washington
	29	11/16/80 vs. San Francisco
	35	10/17/71 vs. New England

MOST ATTEMPTS RUSHING
Season	613	1972
Game	58	10/5/75 at Green Bay
	56	9/12/82 at N.Y. Jets
	55	11/24/77 at St. Louis

FEWEST ATTEMPTS RUSHING
Season	326	1967
Game	9	1/20/85 vs. San Francisco
	16	12/3/67 at Houston

MOST ATTEMPTS OPPONENT
Season	543	1978
	525	1976
Game	59	1/12/86 vs. New England

PASSING

MOST NET YARDS PASSING
Season	5018	1984
Game	435	1/6/85 vs. Pittsburgh
	434	12/2/84 vs. L.A. Raiders
	420	9/30/84 at St. Louis

FEWEST NET YARDS PASSING
Season	1582	1973
Game	22	11/23/69 vs. Houston
	26	12/30/73 vs. Oakland
	26	9/4/83 at Buffalo

MOST NET YARDS PASSING ALLOWED
Season	3511	1985
Game	427	10/1/67 at N.Y. Jets
	426	10/3/76 vs. Los Angeles
	415	1/2/82 vs. San Diego

FEWEST NET YARDS PASSING ALLOWED
Season	1290	1973
Game	1	10/21/73 vs. Buffalo
	11	11/5/79 vs. Houston
	13	12/12/82 vs. New England
	20	11/11/73 vs. Baltimore
	24	10/22/72 vs. Buffalo

MOST GROSS YARDS PASSING
Season	5146	1984
Game	470	12/2/84 vs. L.A. Raiders
	435	1/6/85 vs. Pittsburgh
	429	9/30/84 at St. Louis

FEWEST GROSS YARDS PASSING
Season	1675	1973
Game	34	12/30/73 vs. Oakland
	46	9/4/83 vs. Buffalo

MOST GROSS YARDS PASSING ALLOWED
Season	3789	1985
Game	440	10/1/67 at N.Y. Jets
	436	10/3/76 vs. Los Angeles
	433	1/2/82 vs. San Diego

FEWEST GROSS YARDS PASSING ALLOWED
Season	1604	1973
	2029	1972
Game	13	12/12/82 vs. New England
	25	11/5/79 vs. Houston
	35	12/9/73 at Baltimore
	45	10/22/72 vs. Buffalo

MOST PASS ATTEMPTS
Season	576	1985
Game	57	12/2/84 vs. L.A. Raiders
	52	11/27/66 vs. New England

FEWEST PASS ATTEMPTS
Season	256	1973
Game	6	12/30/73 vs. Oakland
	7	1/13/74 vs. Minnesota

MOST PASS ATTEMPTS OPPONENT
Season	551	1984
Game	56	11/18/84 at San Diego
	55	10/9/83 vs. Buffalo

FEWEST PASS ATTEMPTS OPPONENT
| Season | 320 | 1973 |
| Game | 5 | 12/12/82 vs. New England |

MOST PASS COMPLETIONS
Season	362	1984
Game	35	12/2/84 vs. L.A. Raiders
	31	1/2/82 vs. San Diego

FEWEST PASS COMPLETIONS
Season	133	1973
Game	3	10/15/73 at Cleveland
	3	12/30/73 vs. Oakland

MOST COMPLETIONS OPPONENT
Season	310	1984
Game	38	10/9/83 vs. Buffalo
	37	11/18/84 at San Diego

FEWEST COMPLETIONS OPPONENT
Season	151	1973
Game	2	11/9/69 at New England
	2	12/12/82 at New England
	4	11/14/76 at Pittsburgh

MOST QB SACKS
| Season | 49 | 1983, 363 yards |

	45	1973, 314 yards
Game	9-59	10/21/73 vs. Buffalo
	8-61	9/20/81 at Houston
	7-52	10/17/71 vs. New England
	7-52	11/11/79 vs. Baltimore

MOST QB SACKS ALLOWED

Season	53	1969, 481 yards
	52	1968, 441 yards
Game	8-83	11/16/69 at Buffalo
	8-80	9/20/70 at New England
	7-61	9/9/66 vs. N.Y. Jets

INTERCEPTIONS

MOST INTERCEPTIONS

Season	32	1978, 458 yards
	31	1966, 522 yards
Game	6	12/3/73 vs. Pittsburgh
	6	10/19/75 at N.Y. Jets
	6	9/10/78 at Baltimore
	6	11/21/82 at Buffalo
	6	10/16/83 at N.Y. Jets

FEWEST INTERCEPTIONS

| Season | 11 | 1976, 144 yards |
| | 15 | 1977, 124 yards |

MOST INTERCEPTIONS OPPONENT

Season	32	1966, 370 yards
	29	1969, 596 yards
Game	6	11/13/66 at Kansas City

FEWEST INTERCEPTIONS OPPONENT

| Season | 10 | 1971, 166 yards |
| | 11 | 1983, 205 yards |

PENALTIES

MOST PENALTIES

Season	79	1979, 651 yards
Game	11	10/3/70 vs. Oakland
	11	12/3/72 vs. New England

MOST YARDS PENALIZED

Season	834	1970 on 77
Game	135	10/3/70 vs. Oakland
	126	11/30/69 vs. New England
	124	10/30/83 vs. L.A. Rams

MOST PENALTIES OPPONENT

Season	108	1980, 923 yards
Game	15	10/11/69 vs. San Diego
	15	10/9/83 vs. Buffalo
	12	9/21/68 vs. Oakland
	12	9/12/82 vs. N.Y. Jets

MOST YARDS PENALIZED OPPONENT

Season	923	1980 on 108
Game	156	9/20/69 at Oakland
	144	11/5/67 at Buffalo
	117	12/16/83 vs. N.Y. Jets

FEWEST PENALTIES

Season	48	1968, 485 yards
Game	0	12/23/67 vs. Houston
	0	12/8/68 vs. New England

FEWEST YARDS PENALIZED

| Season | 416 | 1973 on 52 |
| Game | 0 | two times |

FEWEST PENALTIES OPPONENT

| Season | 59 | 1967, 691 yards |
| Game | 1 | seven times |

FEWEST YARDS PENALIZED OPPONENT

| Season | 525 | 1974 on 67 |
| Game | 5 | four times |

MOST YARDS PENALIZED BOTH TEAMS

Season	1538	1970 on 145
Game	230	10/3/70 vs. Oakland
	227	11/30/69 vs. New England

MOST PENALTIES BOTH TEAMS

Season	186	1979, 1485 yards
Game	20	9/12/82 vs. N.Y. Jets
	19	four times

FEWEST PENALTIES BOTH TEAMS

Season	112	1967, 1181 yards
Game	2	12/23/67 vs. Houston
	2	11/11/73 vs. Baltimore
	2	12/12/82 vs. New England

FEWEST YARDS PENALIZED BOTH TEAMS

| Season | 1032 | 1973 on 113 |

Game	10	11/11/73 vs. Baltimore
	10	12/12/82 vs. New England
	20	12/8/66 vs. New England

PUNTING

MOST PUNTS

Season	85	1969
Game	10	9/9/66 vs. N.Y. Jets
	10	10/12/80 at New England

MOST PUNT YARDS

Season	3451	1969, 40.6 avg.
Game	483	9/9/66 vs. N.Y. Jets
	445	10/12/80 at New England

MOST OPPONENT PUNTS

| Season | 90 | 1983 |
| Game | 11 | 11/11/73 vs. Baltimore |

MOST PUNT YARDS OPPONENT

| Season | 3674 | 1983, 40.8 avg. |
| Game | 413 | 11/15/81 vs. Oakland |

HIGHEST AVERAGE

| Season | 44.7 | 1984, 51 punts |
| x- Game | 52.0 | 10/7/73 vs. N.Y. Jets |

HIGHEST OPPONENT AVERAGE

| Season | 44.1 | 1969, 80 punts |
| Game | 55.5 | 9/28/68 vs. Kansas City |

x-minimum 4 punt

PUNT RETURNS

MOST PUNT RETURNS

| Season | 55 | 1983 |
| Game | 7 | 10/19/69 at Kansas City |

MOST PUNT RETURN YARDS

Season	581	1983
Game	123	10/19/69 at Kansas City
	115	12/5/76 vs. Buffalo

MOST PUNT RETURNS OPPONENT

| Season | 45 | 1981, 286 yards |
| Game | 8 | 9/9/66 vs. N.Y. Jets |

MOST PUNT RETURN YARDS OPPONENT

Season	373	1975, 34 returns
Game	115	10/12/80 at New England
	110	11/1/70 at Baltimore

KICKOFF RETURNS

MOST KICKOFF RETURNS

| Season | 67 | 1967, 1443 yards |
| Game | 9 | 9/18/66 at Buffalo |

MOST KICKOFF RETURN YARDS

Season	1507	1966, 65 returns
Game	245	12/5/71 at New England
	229	11/13/66 at Kansas City

MOST KICKOFF RETURNS OPPONENT

Season	70	1978, 1459 yards
	69	1979, 1518 yards
Game	9	11/24/77 at St. Louis

MOST KICKOFF RETURN YARDS OPPONENT

Season	1549	1975, 65 returns
Game	207	9/17/67 vs. Denver
	200	11/24/77 at St. Louis

FUMBLES

MOST FUMBLES

| Season | 36 | 1967 |
| Game | 5 | eight times |

MOST FUMBLES LOST

Season	16	1967, 1973, 1980, 1983
Game	5-5	9/25/83 vs. Kansas City
	5-4	11/5/70 vs. New Orleans
	5-4	1/12/86 vs. New England

MOST OPPONENT FUMBLES

Season	39	1983
Game	7	11/7/71 vs. Buffalo
	7	9/18/77 at Buffalo
	7	10/23/83 at Baltimore

MOST OPPONENT FUMBLES LOST

Season	21	1971, 1978 of 37
Game	4-4	10/18/70 at Buffalo
	4-4	12/10/72 at N.Y. Giants
	4-4	9/26/76 vs. N.Y. Jets
	4-4	11/29/79 vs. New England

THE LAST TIME . . .
(Regular Season)

KICKOFF RETURNED FOR A TOUCHDOWN
 By Dolphins — Fulton Walker at Buffalo (90 yards), 10/12/81
 By Opponents — Harold Hart, Oakland (102 yards), 9/22/75

PUNT RETURNED FOR A TOUCHDOWN
 By Dolphins — Mark Clayton vs. Baltimore (60 yards), 11/20/83
 By Opponents — Billy Johnson, at Houston (83 yards), 11/16/75

INTERCEPTED PASS RETURNED FOR A TOUCHDOWN
 By Dolphins — William Judson at Houston (61 yards), 9/8/85
 By Opponents — Mike Haynes, L.A. Raiders (97 yards), 12/2/84

FUMBLE RETURNED FOR A TOUCHDOWN
 By Dolphins — Bob Brudzinski at Detroit (7 yards), 10/27/85
 By Opponents — Cedric Jones, New England (15 yards), 12/16/85

BLOCKED PUNT RETURNED FOR A TOUCHDOWN
 By Dolphins — Tim Foley vs. Baltimore (5 yards), 11/11/73
 By Opponents — Jewerl Thomas, L.A. Rams (recovered in end zone), 11/9/80

SAFETY SCORED
 By Dolphins — Mike Charles at N.Y. Jets (Pat Ryan), 10/16/83
 By Opponents — Reggie Williams, Cincinnati (Steve Howell), 9/14/80

SHUTOUT
 By Dolphins — at Miami 28, Buffalo 0, 12/22/85
 By Opponents — at New England 3, Miami 0, 12/12/82

200 YARDS RUSHING
 By Dolphins — None
 By Opponents — O.J. Simpson, Buffalo (203 yards), 12/5/76

100 YARDS RUSHING
 By Dolphins — Joe Carter vs. Houston (105 yards), 10/28/84
 By Opponents — Walter Payton, Chicago (121 yards), 12/2/85

400 YARDS PASSING
 By Dolphins — Dan Marino, at Indianapolis (404 yards), 12/9/84
 By Opponents — Joe Ferguson, Buffalo (419 yards), 10/9/83

300 YARDS PASSING
 By Dolphins — Dan Marino, at Green Bay (345 yards), 12/8/85
 By Opponents — Ken O'Brien, N.Y. Jets (393 yards), 11/10/85

200 YARDS RECEIVING
 By Dolphins — Mark Duper vs. N.Y. Jets (217 yards), 11/10/85
 By Opponents — Ron Jessie, L.A. Rams (220 yards), 10/3/76

100 YARDS RECEIVING
 By Dolphins — Mark Duper vs. Chicago (107 yards), 12/2/85
 By Opponents — Al Toon, N.Y. Jets (156 yards), 11/10/85

FIVE TOUCHDOWN PASSES
 By Dolphins — Dan Marino, at Green Bay, 12/8/85
 By Opponents — Joe Ferguson, Buffalo, 10/9/83

FOUR TOUCHDOWN PASSES
 By Dolphins — Dan Marino vs. Dallas, 12/17/84
 By Opponents — Steve DeBerg, Tampa Bay, 10/20/85

THREE TOUCHDOWN PASSES
 By Dolphins — Dan Marino vs. Chicago, 12/2/85
 By Opponents — Eric Hipple, at Detroit, 10/27/85

FOUR TOUCHDOWN RECEPTIONS
 By Dolphins — Paul Warfield vs. Detroit, 12/15/73
 By Opponents — Jimmie Giles, Tampa Bay, 10/20/85

THREE TOUCHDOWN RECEPTIONS
 By Dolphins — Mark Clayton vs. Dallas, 12/17/84
 By Opponents — Sammy White, Minnesota, 12/11/76

TWO TOUCHDOWN RECEPTIONS
 By Dolphins — Bruce Hardy vs. Buffalo, 12/22/85
 By Opponents — Eric Sievers, at San Diego, 11/18/84

THREE TOUCHDOWNS RUSHING
 By Dolphins — Larry Csonka vs. New England, 11/29/79
 By Opponents — Marcus Allen, L.A. Raiders, 12/2/84

FOUR FIELD GOALS
 By Dolphins — Uwe von Schamann, at Buffalo, 9/4/83
 By Opponents — Rick Danmeier, Minnesota, 9/16/79

THREE FIELD GOALS
 By Dolphins — Fuad Reveiz vs. New England, 12/16/85
 By Opponents — Pat Leahy, at N.Y. Jets, 10/14/85

THREE INTERCEPTIONS
 By Dolphins — William Judson, at N.Y. Jets, 10/16/83
 By Opponents — Jeff Nixon, at Buffalo, 9/7/80

TWO INTERCEPTIONS
 By Dolphins — Glenn Blackwood vs. New England, 12/16/85
 By Opponents — Steve Brown, at Houston, 9/8/85

DOLPHIN CONSECUTIVES

(Includes Playoff Games)

INDIVIDUAL

PRO BOWL APPEARANCES
 6 Jim Langer (1973-78)
GAMES PLAYED
 139 Garo Yepremian (1970-78)
 134 Jim Langer (1970-79)
GAMES STARTED
 117 Jim Langer (1972, 1st to 1979, 9th)
 102 Norm Evans (1969, 3rd, to 1975, 9th)
GAMES, SCORING POINTS
 133 Garo Yepremian (8th in 1970 to 17th in 1978)
GAMES, SCORING TOUCHDOWN
 7 Mark Clayton (1984, 12th to 18th)
GAMES, SCORING FIELD GOAL
 15 Garo Yepremian (1971, 1st to 15th)
GAMES, RUSHING TOUCHDOWN
 5 Mercury Morris (1972, 6th to 10th)
 5 Don Nottingham (1975, 2nd to 6th)
 5 Pete Johnson (1984, 8th to 12th)
GAMES, PASSING TOUCHDOWN
 23 Dan Marino (1983, 12th to 14th, inj. 15-16, 17th; 1984, 1st to 19th)
GAMES, RECEIVING TOUCHDOWN
 7 Mark Clayton (1984, 12th to 18th)
GAMES, NO PASSES INTERCEPTED
 4 Bob Griese (1971, 5th to 8th)
GAMES, PASS RECEPTION
 37 Nat Moore (1974, 3rd, to 1977, 2nd)
   (injured for 13th in 1974, 10th to 14th in 1976)
GAMES, INTERCEPTIONS
 5 Dick Westmoreland (1967, 9th to 13th)
SEASONS, RUSHING 1,000 YARDS
 3 Larry Csonka (1971, 1972, 1973)
POINTS AFTER TOUCHDOWN
 125 Garo Yepremian (1972, 7th to 1974, 15th)
FIELD GOALS MADE
 16 Garo Yepremian (1978, 8th to 16th)
 15 Garo Yepremian (1974, 12th, to 1975, 7th)
PASSES, NONE INTERCEPTED
 122 Bob Griese (1967, 10th to 14th)
PASS COMPLETIONS
 13 Earl Morrall (12/1/75 vs. New England)
 12 Don Strock (1/2/82 vs. San Diego)

TEAM

WINS, ALL GAMES
 18 (all of 1972; 1973, 1st)
WINS, REGULAR SEASON
 16 (1971, 14th; all of 1972; 1973, 1st)
 16 (1983, 12th to 16th to 1984, 1st to 11th)
WINS, PRE-SEASON
 11 (1975, 5th and 6th; all of 1976; 1977, 1st to 3rd)
LOSSES, REGULAR SEASON
 8 (1967, 3rd to 10th)
WINS, HOME GAMES
 31 (Oct. 17, 1971 to Dec. 15, 1974)
WINS, ROAD GAMES
 9 (all of 1972)
LOSSES, HOME GAMES
 4 (Dec. 23, 1967 to Sept. 28, 1968)
SERIES GAMES, DOLPHIN WINS
 20 Buffalo (1970 to 1979)
SERIES GAMES, DOLPHIN LOSSES
 8 New York Jets (1966 to 1969)
QUARTERS, OPPONENT SCORELESS
 13 (1973, 8th to 11th)
QUARTERS, DOLPHINS SCORELESS
 11 (1970, 6th to 8th)

PLAYOFF HISTORY

1970 AFC PLAYOFF
Raiders Sink Dolphins With 82-Yard Bomb
OAKLAND 21, MIAMI 14

OAKLAND, DEC. 27 — Quarterback Daryle Lamonica unloaded an 82-yard touchdown pass to Rod Sherman with 9:34 to play as Oakland spoiled the Dolphins' first appearance in the playoffs, 21-14, on a field oozing with mud.

The Dolphins, who had won six consecutive games to finish 10-4 and gain a wild-card berth, had taken a 7-0 lead in the second quarter when Bob Griese fired a 16-yard strike to Paul Warfield in the end zone. Lamonica matched that TD with a 22-yard toss to Fred Biletnikoff only 1:50 before halftime.

Raider right cornerback Willie Brown intercepted a wet and wobbly pass by Griese and fled 50 yards along the sideline for the tie-breaking TD. It came minutes after Jake Scott recovered an Oakland fumble at the Miami 10-yard line.

The heave to Sherman was insurance. Only three plays earlier, Dolphin kicker Garo Yepremian missed a 24-yard field-goal attempt for the second time in the game. Oakland's George Blanda also missed a 23-yarder.

| Miami | 0 | 7 | 0 | 7 | — | 14 |
| Miami | 0 | 7 | 7 | 7 | — | 21 |

Miami — Warfield 16 pass from Griese (Yepremian kick)
Oakland — Biletnikoff 22 pass from Lamonica (Blanda kick)
Oakland — Brown 50 interception return (Blanda kick)
Oakland — Sherman 82 pass from Lamonica (Blanda kick)
Miami — Richardson 7 pass from Griese (Yepremian kick)

	Miami	Oakland
First Downs	16	12
Rushes · Yards	33-118	36-114
Passing Yards	124	187
Total Yards	242	301
Had QB Sacked	3-31	0-0
Passes	27-13-1	16-8-0
Punts	5-39.2	4-32.2
Fumbles/Lost	2-0	4-2
Penalties/Yards	0-0	4-30

A — 54,401 actual, 52,594 paid

INDIVIDUAL LEADERS

RUSHING — Miami: Csonka 10-23, Kiick 14-64, Morris 8-29, Griese 1-2. Oakland: Dixon 8-31, Smith 9-37, Hubbard 1-8, Banaszak 1-(-6).
PASSING — Miami: Griese 27-13-1, 155 yards, two TDS. Oakland: Lamonica 16-8-0, 187 yards, two TDs
RECEIVING — Miami: Twilley 1-14, Warfield 4-62, Kiick 4-34, Morris 2-15, Richardson 2-30. Oakland: Biletinkoff 3-46, Chester 2-47, Dixon 1-3, Smith 1-9, Sherman 1-82.

1971 AFC PLAYOFF
Dolphins Outlast Chiefs In Longest Game
MIAMI 27, KANSAS CITY 24

KANSAS CITY, DEC. 25 — Garo Yepremian ended 82 minutes and 40 seconds of an epic struggle by thumping a 37-yard field goal with 7:40 elapsed in the second overtime, lifting the Dolphins past Kansas City, 27-24, on Christmas Day.

The Dolphins battled from behind three times to tie the AFC West champions, the third time on Bob Griese's five-yard pass to tight end Marv Fleming with 96 seconds remaining in regulation.

Kansas City running back Ed Podolak, who amassed 350 yards of all-purpose running, returned the ensuing kickoff 78 yards to the Dolphin 22 where Curtis Johnson made a desperation tackle. With 35 seconds on the clock, Jan Stenerud missed a 32-yard field-goal try.

Stenerud had a 42-yarder blocked by Nick Buoniconti in the fifth quarter, and Yepremian was short with a 45-yard effort. But Larry Csonka crashed 29 yards to the Chiefs 36, and that put Yepremian, the NFL's scoring leader, in position to win it. Goal posts were on the goal line; in 1974 the uprights were moved to the end line.

| Miami | 0 | 10 | 7 | 7 | 0 | 3 | 27 |
| Kans. City | 10 | 0 | 7 | 7 | 0 | 0 | 24 |

Kans. City — FG Stenerud 24
Kans. City — Podolak 7 pass from Dawson (Stenerud kick)
Miami — Csonka 1 run (Yepremian kick)
Miami — FG Yepremian 14
Kans. City — Otis 1 run (Stenerud kick)
Miami — Kiick 1 run (Yepremian kick)
Kans. City — Podolak 3 run (Stenerud kick)
Miami — Fleming 5 pass from Griese (Yepremian kick)
Miami — FG Yepremian 37

	Miami	K. City
First Downs	22	23
Rushes · Yards	43-144	44-213
Passing Yards	263	238
Total Yards	407	451
Had QB Sacked	0-0	1-8
Passes	35-20-2	26-18-2
Punts	6-40.0	2-51.0
Fumbles/Lost	1-0	3-2
Penalties/Yards	5-26	6-44

INDIVIDUAL LEADERS

RUSHING — Miami: Kiick 15-56, Csonka 24-86, Griese 2-9, Warfield 2-(-7). Kansas City: Hayes 22-100, Podolak 17-85, Wright 2-15, Otis 3-13
PASSING — Miami: Griese 35-20-2, 263 yards, one TD. Kansas City: Dawson 26-18-2, 246 yards, one TD
RECEIVING — Miami: Warfield 7-140, Fleming 4-37, Kiick 3-24, Mandich 1-4, Twilley 5-58. Kansas City: Podolak 8-110, Hayes 3-6, Wright 3-104, Taylor 3-12

1971 AFC CHAMPIONSHIP
Anderson, No-Names Stymie Colts
MIAMI 21, BALTIMORE 0

MIAMI, JAN 2, 1972 — Three lightning plays and a persistent defense propelled the Dolphins into Super Bowl VI with a 21-0 rout of Baltimore before an all-time Orange Bowl record crowd of 78,939.

Strong safety Dick Anderson intercepted a John Unitas pass which was deflected by Curtis Johnson, and behind a wall of six open-field blocks, Anderson weaved 62 yards for a third-quarter touchdown. "My eyes were popping as I ran," Anderson said. "I've never seen so many people land on their heads."

Before Anderson's convoy made it 14-0, the Dolphins staggered the defending Super Bowl champions when Bob Griese and Paul Warfield hooked up for a 75-yard TD pass. Warfield applied the clincher when he escaped 50 yards with a Griese pass, setting up a five-yard TD slam by fullback Larry Csonka.

The Colts hadn't been held scoreless for 97 games over seven seasons. They were stopped at the Dolphin 9 in the second quarter. Jim O'Brien missed two field-goal attempts and had another blocked by Lloyd Mumphord.

| Baltimore | 0 | 0 | 0 | 0 | — | 0 |
| Miami | 7 | 0 | 7 | 7 | — | 21 |

Miami — Warfield 75 pass from Griese (Yepremian kick)
Miami — Anderson 62 interception return (Yepremian kick)
Miami — Csonka 5 run (Yepremian kick)

	Balt	Miami
First Downs	16	13
Rushes · Yards	30-89	35-144
Passing Yards	213	142
Total Yards	302	286
Had QB Sacked	2-11	2-16
Passes	36-20-3	8-4-1
Punts	3-45.3	6-42.7
Fumbles/Lost	1-0	0-0
Penalties/Yards	1-5	2-27

A — 78,939 actual, 78,629 paid

INDIVIDUAL LEADERS

RUSHING — Baltimore: McCauley 15-50, Nottingham 11-33, Unitas 2-1, Nowatzke 2-5. Miami: Kiick 18-66, Csonka 15-63, Griese 1-12, Morris 1-3.
PASSING — Baltimore: Unitas 36-20-3, 224 yards, no TD. Miami: Griese 8-4-1, 158 yards, one TD
RECEIVING — Baltimore: Hinton 6-98, Nottingham 4-26, McCauley 2-24, Mitchell 1-14, Perkins 3-19, Havrilak 2-31, Matte 1-6, Mackey 1-6. Miami: Warfield 2-125, Twilley 2-33.

SUPER BOWL VI
Cowboys Flatten Luckless Dolphins
DALLAS 24, MIAMI 3

NEW ORLEANS, JAN. 16, 1972 — A 252-yard rushing attack and sharp passing by Roger Staubach spurred the Dallas Cowboys to a 24-3 victory over the Dolphins at Tulane Stadium.

Duane Thomas pranced 95 yards on 19 carries, fullback Walt Garrison added 74 yards on 14 carries and Staubach passed twice for touchdowns to Lance Alworth and Mike Ditka. Staubach, who was sacked twice in the first quarter, bounced back to complete 12 of 19 passes, and he scrambled from the Dolphin pass rush five times.

The Dolphins were frustrated all day; in the first quarter, Larry Csonka lost a fumble and Bob Griese was chased by tackle Bob Lily for a 29-yard loss. Griese fumbled away a snap at the Dallas 16 in the fourth period.

Although it was an intriguing 10-3 at halftime, the Cowboys marched 71 yards in seven plays after kickoff, and Thomas swept three yards for the TD.

| Dallas | 3 | 7 | 7 | 7 | — | 24 |
| Miami | 0 | 3 | 0 | 0 | — | 3 |

Dallas — FG Clark 9
Dallas — Alworth 7 pass from Staubach (Clark kick)
Miami — FG Yepremian 31
Dallas — D. Thomas 3 run (Clark kick)
Dallas — Ditka 7 pass from Staubach (Clark kick)

	Dallas	Miami
First Downs	23	10
Rushes · Yards	48-252	20-80
Passing Yards	100	105
Total Yards	352	185
Had QB Sacked	2-19	1-29
Passes	19-12-0	23-12-1
Punts	5-37.2	5-40.0
Fumbles/Lost	1-0	0-0
Penalties/Yards	3-15	0-0

A — 80,591 actual, 81,023 paid

INDIVIDUAL LEADERS

RUSHING — Dallas: Thomas 19-95, Garrison 14-74, Staubach 5-18, Hill 7-25, Hayes 1-16, Reeves 1-7, Ditka 1-17. Miami: Kiick 10-40, Csonka 9-40, Griese 1-0
PASSING — Dallas: Staubach 19-12-0, 119 yards, two TDs. Miami: Griese 23-12-1, 134 yards, no TDs
RECEIVING — Dallas: Hayes 2-23, D. Thomas 3-17, Garrison 2-11, Alworth 2-28, Hill 1-12, Ditka 2-28. Miami: Twilley 1-20, Kiick 3-21, Warfield 4-39, Csonka 2-18, Fleming 1-27, Mandich 1-9.

1972 AFC PLAYOFF
Late TD Drive Rescues Unbeaten Dolphins
MIAMI 20, CLEVELAND 14

MIAMI, DEC. 24 — On the ropes in the fourth quarter after an unprecedented

14 victories, the Dolphins responded to poised Earl Morrall and drove 80 yards for a touchdown with 4:56 to play for a 20-14 victory over the Cleveland Browns.

Morrall, the NFL's leading passer as he replaced injured Bob Griese 10 weeks earlier, had completed only four passes for 38 yards. But he threw 15 and 35 yards to Paul Warfield, reaching the Browns' 20, and a pass interference call against linebacker Billy Andrews put the ball at the 8.

Halfback Jim Kiick then bulled eight yards up the middle on a trap for the winning points. The triumph was sealed with a minute to play when linebacker Doug Swift intercepted quarterback Mike Phipps at the Dolphin 20.

Despite stealing five of Phipps' passes, the Dolphins were stung by a 27-yard TD pass to Fair Hooker and trailed, 14-13 with 8:11 to play.

							Cleve.	Miami
Cleveland	0	0	7	7	—	14		
Miami	10	0	0	10	—	20		

	Cleve.	Miami
First Downs	15	17
Rushes · Yards	32-165	47-198
Passing Yards	118	74
Total Yards	283	272
Had QB Sacked	2-13	4-14
Passes	23-9-5	13-6-0
Punts	6-34.7	5-42.0
Fumbles/Lost	2-0	2-2
Penalties/Yards	3-25	3-25

Miami—Babb 5 recovery of blocked punt (Yepremian kick)
Miami—FG Yepremian 40
Cleveland—Phipps 5 run (Cockroft kick)
Miami—FG Yepremian 46
Cleveland—Hooker 27 pass from Phipps (Cockroft kick)
Miami—Kiick 8 run (Yepremian kick)

A—78,196 actual, 78,916 paid

INDIVIDUAL LEADERS

RUSHING — Cleveland: Scott 16-94, Phipps 8-47, Brown 4-13, Kelly 4-11
Miami: Morris 15-72, Kiick 14-50, Warfield 2-41, Csonka 12-32, Morrall 4-3
PASSING — Cleveland: Phipps 23-9-5, 131 yards, one TD
Miami: Morrall 13-6-0, 88 yards, no TD
RECEIVING — Cleveland: Scott 4-30, Hooker 3-53, Kelly 1-27, Morin 1-21
Miami: Twilley 3-33, Warfield 2-60, Kiick 1-5

1972 AFC CHAMPIONSHIP
Griese Comes Off Bench to Rally Win
MIAMI 21, PITTSBURGH 17

PITTSBURGH, DEC. 31 — Quarterback Bob Griese, playing 11 weeks after he had broken his right leg, ignited a third-quarter touchdown drive with a 52-yard pass to Paul Warfield, and the Dolphins overtook the Pittsburgh Steelers, 21-17, in unusually warm 63-degree weather.

Griese was given the nod in the second half after Earl Morrall had flipped a nine-yard touchdown pass to Larry Csonka for a 7-7 halftime deadlock. Punter Larry Seiple broke loose on a daring 37-yard run to set up that TD.

Trailing 10-7, Griese directed TD drives of 80 and 49 yards with Jim Kiick blasting two and three yards for the scores. Steeler quarterback Terry Bradshaw, who closed the gap with four straight completions on a 71-yard TD drive, was intercepted by Nick Buoniconti at midfield with 2½ minutes to play.

In addition to Seiple's dash, the Dolphins converted fourth-down situations on both Griese-led drives.

							Miami	Pitts
Miami	0	7	7	7	—	21		
Pittsburgh	7	0	3	7	—	17		

	Miami	Pitts
First Downs	19	13
Rushes · Yards	49-193	26-128
Passing Yards	121	122
Total Yards	314	250
Had QB Sacked	0-0	2-15
Passes	16-10-1	20-10-2
Punts	4-35.5	4-51.3
Fumbles/Lost	0-0	2-0
Penalties/Yards	2-19	4-30

Pittsburgh—Mullins recovery Bradshaw fumble (Gerela kick)
Miami—Csonka 9 pass from Morrall (Yepremian kick)
Pittsburgh—FG Gerela 14
Miami—Kiick 2 run (Yepremian kick)
Miami—Kiick 3 run (Yepremian kick)
Pittsburgh—Young 12 pass from Bradshaw (Gerela kick)

A—50,350 actual, 50,845 paid

INDIVIDUAL LEADERS

RUSHING — Miami: Csonka 24-68, Morris 16-76, Kiick 8-12, Seiple 1-37
Pittsburgh: Harris 16-76, Fuqua 8-47, Bradshaw 2-5.
PASSING — Miami: Morrall 11-7-1, 51 yards one TD; Griese 5-3-0, 70 yards, no TD
Pittsburgh: Bradshaw 10-5-2, 80 yards, one TD; Hanratty 10-5-0, 57 yards
RECEIVING — Miami: Morris 1-(-6), Mandich 1-5, Fleming 5-50, Csonka 1-9, Warfield 6-23
Pittsburgh: Young 4-54, Harris 2-3, McMakin 1-22, Shanklin 2-49, Brown 1-9

SUPER BOWL VII
Dolphins Achieve Perfection in 17th Win
MIAMI 14, WASHINGTON 7

LOS ANGELES, JAN. 14, 1973 — "This is the ultimate," Coach Don Shula said quietly after his unbeaten Dolphins dominated the Washington Redskins, 14-7, to cap a perfect season. It was Shula's first Super Bowl triumph in three tries.

A record Super Bowl crowd of 90,182 saw the Dolphins surge to a 14-0 halftime lead even as one touchdown was nullified by an offsides penalty. Miami intercepted three of Bill Kilmer's passes, and Manny Fernandez scuttled the Redskin running game with 17 tackles.

An original Dolphin, Howard Twilley, eluded cornerback Pat Fischer to snare a 28-yard touchdown pass from Bob Griese in the first quarter. Griese's 57-yard TD bomb to Paul Warfield was erased by the penalty, but a 32-yard interception return by linebacker Nick Buoniconti set up the Dolphins' second score.

Safety Jake Scott thwarted Kilmer with an end zone interception and 55-yard runback. The Redskins finally scored on a bizarre 49-yard fumble recovery by Mike Bass after a blocked field goal and attempted pass by kicker Garo Yepremian. Scott was named MVP.

							Miami	Wash.
Miami	7	7	0	0	—	14		
Wash.	0	0	0	7	—	7		

	Miami	Wash.
First Downs	12	16
Rushes · Yards	37-184	36-141
Passing Yards	69	87
Total Yards	253	228
Had QB Sacked	2-19	2-17
Passes	11-8-1	28-14-3
Punts	7-43.0	5-31.2
Fumbles/Lost	2-1	1-0
Penalties/Yards	3-35	3-25

Miami—Twilley 28 pass from Griese (Yepremian kick)
Miami—Kiick 1 run (Yepremian kick)
Washington—Bass 49 fumble recovery (Knight kick)

A—90,182 paid

INDIVIDUAL LEADERS

RUSHING — Miami: Kiick 12-38, Csonka 15-112, Morris 10-34.
Washington: Brown 22-72, Harraway 10-37, C. Taylor 1-8, Smith 1-6, Kilmer 2-18
PASSING — Miami: Griese 11-8-1, 88 yards, one TD.
Washington: Kilmer 28-14-3, 104 yards no TD
RECEIVING — Miami: Csonka 1-(-1), Warfield 3-36, Twilley 1-28, Kiick 2-6, Mandich 1-19.
Washington: Brown 5-26, Jefferson 5-50, Harraway 1-(-3), Smith 1-11, C. Taylor 2-20.

1973 AFC PLAYOFF
Stout Defense Cages Bengals
MIAMI 34, CINCINNATI 16

MIAMI, DEC. 23 — A defense which had allowed only 15 touchdowns all season kept the Cincinnati Bengals out of the end zone while the Dolphins hammered 241 yards on the ground for a convincing 34-16 victory.

Mercury Morris scooted 106 yards on 20 carries and Bob Griese completed 11 of 18 passes including TDs of 13 yards to Paul Warfield and seven yards to Jim Mandich. Garo Yepremian converted long field goals of 50 and 46 yards in the second half to widen the winning margin.

The Dolphins led 21-3 when a lapse just before halftime gave life to the Bengals. Safety Neal Craig intercepted Griese and returned 45 yards for a score, and Horst Muhlman booted field goals for 46 and 12 yards — the second coming after Morris fumbled a kickoff — to make it 21-16.

							A—75,770 actual, 78,928 paid
Cincinnati	3	13	0	0	—	16	
Miami	14	7	10	3	—	34	

	Cin.	Miami
First Downs	11	27
Rushes · Yards	20-97	52-241
Passing Yards	97	159
Total Yards	194	400
Had QB Sacked	3-16	0-0
Passes	27-14-1	19-11-2
Punts	7-36.3	2-49.0
Fumbles/Lost	0-0	2-1
Penalties/Yards	2-19	1-5

Miami—Warfield 13 pass from Griese (Yepremian kick)
Cincinnati—FG Muhlman 24
Miami—Csonka 1 run (Yepremian kick)
Miami—Morris 4 run (Yepremian kick)
Cincinnati—Craig 45 interception return (Muhlman kick)
Cincinnati—FG Muhlman 46
Cincinnati—FG Muhlman 12
Miami—Mandich 7 pass from Griese (Yepremian kick)
Miami—FG Yepremian 50
Miami—FG Yepremian 46

INDIVIDUAL LEADERS

RUSHING — Cincinnati: Clark 7-40, E. Johnson 2-17, Elliott 7-15, Curtis 1-(-1), Anderson 3-26
Miami: Morris 20-106, Csonka 20-71, Kiick 10-51, Nottingham 1-5, Leigh 1-8
PASSING — Cincinnati: Anderson 27-14-1, 113 yards, no TD
Miami: Griese 18-11-1, 159 yards, two TDs; Briscoe 1-0-1.
RECEIVING — Cincinnati: Clark 2-18, Curtis 1-9, Elliott 9-53, Joiner 2-33.
Miami: Kiick 3-19, Warfield 4-95, Mandich 3-28, Briscoe 1-17.

1973 AFC CHAMPIONSHIP
Dolphins Grind Raiders With 266 Rushing
MIAMI 27, OAKLAND 10

MIAMI, DEC. 30 — A relentless running attack with Larry Csonka and Mercury Morris accounting for 203 of the 266 yards powered the Dolphins to a 27-10 triumph over the Oakland Raiders for a third straight American Conference title.

Csonka, a 237-pound battering ram who had his third consecutive 1,000-yard season, scored three touchdowns with his 117 yards on 29 carries. The Dolphins covered 64 and 63 yards exclusively on the ground for a 14-0 halftime lead.

Then as the Raiders battled within 17-10, Bob Griese directed ground assaults of 63 yards culminating in a field goal and 40 yards ending in Csonka's third TD.

Defensively, safety Dick Anderson forced a fourth-down fumble by Marv Hubbard at midfield, and the Dolphins took possession with a 20-10 lead and six minutes to play.

Oakland had stopped Miami's 218-game winning streak, 12-7, three months earlier.

							Oakland	Miami
Oakland	0	0	10	0	—	10		
Miami	7	7	3	10	—	27		

	Oakland	Miami
First Downs	15	21
Rushes · Yards	26-107	53-266
Passing Yards	129	26
Total Yards	236	292
Had QB Sacked	0-0	1-8

Miami—Csonka 11 run (Yepremian kick)
Miami—Csonka 2 run (Yepremian kick)
Oakland—FG Blanda 21

Miami—FG Yepremian 42
Oakland—Siani 25 pass from Stabler
   (Blanda kick)
Miami—FG Yepremian 26
Miami—Csonka 2 run (Yepremian kick)

	Passes	25-15-1	6-3-1
	Punts	2-51.0	1-39.0
	Fumbles/Lost	1-0	1-0
	Penalties/Yards	3-35	3-26

A—75,105 actual, 79,325 paid

INDIVIDUAL LEADERS

RUSHING — Oakland: Hubbard 10-54, C. Smith 10-35, Davis 4-15, Banaszak 2-3
   Miami: Csonka 29-117, Morris 14-86, Kiick 6-12, Griese 3-39, Nottingham 1-12
PASSING — Oakland: Stabler 23-15-1, 129 yards, one TD
   Miami: Griese: 6-3-1, 34 yards, no TD
RECEIVING — Oakland: Hubbard 2-11, C. Smith 5-43, Moore 2-9, Siani 3-45, Biletnikoff
   2-15, C. Davis 1-6
   Miami: Briscoe 1-6, Warfield 1-27, Kiick 1-1.

SUPER BOWL VIII
Dolphins Demolish Vikings
MIAMI 24, MINNESOTA 7

HOUSTON, JAN. 13, 1974 — Winning for the 32nd time in 34 games, the Dolphins repeated as Super Bowl champions and proved themselves "Best Ever" with a 24-7 rout of the Minnesota Vikings at Rice Stadium.

There was no doubt from the beginning. The Dolphins swept 62 yards in 10 plays with the opening kickoff, scoring on Larry Csonka's five-yard smash. Minnesota punted, and the onslaught resumed with a 56-yard, 10-play Dolphin drive capped by Jim Kiick's one-yard plunge.

It was 17-0 before the Vikings crossed their 40, and a fourth-down fumble by Oscar Reed was recovered by safety Jake Scott at the Dolphin six-yard line.

A brilliant, diving catch by Paul Warfield netted 27 yards on a third-quarter TD drive that hiked it to 24-0. Csonka finished with his best-ever total of 145 yards on 33 carries. The Dolphins rushed for 703 yards and outscored opponents, 85-33, in the three-game playoff blitz. Csonka gained a Super Bowl record 145 yards and was named MVP.

								Minn.	Miami
Minnesota	0	0	0	7	—	7	First Downs	14	21
Miami	14	3	7	0	—	24	Rushes · Yards	24-72	53-196

	Minn.	Miami
Passing Yards	166	63
Total Yards	238	259
Had QB Sacked	2-16	1-10
Passes	28-18-1	7-6-0
Punts	5-42.2	3-39.0
Fumbles/Lost	2-1	1-0
Penalties/Yards	7-65	1-4

Miami—Csonka 5 run (Yepremian kick)
Miami—Kiick 1 run (Yepremian kick)
Miami—FG Yepremian 28
Miami—Csonka 2 run (Yepremian kick)
Minnesota—Tarkenton 4 run (Cox kick)

A—68,142 actual, 71,882 paid

INDIVIDUAL LEADERS

RUSHING — Minnesota: Foreman 7-18, Reed 11-31, Tarkenton 4-17, Marinaro 1-3
   Brown 1-2
   Miami: Csonka 33-145, Morris 11-34, Kiick 7-10, Griese 2-7
PASSING — Minnesota: Tarkenton 28-18-1, 182 yards, no TD
   Miami: Griese 7-6-0, 73 yards, no TD
RECEIVING — Minnesota Foreman 5-27, Kingsriter 1-9, Lash 1-9, Voight 3-46, Gilliam
   4-44, Marinaro 2-39, Brown 1-9, Reed 1-(-1)
   Miami: Mandich 2-21, Briscoe 2-19, Warfield 2-33.

1974 AFC PLAYOFF
Dream of 'Triple Crown' Shattered
OAKLAND 28, MIAMI 26

OAKLAND, DEC. 21 — Oakland quarterback Ken Stabler, falling in the clutches of Vern Den Herder, unloaded a wobbly eight yard pass that Clarence Davis wrested from three defenders in the end zone, and the Raiders scored a stunning 28-26 victory over the defending champion Dolphins.

Stabler, who had spent the last of his timeouts, appeared to have thrown an interception. But running back Davis clutched the football when bodies were untangled with 26 seconds remaining.

It was the fourth TD pass for lefthander Stabler and his second "freak" score. Four minutes earlier, Cliff Branch fell while catching a pass at the Dolphin 27, but defender Henry Stuckey also slipped, and Branch got up and escaped for a 72-yard TD.

The Dolphins, trailing by two points, went ahead with 2:08 remaining as rookie Benny Malone broke two tackles on a 23-yard touchdown run along the sideline.

Miami	7	3	6	10	—	26
Oakland	0	7	7	14	—	28

Miami—Moore 89 kickoff return
   (Yepremian kick)
Oakland—C. Smith 31 pass from Stabler
   (Blanda kick)
Miami—FG Yepremian 33
Oakland—Biletnikoff 13 pass from Stabler
   (Blanda kick)
Miami—Warfield 16 pass from Griese
   (Yepremian kick)
Miami—FG Yepremian 46
Oakland—Branch 72 pass from Stabler
   (Blanda kick)
Miami—Malone 23 run (Yepremian kick)

Oakland—Davis 8 pass from Stabler
   (Blanda kick)

A—52,817 actual, 53,023 paid

	Miami	Oakland
First Downs	18	19
Rushes · Yards	41-213	32-135
Passing Yards	81	276
Total Yards	294	411
Had QB Sacked	2-20	2-17
Passes	14-7-1	30-20-1
Punts	6-33.2	7-42.7
Fumbles/Lost	0-0	0-0
Penalties/Yards	3-15	3-59

INDIVIDUAL LEADERS

RUSHING — Miami: Csonka 24-114, Malone 14-83, Griese 2-14, Kiick 1-2

Oakland: C. Davis 12-59, Hubbard 14-55, Banaszak 3-14, Stabler 3-7
PASSING — Miami: Griese 14-7-1, 101 yards, one TD
   Oakland: Stabler 30-20-1, 2932yards, four TDs
RECEIVING — Miami: Warfield 3-47, Moore 2-40, Nottingham 1-9, Kiick 1-5
   Oakland: Biletnikoff 8-122, Branch 3-84, Moore 3-22, Smith 2-35, Davis 2-16,
   Hubbard 1-9, Pitts 1-5

1978 AFC "WILD-CARD" PLAYOFF
Oilers Jolt Erring Dolphins
HOUSTON 17, MIAMI 9

MIAMI, DEC. 24 — The Houston Oilers amassed a 455-209 margin in total yardage and, aided by five Dolphin turnovers, gained a 17-9 victory in a battle of AFC "wild-card" entries at the Orange Bowl.

Toni Fritsch kicked a 35-yard field goal with 7:25 remaining to snap a 7-7 tie that existed since the first quarter. An interception by linebacker Greg Bingham led to a clinching 50-yard touchdown drive capped by Earl Campbell's one-yard dive with 1:55 to go. Campbell, the NFL rushing leader with 1,450 yards as a rookie, had been checked for only 16 yards on 13 carries in the first half.

Dolphin quarterback Bob Griese, playing with very sore ribs, connected with tight end Andre Tillman for a 13-yard TD after Earnest Rhone had recovered a fumbled punt at the Houston 21. But Griese completed only 13 of 28 passes. Twice the Dolphins lost the ball inside the Oiler 10-yard line when the game was tied.

Houston's Dan Pastorini wore a flak jacket to protect three broken ribs, and he passed for 261 of his 306-yard total in the first half.

								Houston	Miami
Houston	7	0	0	10	—	17	First Downs	23	14
Miami	7	0	0	2	—	9	Rushes · Yards	45-165	25-91

	Houston	Miami
Passing Yards	290	118
Total Yards	455	209
Had QB Sacked	2-16	2-19
Passes	30-20-0	30-12-3
Punts	5-44.0	5-48.6
Fumbles/Lost	3-1	2-2
Penalties/Yards	5-37	1-5

Miami—Tillman 13 pass from Griese
   (Yepremian kick)
Houston—T. Wilson 13 pass from Pastorini
   (Fritsch kick)
Houston—Campbell 1 run (Fritsch kick)
Miami—Safety, Pastorini runs out of end
   zone

A—70,036 actual, 73,945 paid

INDIVIDUAL LEADERS

RUSHING — Houston: Campbell 26-84, Wilson 14-76, Poole 1-12, Coleman 1-2
   Pastorini 3(-9)
   Miami: Williams 13-41, L. Harris 9-43, Moore 1-7, Bulaich 2-0
PASSING — Houston: Pastorini 29-20-0, 306 yards, one TD. Barber 1-0-0
   Miami: Griese 28-11-2, 114 yards, one TD. Strock 2-1-1, 23 yards, no TD
RECEIVING — Houston: Burrough 6-103, Barber 4-112, Wilson 5-40, Woods 2-22
   Campbell 1-13, Caster 1-11, Coleman 1-5
   Miami: D. Harris 4-42, Moore 2-28, Tillman 2-24, L. Harris 1-21, Bulaich 2-14,
   Williams 1-8.

1979 AFC PLAYOFF
Steelers Blitz Dolphins in First Quarter
PITTSBURGH 34, MIAMI 14

PITTSBURGH, DEC. 30 — Launching a drive to their fourth Super Bowl title in six years, the Pittsburgh Steelers scored touchdowns on their first three possessions and coasted to a 34-14 victory at Three Rivers Stadium.

Miami managed only 25 yards rushing against the Steel Curtain and was stopped twice in the second quarter after achieving a first down inside the Steeler 10-yard line. The Dolphins got as close as 20-7 with a seven-yard TD pass from Bob Griese to Duriel Harris in the third period, but Pittsburgh responded with a 69-yard TD drive.

The Steelers marched 62, 62 and 56 yards for their first-quarter scores when quarterback Terry Bradshaw completed 8 of 10 passes including touchdowns to John Stallworth and Lynn Swann, who was standing alone in the end zone.

Don Strock directed a 13-play, 76-yard TD drive after relieving Griese in the fourth quarter.

								Miami	Pitt.
Miami	0	0	7	7	—	14	First Downs	16	27
Pittsburgh	20	0	7	7	—	34	Rushes · Yards	22-25	40-159

	Miami	Pitt.
Passing Yards	224	220
Total Yards	249	379
Had QB Sacked	3-19	1-10
Passes	40-22-2	31-21-0
Punts	4-36.3	2-29.5
Fumbles/Lost	0-0	3-3
Penalties/Yards	4-35	8-41

Pittsburgh—Thornton 1 run (Bahr kick)
Pittsburgh—Stallworth 17 pass from Bradshaw
   (kick blocked)
Pittsburgh—Swann 20 pass from Bradshaw
   (Bahr kick)
Miami—Harris 7 pass from Griese (von
   Schamann kick)
Pittsburgh—Bleier 1 run (Bahr kick)
Pittsburgh—Harris 5 run (Bahr kick)
Miami—Csonka 1 run (von Schamann kick)

A—50,214 actual, 50,320 paid

INDIVIDUAL LEADERS

RUSHING — Miami: Csonka 10-20, Williams 8-1, Davis 2-12, Griese 1-1, Roberts 1-(-9)
   Pittsburgh: Harris 21-83, Thornton 12-52, Bleier 4-13, Hawthorne 2-15
PASSING — Miami: Griese 26-14-1, 118 yards, one TD; Strock 14-8-1, 125 yards, no TD
   Pittsburgh: Bradshaw 31-21-0, 230 yards, 2 TDs
RECEIVING — Miami: Moore 5-93, Williams 6-26, Harris 3-61, Nathan 3-27, Davis 2-24
   Hardy 2-12, Torrey 1-0
   Pittsburgh: Stallworth 6-86, Harris 5-32, Smith 4-41, Swann 3-37, Thornton 3-34.

1981 AFC PLAYOFF
Chargers Survive Dolphins' Comeback
SAN DIEGO 41, MIAMI 38

MIAMI, JAN. 2, 1982 — A record-setting showcase of the passing game resulted in NFL playoff marks for most points (79), most total yards (1,036) and most drama as the San Diego Chargers outlasted the Dolphins 41-38, in overtime.

"The Miracle That Died" was the Miami Herald headline after the Dolphins rallied behind reserve quarterback Don Strock to overcome a 24-point deficit. Strock completed 29 of 43 passes for 403 yards and four touchdowns, spurring the Dolphins to a 38-31 lead. A 12-yard sweep by Tony Nathan on the first play of the fourth quarter put the Dolphins on top. But Chargers' quarterback Dan Fouts, who passed for an NFL-record 4,802 yards during the season, led an 82-yard drive capped by a 9-yard pass to James Brooks to tie the game with 58 seconds remaining. Five players had more than 100 yards in receptions topped by Chargers' tight end Kellen Winslow with 13 catches for 166 yards.

Fouts, who finished with 433 yards on 33-of-53 marksmanship, hooked up with Charlie Joiner for 39 yards to the Dolphin 10-hard line. Rolf Benirschke then kicked a 29-yard field goal to end the struggle after 13:52 of overtime. Benirschke had missed a 27-yard attempt eight minutes earlier, and Miami's Uwe von Schamann had two attempts blocked — a 43-yarder on the last play of regulation and a 35-yarder after 11:27 of overtime.

It was the only game in NFL history in which two quarterbacks passed for more than 400 yards.

S. Diego	24	0	7	7	3	41
Miami	0	17	14	7	0	38

San Diego—FG Benirschke 32
San Diego—Chandler 56 punt return (Benirschke kick)
San Diego—Munice 1 run (Benirschke kick)
San Diego—Brooks 8 pass from Fouts (Benirschke kick)
Miami—FG von Schmann 34
Miami—Rose 1 pass from Strock (von Schamann kick)
San Diego—Brooks 9 pass from Fouts (Benirschke kick)
San Diego—FG Benirschke 29

Miami—Nathan 40 pass play, Harris 15 pass from Strock, Nathan 25 lateral from Harris (von Schamann kick)
Miami—Rose 15 pass from Strock (von Schamann kick)
San Diego—Winslow 25 pass from Fouts (Benirschke kick)
Miami—Hardy 50 pass from Strock (von Schamann kick)
Miami—Nathan 12 run (von Schamann kick)
(cont.)

A—73,735 actual, 74,233 paid

	S. Diego	Miami
First Downs	34	25
Rushes - Yards	29-149	28-78
Passing Yards	415	394
Total Yards	564	472
Had QB Sacked	2-18	3-29
Passes	54-33-1	48-31-2
Punts	4-40.3	5-42.0
Fumbles/Lost	3-3	2-1
Penalties/Yards	9-55	7-50

INDIVIDUAL LEADERS

RUSHING — San Diego: Muncie 24-120, Brooks 3-19, Fouts 2-10.
Miami: Nathan 14-48, Franklin 9-6, Hill 3-8, Woodley 1-10, Vigorito 1-6.
PASSING — San Diego: Fouts 53-33-1, 433 yards, 3 TDs, Muncie 1-0-0.
Miami: Woodley 5-2-1, 20 yards, no TD; Strock 43-29-1, 403 yards, 4 TDs.
RECEIVING — San Diego: Winslow 13-166, Joiner 7-108, Chahdler 6-106, Brooks 4-31, Scales 1-17, Muncie 2-5.
Miami: Nathan 9-114, Harris 6-106, Hardy 5-89, Cefalo 3-62, Vigorito 2-12, Hill 2-3, Rose 4-37.

1982 AFC PLAYOFF (First Round)
Woodley Keys Dolphin Revenge
MIAMI 28, NEW ENGLAND 13

MIAMI, JAN. 8, 1983—For the first time in 9 years, the Miami Dolphins won a play-off game — defeating the New England Patriots 28-13. Dolphin QB David Woodley had one of his finest games, completing 16-of-19 passes for 246 yards and two TD's. He was a perfect 8-for-8 in the second half. The Dolphins, now 8-2 including this playoff game and winners of four straight, had not experienced a playoff win since January 13, 1974 when they downed Minnesota in Super Bowl VIII. The Dolphins took command in the second quarter gaining back-to-back TD drives of 76 and 79 yards that turned a 3-0 deficit into a 14-3 halftime advantage. The four Miami TD's came on a pair of two-yard passes from David Woodley to tight end Bruce Hardy, a one-yard run by Andra Franklin and Woody Bennett's two-yard burst up the middle. Franklin finished with 112 yards on 26 carries, but lost the ball three times on fumbles. Two of those fumbles resulted in John Smith field goals of 23 and 43 yards.

New Eng.	0	3	3	7	— 13
Miami	0	14	7	7	— 28

New England—FG Smith 23
Miami—Hardy 2 pass from Woodley (von Schamann kick)
Miami—Franklin 1 run (von Schamann kick)
New England—FG Smith 42
Miami—Bennett 2 run (von Schamann kick)
Miami—Hardy 2 pass from Woodley (von Schamann kick)
New England—Hasselbeck 22 pass from Grogan (Smith kick)

A—68,842 actual 70,881 paid

	N.Eng.	Miami
First Downs	14	27
Rushes - Yards	18-77	45-214
Passing Yards	160	234
Total Yards	237	448
Had QB Sacked	4-29	2-12
Passes	16-30-2	16-19-0
Punts	5-43.6	1-51.0
Fumbles-Lost	1-1	3-3
Penalties/Yards	4-27	2-15

INDIVIDUAL LEADERS

RUSHING — NE: van Eeghen 9-40, Collins 7-35.
Miami: Franklin 26-112, Nathan 12-71.
PASSING — NE: Grogan 30-16-2, 189 yards, 1 TD.
Miami: Woodley 19-16-0, 246 yards, 2 TDs.
RECEIVING — NE: Hasselbeck 7-87, Dawson 4-49.
Miami: Nathan 5-68, Hardy 3-23, Rose 2-47, Vigorito 2-40.

1982 AFC PLAYOFF (Second Round)
"Killer B's" Stymie Fouts and Co.
MIAMI 34, SAN DIEGO 13

Miami, Jan. 16, 1983—The Dolphins, on their way to a five game victory roll, choked off the famed Charger offense and won 34-13. The Dolphin defense stopped the San Diego Chargers' offense with a total 247 yards — 203 yards below their league-leading average, while holding them scoreless in the second half. Dolphin defenders intercepted QB Dan Fouts five times, sacked him three times and held the Chargers to 15 completions for 191 yards — their lowest output since last January's playoff game in the ice at Cincinnati. The Dolphins' offense kept Fouts and Company on the sideline utilizing ball control that produced 80 plays to San Diego's 54 and an overwhelming time of possession advantage. The Dolphins had the ball for 40:46; the Chargers for 19:14. Dolphins' QB David Woodley guided his team to a 214-yard ground attack while connecting on 17-22 passes for 195 yards and two TD's. Woodley opened the scoring with a three-yard pass to Nat Moore in the first quarter, and made it 14-0 by directing Miami 89 yards on 13 plays. Chargers' kickoff returner Hank Bauer fumbled a kickoff which was recovered by Uwe von Schamann at the Chargers' 23-yard line. Seven plays later Woodley hit tight end Ronnie Lee on a six-yard look-in pass for the score. On the next kickoff, Dolphin's rookie Rich Diana recovered a fumble by the Chargers' Brooks, but this time had to settle for a 29-yard von Schamann field goal. The Chargers scored two late TD's, one on a 28-yard pass to Charlie Joiner and the other on Chuck Muncie's one-yard dive that ended the Chargers' scoring. Von Schamann added a second field goal shortly before the end of the first half, and Woodley scored on a two-yard QB draw early in the fourth quarter.

San Diego	0	13	0	0	— 13
Miami	7	20	0	7	— 34

Miami—Moore 3 pass from Woodley (von Schamann kick)
Miami—Franklin 3 run (von Schamann kick)
Miami—Lee 6 pass from Woodley (von Schamann kick)
Miami—FG von Schamann 24
San Diego—Joiner 28 pass from Fouts (Benirschke kick wide right)
Miami—FG von Schamann 23
San Diego—Muncie 1 run (Benirschke kick)
Miami—Woodley 7 run (von Schamann kick)

A — 71,383 actual, 73,772 paid

	San Diego	Miami
First Downs	17	29
Rushes - Yards	17-79	56-214
Passing Yards	168	199
Total Yards	247	413
Had QB Sacked	3-23	1-16
Passes	34-15-5	23-18-1
Punts	4-41.3	3-40.3
Fumbles/Lost	3-2	2-1
Penalties/Yards	7-62	6-70

INDIVIDUAL LEADERS

RUSHING — San Diego: Muncie 11-62, Brooks 3-9.
Miami: Franklin 23-96, Nathan 19-83, Bennett 7-14, Woodley 3-14.
PASSING — San Diego: Fouts 34-15-5, 191 yards, 1 TD.
Miami: Woodley 22-17-1, 195 yards, 2 TD.
RECEIVING — San Diego: Muncie 6-53, Chandler 2-38, Sievers 2-21, Brooks 2-25.
Miami: Nathan 8-55, Hardy 3-45, Vigorito 2-22, Cefalo 2-69.

1982 AFC CHAMPIONSHIP
Dolphin Defense, Rain White-Wash Jets
MIAMI 14, NEW YORK JETS 0

MIAMI, JAN. 23, 1983 — For the third time in as many games the Miami Dolphins defeated the New York Jets, this time on a rainy, mud soaked Orange Bowl field. The Dolphins set an AFC Championship game record by holding the Jets to 139 total yards. A.J. Duhe set an AFC playoff record with three interceptions including one he returned for a 35-yard TD. The Dolphins set an NFL record by being the first team to have defeated the same team three times in a season — two times during regular season and once in a playoff. On nine occasions since the leagues' merger, teams have met three times in a season — but no team has won all three games. Before a crowd of 67,396, the Dolphins' Woody Bennett rumbled seven yards up the middle to score the only points the Dolphins would need. That came in the third quarter, after the teams had slogged through a scoreless first half on the soggy Prescription Athletic Turf.

NY Jets	0	0	0	0	— 0
Miami	0	0	7	7	— 14

Miami—Bennett 7 run (von Schamann kick)
Miami—Duhe 35 interception return (von Schamann kick)

A—67,396 actual, 74,918 paid

	NYJ	Miami
First Downs	10	13
Rushes - Yards	24-62	41-138
Passing Yards	77	60
Total Yards	139	198
Had QB Sacked	4-26	4-27
Passes	37-15-5	21-9-3
Punts	10-35.7	10-33.3
Fumbles/Lost	1-0	3-1
Penalties/Yards	6-42	3-15

INDIVIDUAL LEADERS

RUSHING — NYJ: McNeil 17-46, Todd 4-10.
Miami: Woodley 8-46, Franklin 13-44, Bennett 13-24, Nathan 7-24.
PASSING — NYJ: Todd 37-15-5, 103 yards, no TD.
Miami: Woodley 21-9-3, 87 yards, no TD.
RECEIVING — NYJ: Harper 4-14, Jones 3-35, Barkum 2-20, Augustyniak 2-12.
Miami: Vigorito 3-29, Harris 2-28, Nathan 2-4.

SUPER BOWL XVII
Redskins' Riggins Runs Past Miami
WASHINGTON 27, MIAMI 17

Pasadena, Jan. 30, 1983—The Washington Redskins, behind the power running of John Riggins, came from behind to win Super Bowl XVII in the famed Rose Bowl. Before the second largest crowd for a Super Bowl — 103,667 fans — the Redskins took the lead for the first time with a little more than ten minutes left on the playing clock. The game was marked by a Super Bowl record performance by Fulton Walker, who returned four kickoffs 190 yards, including a 98-yard TD that gave Miami a 17-10 halftime lead. It was the first kickoff returned for a TD in Super Bowl history and the longest kickoff return in playoff history. Riggins ran up 166 yards on 38 runs, both Super Bowl records. On a short-yardage play — fourth and one from the Redskins' 43 with 10:01 to play — Riggins broke a tackle and scored on a 43-yard run. Riggins accounted for 181 total yards, five more than the entire Miami offense could manage in the game. In the first quarter, Miami jumped to a quick lead with a 76-yard Woodley to Cefalo pass for a TD.

Miami	7	10	0	0	—	17
Wash.	0	10	3	14	—	27

Miami—Cefalo 76 pass from Woodley (von Schamann kick)
Washington—FG Moseley 31
Miami—FG von Schamann 20
Washington—Garrett 4 pass from Theismann (Moseley kick)
Miami—Walker 98 kickoff return (von Schamann kick)
Washington—FG Moseley 20
Washington—Riggins 43 run (Moseley kick)
Washington—Brown 6 pass from Theismann (Moseley kick)
A — 103,667 actual

	Miami	Wash.
First Downs	9	24
Rushes · Yards	29-96	52-276
Passing Yards	80	124
Total Yards	176	400
Had QB Sacked	1-17	3-19
Passes	17-4-1	23-15-2
Punts	6-37.8	4-42.0
Fumbles/Lost	2-1	0-0
Penalties/Yards	4-55	5-36

INDIVIDUAL LEADERS

RUSHING — Miami: Franklin 16-49, Nathan 7-26, Woodley 4-16
Washington: Riggins 38-166, Harmon 9-40, Garrett 1-44, Theismann 3-20
PASSING — Miami: Woodley 14-4-1, 97 yards, 1 TD
Washington: Theismann 23-15-2, 143 yards, 2 TD
RECEIVING — Miami: Cefalo 2-82, Harris 2-15
Washington: Brown 6-60, Warren 5-28, Garrett 2-13

1983 AFC PLAYOFF
Warner Keys Seahawk Upset
SEATTLE 27, MIAMI 20

MIAMI, DEC. 31 — The Miami Dolphins saw 1983 and their season end on a sour note as they lost a 27-20 decision to the Seattle Seahawks in the semi-final round of the AFC playoffs. Before 71,032 fans in the Orange Bowl, Dolphin rookie quarterback Dan Marino returned from his December 4 knee injury. On their second possession, the Dolphins launched a 12-play, 80-yard drive ending with a 19-yard TD pass from Marino to tight end Dan Johnson (PAT missed). A 59-yard return by Zachary Dixon on the ensuing kickoff led to a six-yard scoring toss from Seattle's Dave Krieg to Cullen Bryant, with the extra point giving the Seahawks a one point lead. Miami immediately retaliated, using a 17-yard Marino to Mark Duper hook-up to pave the way for a 32-yard circus catch by Duper for the touchdown. Early in the third quarter, a David Overstreet fumble in Seahawk territory set Seattle up for a 55-yard TD march featuring a 28-yard completion from Krieg to Paul Johns, and culminating in a one-yard run by Curt Warner. Norm Johnson's 27-yard field goal early in the fourth quarter gave Seattle a 17-13 lead. The Dolphins managed to regain the lead at 20-17 following a Gerald Small interception (18-yard return) and Woody Bennett's two-yard jaunt with only 3:43 remaining. However, the lead was shortlived as the Seahawks came right back to score on Warner's short run following a pair of Krieg to Steve Largent completions for a total of 56 yards. Miami's Fulton Walker then fumbled the Seattle kickoff, thus leading to a 37-yard Johnson three-pointer. Another Walker kickoff fumble iced the game for the Seahawks, participating in the playoffs for the first time in their eight-year history.

Seattle	0	7	7	13	—	27
Miami	0	13	0	7	—	20

Miami—Johnson 19 pass from Marino (kick failed)
Seattle—Bryant 6 pass from Krieg (Johnson kick)
Miami—Duper 32 pass from Marino (von Schamann kick)
Seattle—Warner 1 run (Johnson kick)
Seattle—FG Johnson 27
Miami—Bennett 2 run (von Schamann kick)
Seattle—Warner 2 run (Johnson kick)
Seattle—FG Johnson 37
A—71,032 actual, 75,116 paid

	Seattle	Miami
First Downs	21	21
Rushes · Yards	42-151	30-128
Passing Yards	183	193
Total Yards	334	321
Had QB Sacked	1-9	0-0
Passes	29-15-1	26-15-2
Punts	4-38.0	4-35.5
Fumbles/Lost	0-0	3-3
Penalties/Yards	2-15	5-30

INDIVIDUAL LEADERS

RUSHING — Seattle: Warner 29-113, Bryant 5-22, Hughes 4-21
Miami: Overstreet 9-50, Bennett 7-31, Franklin 6-28, Nathan 8-19
PASSING — Seattle: Krieg 28-15-1, 192 yards, 1 TD
Miami: Marino 25-15-2, 193 yards, 2 TDs
RECEIVING — Seattle: Warner 5-38, Johns 4-60, Largent 2-56
Miami: Duper 9-117, Johnson 2-29, Moore 2-26

1984 AFC PLAYOFF
Dolphins Atone For '83 Post-Season Loss
MIAMI 31, SEATTLE 10

MIAMI, DEC. 29 — The Miami Dolphins, led by quarterback Dan Marino's three touchdown passes and a defense that shut out the opposition in three of four quarters, defeated the Seattle Seahawks 31-10 before 73,469 fans in the Orange Bowl. The Dolphins moved in front on their second possession and stayed there. Running back Tony Nathan keyed the 68-yard drive by gaining 38 yards on four carries, including the touchdown on a 14-yard run. A 26-yard Marino to Mark Clayton completion was the long play of the scoring march. A 32-yard interception return by Seattle's John Harris and a 25-yard pass from Dave Krieg to Steve Largent paved the way for Norm Johnson's 27-yard field goal that cut Miami's lead to 7-3. The Dolphins, however, came right back to score on their next series as a 20-yard reception by Woody Bennett preceded Marino's 34-yard scoring hook-up with Jimmy Cefalo. The Seahawks made it 14-10 when Largent scored on a 56-yard catch-and-run play. After Miami's defense had stopped Seattle on the Dolphin 24-yard line to open the second half, the Dolphins embarked on a 13-play, 76-yard TD drive that included a Bruce Hardy touchdown catch from three yards out. After the Seahawk's Jeff West managed just a seven-yard punt, Clayton made an acrobatic catch on a tipped ball in the end zone for a 33-yard TD. Miami closed out the scoring on Uwe von Schamann's 37-yard field goal in a drive that featured a 32-yard Marino to Hardy pass.

Seattle	0	10	0	0	—	10
Miami	7	7	14	3	—	31

Miami—Nathan 14 run (von Schamann kick)
Seattle—FG Johnson 27
Miami—Cefalo 34 pass from Marino (von Schamann kick)
Seattle—Largent 56 pass from Krieg (Johnson kick)
Miami—Hardy 3 pass from Marino (von Schamann kick)
Miami—Clayton 33 pass from Marino (von Schamann kick)
Miami—FG von Schamann 37
A—73,469 actual, 74,291 paid

	Seattle	Miami
First Downs	8	22
Rushes · Yards	18-51	36-143
Passing Yards	216	262
Total Yards	267	405
Had QB Sacked	2-18	0-0
Passes	35-20-0	34-21-2
Punts	7-37.0	3-37.0
Fumbles/Lost	1-1	0-0
Penalties/Yards	4-20	1-5

INDIVIDUAL LEADERS

RUSHING — Seattle: Doornink 10-35, Hughes 7-14
Miami: Nathan 18-76, Bennett 11-41, P. Johnson 6-22
PASSING — Seattle: Krieg 35-20-0, 234 yards, 1 TD
Miami: Marino 34-21-2, 262 yards, 3 TDs
RECEIVING — Seattle: Largent 6-128, Doornink 6-23, Turner 3-38
Miami: Clayton 5-75, Nathan 4-20, Hardy 3-48, Duper 3-32, Cefalo 2-43

1984 AFC CHAMPIONSHIP
Marino's 421 Yds., 4 TDs Pace Win
MIAMI 45, PITTSBURGH 28

MIAMI, JAN. 6 — The Miami Dolphins, led by Dan Marino's 421 yards passing (four touchdowns) and Mark Duper's 148 yards receiving, advanced to Super Bowl XIX by defeating the Pittsburgh Steelers 45-28 in the AFC Championship Game before 76,029 fans in the Orange Bowl. The Dolphins scored on their first offensive series as they moved 67 yards in four plays following a William Judson interception, with the TD coming on a 40-yard pass from Marino to Clayton. Pittsburgh's first score came on Rich Erenberg's seven-yard run that had been set up by Walter Abercrombie's 38 yards gained in the 66-yard march. A 26-yard Uwe von Schamann field goal preceded a 65-yard toss from the Steelers' Mark Malone to John Stallworth that gave Pittsburgh a 14-10 lead. The Dolphins then scored two TDs in the first half's final 2:52, first on a 41-yard reception by Mark Duper. After Lyle Blackwood's interception, Marino hit TE Joe Rose for a 28-yard gain before Tony Nathan gave the Dolphins a 24-14 lead on a two-yard run. Miami then scored on its first three second half possessions, leading off with Marino's 36-yard scoring strike to Duper. The Steelers closed the gap to 31-21 on Malone's 19-yarder to Stallworth (33-yarder to Louis Lipps in drive). Completions to Duper (41 yards), Nathan (20 yards), and Nat Moore (28 yards) then led to a one-yard TD dive by Woody Bennett. Moore then caught a six-yard touchdown throw before Wayne Capers closed out the scoring with a 29-yard reception.

Pittsburgh	7	7	7	7	—	28
Miami	7	17	14	7	—	45

Miami—Clayton 40 pass from Marino (von Schamann kick)
Pittsburgh—Erenberg 7 run (Anderson kick)
Miami—FG von Schamann 26
Pittsburgh—Stallworth 65 pass from Malone (Anderson kick)
Miami—Duper 41 pass from Marino (von Schamann kick)
Miami—Nathan 2 run (von Schamann kick)
Miami—Duper 36 pass from Marino (von Schamann kick)

	Pittsburgh	Miami
First Downs	22	28
Rushes · Yards	32-143	38-134
Passing Yards	312	435
Total Yards	455	569
Had QB Sacked	0-0	0-0
Passes	36-20-3	33-22-1
Punts	3-43.7	2-42.5
Fumbles/Lost	2-1	1-1
Penalties/Yards	3-30	3-25

Pittsburgh—Stallworth 19 pass from Malone
(Anderson kick)
Miami—Bennett 1 run (von Schamann kick)
Miami—Moore 6 pass from Marino (von
Schamann kick)
Pittsburgh—Capers 29 pass from Malone
(Anderson kick)

A—76,029 actual, 76,029 paid

INDIVIDUAL LEADERS

RUSHING — Pittsburgh: Abercrombie 15-68, Pollard 11-48, Erenberg 6-27
  Miami: Nathan 19-64, P. Johnson 10-39, Bennett 8-33
PASSING — Pittsburgh: Malone 36-20-3, 312 yards, 3 TDs
  Miami: Marino 32-21-1, 421 yards, 4 TDs; Nathan 1-1-0, 14 yards, no TD
RECEIVING — Erenberg 5-59, Stallworth 4-111, Lipps 3-45, Sweeney 3-42, Pollard 3-13
  Miami: Nathan 8-114, Duper 5-148, Clayton 4-95, Moore 2-34, Hardy 2-16

SUPER BOWL XIX
49ers' 537 Yards Buries Dolphins
SAN FRANCISCO 38, MIAMI 16

PALO ALTO, JAN. 20 — The Miami Dolphins, unable to score in the game's final two quarters, dropped a 38-16 decision to the San Francisco 49ers in Super Bowl XIX before 84,059 fans in Stanford Stadium. The Dolphins were outgained in the contest by a 537-314 margin with the 49ers maintaining possession for 37:11. Miami opened the scoring on its first possession as Uwe von Schamann converted a 37-yard field goal (key play – Dan Marino's 25-yard completion to Tony Nathan). San Francisco jumped ahead 7-3 when QB Joe Montana led the Niners on an eight-play, 78-yard drive that culminated in a 33-yard TD toss to Carl Monroe. The Dolphins scored their only touchdown of the game on their next series as two Marino completions to Mark Clayton (18, 13 yards) and a 21-yarder to Dan Johnson paved the way for Johnson's two-yard scoring catch. Touchdown runs of eight and two yards by Roger Craig and Montana's six-yard scamper gave San Francisco a 28-10 lead. Von Schamann then connected on two field goals of 31 and 30 yards in the final 12 seconds of the first half to close the Dolphin deficit to 28-16. The 49ers upped their lead on their intial second half possession on Ray Wersching's 27-yard field goal before closing out the scoring on Craig's 16-yard scoring reception (key play – 40-yard Montana to Wendell Tyler pass play).

							First Downs	Miami	San Fran
Miami	10	6	0	0	—	16	First Downs	19	31
San Fran.	7	21	10	0	—	38	Rushes - Yards	9-25	40-211
							Passing Yards	289	326
							Total Yards	314	537
							Had QB Sacked	4-29	1-5
							Passes	50-29-2	35-24-0
							Punts	6-39.3	3-32.7
							Fumbles/Lost	1-0	2-2
							Penalties/Yards	1-10	2-10

Miami —FG von Schamann 37
San Fran —Monroe 33 pass from Montana
(Wersching kick)
Miami —D. Johnson 2 pass from Marino (von
Schamann kick)
San Fran —Craig 8 pass from Montana
(Wersching kick)
San Fran —Montana 6 run (Wersching kick)
San Fran —Craig 2 run (Wersching kick)
Miami —FG von Schamann 31
Miami —FG von Schamann 30
San Fran —FG Wersching 27
San Fran —Craig 16 pass from Montana
(Wersching kick)

A—84,059 actual

INDIVIDUAL LEADERS

RUSHING — Miami: Nathan 5-18, Bennett 3-7
  San Francisco: Tyler 13-65, Montana 5-59, Craig 15-58, Harmon 5-20
PASSING — Miami: Marino 50-29-2, 318 yards, 1 TD
  San Francisco: Montana 35-24-0, 331 yards, 3 TDs
RECEIVING — Miami: Nathan 10-83, Clayton 6-92, Rose 6-73, D. Johnson 3-28, Moore 2-17
  San Francisco: Craig 8-82, D. Clark 5-72, Francis 5-60, Tyler 4-70, Monroe 1-33

1985 AFC PLAYOFF
Davenport's 2 TDs Lead Second-Half Comeback
MIAMI 24, CLEVELAND 21

MIAMI, JAN. 4 — Most people had not given them much of a chance to win, but the 8-8 Cleveland Browns nearly upset the 12-4 Dolphins in the Orange Bowl. It would take two Ron Davenport touchdowns in the final 17 minutes to send Miami to a 24-21 victory and the AFC Championship game against New England the following week. Fuad Reveiz put the Dolphins on the board early with a 51-yard field goal on Miami's first drive of the game. But Cleveland came back to score 21 unanswered points, and held a 21-3 advantage midway through the third quarter. Cleveland rookie quarterback Bernie Kosar, who had played two college seasons in the Orange Bowl for the University of Miami, hit Ozzie Newsome with a 16-yard touchdown pass for the Browns' first points of the day. Earnest Byner (16-161) ran in from 21 yards out just before the half, and broke a 66-yard touchdown jaunt 3:38 into the second half. Just like that, the improbable began to look possible. Dan Marino connected with Nat Moore for a six-yard touchdown pass just over six minutes later, and Miami had closed the margin to 21-10. Then it was time for Davenport (6-48) to show his stuff. First, he hit the hole for a 31-yard touchdown run late in the third period and then he closed the scoring and put Miami up for good, going over from one yard out with just 1:57 remaining in the game.

							First Downs	Miami	Cleveland
Cleveland	7	7	7	0	—	21	First Downs	20	17
Miami	3	0	14	7	—	24	Rushes — Yards	19-92	37-251
							Passing Yards	238	62
							Total Yards	330	313
							Had QB Sacked	1-4	0-0
							Passes	45-25-1	19-10-1
							Punts	5-41.6	6-37.2
							Fumbles/Lost	1-0	1-0
							Penalties/Yards	2-20	6-49

Miami—FG Reveiz 51
Cleveland—Newsome 16 pass from Kosar
(Bahr kick)
Cleveland—Byner 21 run (Bahr kick)
Cleveland—Byner 66 run (Bahr kick)
Miami—Moore 6 pass from Marino (Reveiz kick)
Miami—Davenport 31 run (Reveiz kick)
Miami—Davenport 1 run (Reveiz kick)
A—75,128 actual, 75,842 paid

INDIVIDUAL LEADERS

RUSHING — Miami: Davenport 6-48, Nathan 7-21, Bennett 4-17, Carter 2-6
  Cleveland: Byner 16-161, Mack 13-56, Dickey 6-28, Kosar 2-6
PASSING — Miami: Marino 45-25-1, 238 yards, 1 TD
  Cleveland: Kosar 19-10-1, 66 yards, 1 TD
RECEIVING — Miami: Nathan 10-101, Hardy 5-51, Moore 4-29, Johnson 2-17, Rose 1-17, Clayton 1-15,
  Bennett 1-6, Carter 1-2
  Cleveland: Byner 4-25, Newsome 2-22, Holt 2-2, Weathers 1-12, Fontenot 1-5

AFC CHAMPIONSHIP
New England Snaps Streak
PATRIOTS 31, MIAMI 14

MIAMI, JAN. 12 — The New England Patriots garnered a bid to their first Super Bowl by snapping an 18-game losing streak to the Dolphins in Miami with a 31-14 triumph at the Orange Bowl. The Patriots' only previous victory in Miami came in the first meeting between the two teams in 1966. New England backs Craig James (22-105) and Robert Weathers (16-87) combined for 192 yards rushing and quarterback Tony Eason was on target with a 10-of-12 performance for 71 yards as the Pats set up a Super Bowl date with the Chicago Bears. After New England got on the board first with a Tony Franklin 23-yard field goal, the Dolphins stormed back for their only lead of the afternoon when Dan Marino passed 10 yards to Dan Johnson early in the second quarter. Eason brought New England right back with three touchdown tosses and the Pats led 24-7 after three quarters. Miami's last score of the day came early in the fourth quarter when Tony Nathan grabbed a 10-yard TD pass from Marino. Pat fullback Mosi Tatupu ended the game's scoring with a one-yard jaunt midway in the fourth quarter.

							First Downs	New England	Miami
New England	3	14	7	7	—	31	First Downs	21	18
Miami	0	7	0	7	—	14	Rushes — Yards	59-255	13-68
							Passing Yards	71	234
							Total Yards	326	302
							Had QB Sacked	0-0	1-14
							Passes	12-10-0	48-20-2
							Punts	5-40.2	4-41.3
							Fumbles/Lost	2-2	5-4
							Penalties/Yards	2-15	4-35

New England—FG Franklin 23
Miami—Johnson 10 pass from Marino (Reveiz kick)
New England—Collins 4 pass from Eason
(Franklin kick)
New England—D. Ramsey 1 pass from Eason
(Franklin kick)
New England—Weathers 2 pass from Eason
(Franklin kick)
Miami—Nathan 10 pass from Marino (Reveiz kick)
New England—Tatupu 1 run (Franklin kick)
A—74,978 actual, 76,270 paid

INDIVIDUAL LEADERS

RUSHING — New England: C. James 22-105, Weathers 16-87, Collins 12-61
  Miami: Carter 6-56, Davenport 3-6, Nathan 2-4
PASSING — New England: Eason 12-10-0, 71 yards, 3 TDs
  Miami: Marino 48-20-2, 248 yards, 2 TDs
RECEIVING — New England: Morgan 2-30, D. Ramsey, 3-18, Collins 3-15
  Miami: Nathan 5-57, Hardy 3-51, Duper 3-45, Clayton 3-41

MIAMI DOLPHINS ALL-TIME ROSTER
(1966-1986)

HEAD COACHES

George Wilson — Northwestern 66-69
Don Shula — John Carroll 70-86

ASSISTANT COACHES

Arnsparger, Bill —
   Miami, Ohio 70-73, 76-83
Bingaman, Les—Illinois 66-69
Clarke, Monte—Southern Cal . 70-75
Costello, Vince—Ohio U 74
Crosby, Steve—Fort Hays 79-82
Doll, Don—Southern Cal ... 75-76
English, Wally—Louisville 82
Hefferle, Ernie—Duquesne ... 66-69
Henning, Dan—Wm. & Mary . 79-80
Idzik, John—Maryland 66-69
Keane, Tom—West Virginia .. 66-85
Matheson, Bob—Duke .. 83-86
McPeak, Bill—Pittsburgh 73-74

Pellegrini, Bob—Maryland 66-67
Phillips, Mel—N. Carol. A&T . 85-86
Sandusky, John—Villanova ... 76-85
Scarry, Mike—Waynesburg ... 70-85
Schnelker, Bob—Bowling Green .. 74
Schnellenberger, Howard—
   Kentucky 70-72, 75-78
Sekanovich, Dan—Tennessee .. 86
Shula, David—Dartmouth .. 82-86
Studley, Chuck—Illinois 84-86
Taseff, Carl—John Carroll 70-86
Wade, Junior—Savannah St. . 83-86
Walston, Bobby—Georgia .. 66-67
Westhoff, Mike—Wichita St. 86

PLAYERS ON ACTIVE ROSTER

A

Alexander, John (DE) Rutgers . 77-78
Allen, Jeff (CB) Cal-Davis 80
Anderson, Dick (SS) Colo . 68-75, 77
Anderson, Terry (WR)
   Bethune-Cookman 77-78
Andrews, John (DE)
   Morgan St. 75-76
Auer, Joe (RB) Georgia Tech . 66-67

B

Babb, Charlie (S) Memphis St. . 72-79
Bachman, Ted (CB) N. Mex. St. .. 76
Bailey, Elmer (WR) Minnesota . 80-81
Baker, Mel (WR) Tex Southern 74
Ball, Larry (LB)
   Louisville 72-74, 77-78
Bannon, Bruce (LB) Penn St. . 73-74
Barber, Rudy (LB)
   Bethune-Cookeman 68
Barnett, Bill (DT) Nebraska ... 80-85
Barisich, Carl (DT) Princeton . 77-80
Barnes, Rodrigo (LB) Rice 75
Baumhower, Bob (DT) Alabama
   77-85
Beaudoin, Doug (S) Minnesota ... 80
Beier, Tom (S) Miami, Fla. ... 67,69
Benjamin, Guy (QB) Stanford . 78-79
Bennett, Woody (FB)
   Miami, Fla. 80-85
Benson, Charles (DE) Baylor . 83-84
Berger, Ron (DE) Wayne St. 73
Bessilleu, Don (S) Ga. Tech. .. 79-81
Betters, Doug (DE) Nev/Reno . 78-85
Bishop, Richard (DE) Louisville .. 82
Blackwood, Glenn (S) Texas . 79-85
Blackwood, Lyle (S) TCU 81-85
Bokamper, Kim (DE)
   San Jose St. 77-85
Bosarge, Wade (S) Tulsa 77
Boutwell, Tom (QB) So. Miss 69
Bowser, Charles (LB) Duke .. 82-85
Boynton, John (T) Tennessee ... 69
Bramlett, John (LB)
   Memphis State 67-68
Branch, Mel (DE) LSU 66-68
Braxton, Jim (RB) W. Va. 78
Briscoe, Marlin (WR) Omaha . 72-74
Brophy, Jay (LB) Miami, Fla. .. 84-85
Brown, Bud (S) So. Miss. 84-85
Brown, Dean (S) Ft. Valley St. .. 70
Brown, Mark (LB) Purdue .. 83-85
Brudzinski, Bob (LB) Ohio St. . 81-85
Bruggers, Bob (LB) Minnesota . 66-68
Bulaich, Norm (RB) TCU 75-79

Buoniconti, Nick (LB)
   Notre Dame 69-74, 76
Burgess, Fernanza (WR)
   Morris Brown 84

C

Canale, Whit (DE) Tennessee 66
Carlton, Darryl (T) Tampa 75-76
Carpenter, Preston (TE) Ark. 66
Carter, Joe (RB) Alabama 84-85
Casares, Rick (RB) Florida 66
Cefalo, Jimmy (WR) Penn St. . 78-84
Cesare, Billy (S) Miami, Fla. 80
Chambers, Rusty (LB) Tulane . 76-80
Charles, Mike (DE) Syracuse . 83-85
Chesser, George (RB)
   Delta State 66-67
Clancy, Jack (WR) Michigan .. 67-69
Clancy, Sean (LB) Amherst 78
Clark, Steve (G) Utah 82-85
Clayton, Mark (WR) Louisville . 83-85
Cole, Terry (RB) Indiana 71
Colzie, Neal (S) Ohio St........... 79
Cooke, Ed (DE) Maryland 66-67
Cornelius, Charles (CB)
   Bethune-Cookman 77-78
Cornish, Frank (DT)
   Grambling 70-71
Cowan, Larry (RB) Jackson St. ... 82
Cox, Jim (TE) Miami, Fla......... 68
Cronin, Bill (TE) Boston College .. 66
Crowder, Randy (DT)
   Penn State 74-76
Crusan, Doug (T)
   Indiana 68-74
Csonka, Larry (FB) Syracuse
   .... 68-74, 79
Current, Mike (T) Ohio St. . 67, 77-79

D

Darnall, Bill (WR) N. Carolina . 68-69
Davenport, Ron (FB) Louisville .. 85
Davis, Gary (RB) Cal Poly .. 76-79
Davis, Ted (LB) Georgia Tech 70
DeMarco, Bob (C) Dayton 70-71
Del Gaizo, Jim (QB) Tampa .. 72, 75
Dellenbach, Jeff (T) Wisconsin ... 85
Den Herder, Vern (DE)
   Central College, Iowa 71-82
Dennard, Mark (C) Tex. A&M .. 79-83
Dennery, Mike (LB) So. Miss 76
Diana, Richard (RB) Yale 82
Dornbrook, Thom (G) Kentucky .. 80
Dotson, Al (DT) Grambling 66
Drougas, Tom (T) Oregon 75-76

Duhe, A.J. (LB) LSU 77-84
Dunaway, Jim (DT) Mississippi ... 72
Duper, Mark (WR) Northwestern St.
   (La.) 82-85
Dvorak, Rick (DE) Wichita St 77

E

Edmunds, Randall (LB)
   Georgia Tech 68-69
Elia, Bruce (LB) Ohio State 75
Ellis, Ken (CB) Southern 76
Emanuel, Frank (LB) Tenn. .. 68-69
Erlandson, Tom (LB) Wash. St. .. 66-67
Evans, Norm (T) TCU 66-75

F

Faison, Earl (DE) Indiana 66
Farley, Dale (LB) W. Virginia 71
Fernandez, Manny (DE) Utah . 68-75
Fleming, Marv (TE) Utah 70-74
Foley, Tim (CB) Purdue 70-80
Foster, Roy (G) USC 82-85
Fowler, Charlie (G) Houston . 67-68
Franklin, Andra (FB)
   Nebraska 81-84
Fultz, Mike (DT) Nebraska 81
Funchess, Tom (T) Jackson St. ... 74

G

Giaquinto, Nick (RB) Conn. .. 80-81
Giesler, Jon (T) Michigan 79-85
Gilchrist, Cookie (RB) None 66
Ginn, Hubert (RB) Fla. A&M . 70-75
Goode, Irv (C-G) Kentucky 73-74
Goode, Tom (C) Miss. State .. 66-69
Gordon, Larry (LB) Ariz. St. .. 76-82
Grady, Garry (S) E. Mich. 69
Green, Cleveland (T)
   Southern 79-85
Green, Hugh (LB) Pittsburgh 85
Griese, Bob (QB) Purdue 67-80
Groth, Jeff (WR) Bowling Green .. 79

H

Hammond, Kim (QB) Fla. St. ... 68
Hampton, Lorenzo (RB) Florida .. 85
Hardy, Bruce (TE) Ariz. St. .. 78-85
Harper, Jack (RB) Florida 67-68
Harris, Duriel (WR) N. Mex. St. . 76-83
Harris, Leroy (RB) Ark. St. .. 77-78
Haynes, Abner (RB) N. Tex.St. .. 67
Heflin, Vince (WR) Central St. . 82-85
Heinz, Bob (DT)
   Pacific 69-74, 76-77
Heath, Clayton (RB)
   Wake Forest 76
Hester, Ron (LB) Florida St. . 82-84
Higgins, Jim (G) Xavier 66
Hill, Barry (S) Iowa State 75-76
Hill, Eddie (RB) Memphis St. .. 81-84
Hill, Ike (WR) Catawba 76
Hines, Jimmy (WR) Texas So. ... 69
Holmes, John (DE) Fla. A&M 66
Holmes, Mike (WR) Texas So. 76
Hopkins, Jerry (LB)
   Tex. A&M 67-68
Howell, Mike (DB) Grambling 72
Howell, Steve (RB) Baylor ... 79-81
Hudock, Mike (C) Miami, Fla. ... 66
Hunter, Billy (RB) Syracuse 66

J

Jackson, Frank (WR) SMU .. 66-67
Jacobs, Ray (DT)
   Howard Payne 67-68
Jaquess, Pete (DB)
   Eastern New Mexico 66-67
Jenkins, Al (T) Tulsa 72
Jenkins, Ed (RB) Holy Cross 72
Jensen, Jim (QB-WR)
   Boston Univ. 81-85
Joe, Billy (RB) Villanova 66
Johnson, Curtis (CB) Toledo . 70-78
Johnson, Dan (TE)
   Iowa State 82-85
Johnson, Pete (FB) Ohio State ... 84
Joswick, Bob (DE) Tulsa 68-69
Judie, Ed (LB) Northern Arizona .. 84
Judson, William (CB)
   S. Carolina St. 82-85

K

Keating, Bill (DT) Michigan 67
Keyes, Jimmy (LB-K) Miss 68-69
Kiick, Jim (RB) Wyoming 68-74
Kindig, Howard (G-C)
   Cal State-Los Angeles 72-73
Kocourek, Dave (TE) Wisconsin .. 66
Kolen, Mike (LB) Auburn .. 70-75, 77
Kozlowski, Mike (S) Colorado . 79-85
Kremser, Karl (K) Tennessee . 69-70
Kuechenberg, Bob (G)
   Notre Dame 70-84

L

Laakso, Eric (T) Tulane 78-84
Lamb, Mack (CB) Tenn. St. . 67-68
Land, Mel (LB) Mich. St. 79
Landry, Ron (FB) McNeese State . 84
Lankford, Paul (CB) Penn St. . 82-85
Langer, Jim (C) S. Dakota St. . 71-79
Lawless, Burton (G) Florida 81
Lee, Larry (G/C) UCLA 82-85
Lee, Ronnie (TE-G) Baylor . 79-82, 84
Leigh, Charles (RB) None 71-73
Little, George (DT) Iowa 85
Little, Larry (G)
   Bethune-Cookman 69-80
Lothridge, Billy (P) Ga. Tech. ... 72
Lusteg, Booth (K) Connecticut ... 67

M

Malone, Benny (RB) Ariz. St. .. 74-78
Mandich, Jim (TE) Michigan .. 70-77
Marino, Dan (QB) Pittsburgh .. 83-85
Mass, Wayne (T) Clemson 71
Matheson, Bob (LB) Duke 71-79
Matthews, Bo (FB) Colorado 81
Matthews, Wes (WR) NE Okla. ... 66
Mauck, Carl (C) So. Illinois 70
McBride, Norm (DE) Utah 69-70
McCreary, Loaird (TE)
   Tennessee St. 76-78
McCullers, Dale (LB) Fla. St. 69
McDaniel, Wahoo (LB) Okla. . 66-68
McFarland, Jim (TE) Nebraska ... 75
McGeever, John (S) Auburn 66
McNeal, Don (CB) Alabama ... 80-85
Mertens, Jim (TE) Fairmont St. ... 69
Michel, Mike (P-K) Stanford 77
Milton, Gene (WR) Fla. A&M .. 68-69
Mingo, Gene (K) None 66-67
Mira, George (QB) Miami,Fla...... 71
Mitchell, Melvin (G) Tenn St. . 76-78
Mitchell, Stan (RB) Tennessee . 66-70
Moore, Mack (DT) Texas A&M 85
Moore, Maulty (DT)
   Bethune-Cookman 72-74
Moore, Nat (WR) Florida 74-85
Moore, Wayne (T) Lamar Univ. . 70-78
Moreau, Doug (TE) LSU 66-69
Morrall, Earl (QB) Mich. St. . 72-76
Morris, Mercury (RB)
   West Texas St. 69-75
Moser, Rick (RB) Rhode Island .. 80
Moyer, Alex (LB) Northwestern ... 85
Mumphord, Lloyd (CB)
   Tex. So. 69-74

N

Nathan, Tony (RB) Alabama .. 79-85
Neff, Bob (S)
   Stephen F. Austin 66-68
Neighbors, Billy(G) Alabama . 66-69
Newman, Ed (G) Duke 73-84
Nomina, Tom (DT)
   Miami, Ohio 66-68
Noonan, Karl (WR) Iowa 66-71
Norton, Rick (QB) Kentucky .. 66-69
Nottingham, Don (RB) Kent St
   73-77

O

Orosz, Tom (P) Ohio St. 81-82
Ortega, Ralph (LB) Florida . 79-80
Overstreet, David (RB) Oklahoma
   83
Owens, Morris (WR) Ariz. St. . 75-76

P

Palmer, Dick (LB) Kentucky 70
Park, Earnie (G) McMurray 66

Pearson, Willie (CB) N.C. A&T .. 69
Pesuit, Wally (T) Kentucky ... 77-78
Petrella, Bob (S) Tennessee .. 66-71
Poole, Ken (DT) NE Louisiana . 81-82
Potter, Steve (LB) Virginia ... 81-82
Powell, Jesse (LB) W. Tex.St. . 69-73
Price, Sam (RB) Illinois 66-68
Pryor, Barry (RB) Boston U . 69-70
Pyburn, Jack (T) Texas A&M . 66-68

R
Rather, Bo (RB) Michigan 73,78
Ray, Ricky (CB) Norfolk St. ... 81-82
Reese, Don (DT) Jackson St. . 74-76
Reveiz, Fuad (PK) Tennessee 85
Rhone, Earnie (LB)
   Henderson, Ark 75-84
Rice, Ken (G) Auburn 66-67
Richardson, Jeff (T) Mich. St. ... 69
Richardson, John (DT) UCLA . 67-71
Richardson, Willie (WR)
   Jackson St. 70
Riley, Jim (DE) Oklahoma ... 67-71
Roberson, Bo (WR) Cornell ... 66
Roberson, Vern (S) Grambling .. 77
Roberts, Archie (QB) Columbia . 67
Roberts, George (P) Va. Tech . 78-80
Roberts, Guy (LB) Maryland ... 77
Robiskie, Terry (FB) LSU 80-81
Roby, Reggie (P) Iowa 83-85
Roderick, John (WR) SMU ... 66-67
Rose, Joe (TE) California 80-85
Rudolph, Jack (LB) Ga. Tech.... 66

S
Salter, Bryant (S) Pittsburgh 76
Scott, Jake (S) Georgia 70-75
Seiple, Larry (P) Kentucky ... 67-77
Selfridge, Andy (LB) Virginia ... 76
Sellers, Ron (WR) Florida St. ... 73
Sendlein, Robin (LB) Texas 85
Shipp, Jackie (LB)Oklahoma . 84-85
Shiver, Sanders (LB)
   Carson-Newman 84
Shull, Steve (LB) Wm/Mary .. 80-83
Simpson, Bob (DE) Colorado ... 78
Small, Gerald (CB)
   San Jose St. 78-83
Smith, Mike (CB) Texas-El Paso . 85
Smith, Tom (RB) Miami, Fla. 73
Solomon, Freddie (WR)
   Tampa 75-77
Sowell, Robert (CB) Howard . 83-85
Speyrer, Cotton (WR)Texas 75
Stanfill, Bill (DE) Georgia 69-76
Stephenson, Dwight (C)
   Alabama 80-85
Stofa, John (QB)
   Buffalo 66-67, 69-70
Stowe, Otto (WR) Iowa State . 71-72
Strock, Don (QB) Va. Tech ... 74-85
Stuckey, Henry (CB) Missouri . 72-74
Swift, Doug (LB) Amherst ... 70-75

T
Tautolo, Terry (LB) UCLA 83-84
Taylor, Ed (CB) Memphis St.... 79-82
Testerman, Don (FB) Clemson 80
Thomas, Norris (CB) So. Miss . 77-79
Thomas, Rodell (LB)
   Alabama St. 81, 83-84
Thornton, Jack(LB) Auburn 66
Tilley, Emmett (LB) Duke 83
Tillman, Andre (TE) Tex Tech . 75-78
Toews, Jeff (G) Washington 79-85
Torczon, LaVerne (DE) Nebraska . 66
Torrey, Bob (FB) Penn St. 79
Towle, Steve (LB) Kansas 75-80
Tucker, Gary (RB) Chatanooga ... 68
Twilley, Howard (WR) Tulsa 66-76

U
Urbanek, Jim (DT) Miss 68

V
Vigorito, Tom (RB) Virginia 81-85

Volk, Rick (S) Michigan 77-78
von Schamann, Uwe (K) Okla.. 79-84

W
Wade, Charley (WR) Tenn. St. 73
Walker, Fulton (CB) West Va. ... 81-84
Walters, Rod (G) Iowa 80
Wantland, Hal (TE) Tenn 66
Warfield, Paul (WR) Ohio State . 70-74
Warren, Jimmy (CB) Illinois 66-69
Washington, Dick (DB)
   Bethune-Cookman 68
Weisacosky, Ed (LB)
   Miami, Fla.................... 68-70
West, Willie (S) Oregon 66-68
Westmoreland, Dick (CB)
   North Carolina A&T 66-69
White, Jeris (CB)Hawaii 74-76
Wickert, Tom (T) Wash. State 74
Williams, Delvin (RB) Kansas .. 78-80
Williams, Maxie (G-T) SE LA .. 66-70
Wilson, George, Jr. (QB) Xavier .. 66
Windauer, Bill (DT) Iowa 75
Winfrey, Stan (RB) Ark. St. 75-77
Wood, Dick (QB) Auburn 66
Woodley, David (QB) LSU 80-83
Woods, Larry (DT) Tenn. State 73
Woodson, Fred (G) Fla. A&M .. 67-69

Y
Yepremian, Garo (K) None 70-78
Young, Steve (T) Colorado 77
Young, Willie (T) Alcorn A&M 73

Z
Zecher, Rich (DT) Utah State .. 66-67

1986 SCHEDULE

REGULAR SEASON

DATE	OPPONENT	TIME
Sun., Sept. 7	at San Diego	4:00 PM
Sun., Sept. 14	INDIANAPOLIS	4:00 PM
Sun., Sept. 21	at N.Y. Jets	1:00 PM
Sun., Sept. 28	SAN FRANCISCO	1:00 PM
Sun., Oct. 5	at New England	1:00 PM
Sun., Oct. 12	BUFFALO	1:00 PM
Sun., Oct. 19	L.A. RAIDERS	1:00 PM
Sun., Oct. 26	at Indianapolis	1:00 PM
Sun., Nov. 2	HOUSTON	1:00 PM
Mon., Nov. 10	at Cleveland	9:00 PM
Sun., Nov. 16	at Buffalo	1:00 PM
Mon., Nov. 24	N.Y. JETS	9:00 PM
Sun., Nov. 30	ATLANTA	1:00 PM
Sun., Dec. 7	at New Orleans	1:00 PM
Sun., Dec. 14	at L.A. Rams	4:00 PM
Mon., Dec. 22	NEW ENGLAND	9:00 PM

All starting times are Eastern time

HISTORICAL HIGHLIGHTS

1965

March 3 — Minneapolis lawyer Joseph Robbie meets AFL Commissioner Joe Foss in Washington, and Foss advises Robbie to apply for an expansion franchise in Miami.

May 6 — Joseph Robbie meets Miami Mayor Robert King High to ascertain the availability of the Orange Bowl stadium, and the mayor agrees to invite the AFL to Miami.

June 7 — AFL Executive Committee votes to expand in 1966 at a meeting in Monmouth Park, N.J.

Aug. 16 — AFL awards its first expansion franchise to Joseph Robbie and television star Danny Thomas for $7.5 million.

Nov. 27 — Miami picks Kentucky QB Rick Norton and Illinois RB Jim Grabowski in first round of AFL's college draft. Tulsa WR Howard Twilley is selected in 12th round.

Dec. 16 — Miami Dolphins, Ltd. organizes as a Florida limited partnership. Joseph Robbie becomes Managing General Partner and Danny Thomas Sports, Inc., becomes the other general partner.

1966

Jan. 15 — Miami picks 31 players from eight teams in AFL expansion draft. One of the draftees, OT Norm Evans of Houston, would play 10 seasons at right tackle.

Jan. 29 — George Wilson becomes first head coach after eight years coaching the Detroit Lions (57-46-6 and NFL champions in 1957) and one year as a Washington assistant.

June 8 — AFL merges into NFL with Pete Rozelle as commissioner. An AFL-NFL championship game is scheduled for the next January followed by a common draft.

July 5 — Dolphins open first training camp at St. Petersburg Beach as 83 players report.

Aug. 7 — Training camp moves to St. Andrews School in Boca Raton, Fla.

Sept. 2 — Joe Auer returns opening kickoff 95 yards for Dolphin TD in first regular-season game, but Oakland wins, 23-14, at Orange Bowl before 26,776 spectators.

Oct. 16 — Dolphins end string of nine losses (four in pre-season) by defeating Denver, 24-7 with a George Wilson, Jr. screen pass to Billy Joe turning into a 67-yard TD. Only 23,393 spectators were at Orange Bowl.

Oct. 23 — QB Rick Norton suffers broken jaw during third quarter of 20-13 victory at Houston, and Norton is lost for the season.

Dec. 18 — QB John Stofa passes for four TDs capped by 14-yard strike to Joe Auer with 38 seconds remaining for 29-28 victory over Houston at Orange Bowl before 20,045 spectators.

1967

March 14 — Miami picks Purdue QB Bob Griese in first round of common draft. Griese is the fourth player selected.

June 1 — Joseph Robbie and W.H. Keland purchase the interest of Danny Thomas and agree to equalize present holdings in Miami Dolphins, Ltd., whenever either acquires outside holdings.

Aug. 19 — Record crowd of 50,822 sees first interleague game which Atlanta wins, 27-17.

Sept. 17 — QB John Stofa breaks his right ankle shortly after scoring a TD, and rookie Bob Griese directs 35-21 victory over Denver at Orange Bowl. RB Abner Haynes gains 151 yards in season opener, Griese throws 68-yard TD pass to Joe Auer.

Nov. 26 — Dolphins end eight-game losing streak by defeating Buffalo, 17-14 on a fourth-down, 31-yard TD pass from Bob Griese to Howard Twilley with 1:01 remaining.

Dec. 17 — CB Dick Westmoreland scores TD with his 10th interception in 41-32 victory over Boston at Orange Bowl. Patriots RB Jim Nance gains 164 yards.

Dec. 27 — Miami trades QB John Stofa to expansion club Cincinnati for 1968 draft picks in first and second rounds.

1968

Jan. 30 — Miami picks Syracuse FB Larry Csonka in first round of draft. Csonka is the eighth player selected.

Aug. 17 — Dolphins gain first interleague victory, 23-7, over Philadelphia at Orange Bowl.

Aug. 31 — AFL-record crowd of 68,125 at Orange Bowl sees Coach Don Shula's Baltimore Colts win interleague game, 22-13. WR Jack Clancy (67 catches as rookie) injures left knee, out for season.

Nov. 24 — Rookie strong safety Dick Anderson returns interception 96 yards for TD in 34-10 victory over Boston at Fenway Park.

Dec. 8 — QB Bob Griese sets then-club records with 2,473 yards, 186 completions and 21 TDs for season after directing 38-7 victory over Boston at Orange Bowl. Griese misses final game due to bruised knee.

1969

Jan. 28 — Miami picks Georgia DE Bill Stanfill in first round of draft. Stanfill is the 11th player selected.

March 24 — Miami obtains all-time AFL middle linebacker Nick Buoniconti from Boston in trade for QB Kim Hammond and LB John Bramlett.

May 10 — Pro football realignment for 1970 places Dolphins in AFC East with Boston, Buffalo, New York Jets and NFL's Baltimore.

May 16 — Joseph Robbie becomes majority owner of Dolphins when he is joined by five Miami businessmen in purchasing the interest of W.H. Keland.

July 2 — Miami obtains RG Larry Little, a native Miamian, from San Diego in trade for CB Mack Lamb.

Sept. 14 — QB Bob Griese passes for a record 327 yards and rookie Mercury Morris returns kickoff 105 yards for TD, but Dolphins lose season opener 27-21, at Cincinnati.

Oct. 26 — Dolphins notch first victory after 0-4-1 start as LB Nick Buoniconti helps restrict rookie O.J. Simpson to 12 yards on 10 carries. Miami wins 24-6 over Buffalo at Orange Bowl.

Nov. 9 — Only 8,374 spectators brave a downpour at Boston College and FB Larry Csonka splashes 54 yards for TD in 17-16 victory over Patriots. QB Bob Griese injures right knee, out for final five games.

1970

Jan. 27 — Miami obtains WR Paul Warfield from Cleveland in trade for 1970 first-round draft pick.

Feb. 18 — Don Shula, 40, becomes head coach and vice president after seven years coaching the Baltimore Colts (71-23-4). He succeeds George Wilson after four years with Dolphins (15-39-2).

April 11 — Dolphins join scouting combine, BLESTO-V.

April 13 — NFL Commissioner Pete Rozelle gives the Dolphins' 1971 first-round draft pick to Baltimore as compensation for loss of Don Shula.

April 20 — Don Shula completes coaching staff with Mike Scarry (defensive line), Monte Clark (offensive line), Bill Arnsparger (defensive coordinator), Howard Schnellenberger (offensive coordinator), Carl Taseff (offensive backs) and holdover Tom Keane (defensive backs).

April 25 — Don Shula meets 47 players for indoctrination camp at University of Miami.

July 12 — Rookies report to new training headquarters at Biscayne College in North Miami.

Aug. 10 — Dolphins cut QB Rick Norton who signed four-year $350,000 contract as club's first draftee in 1966.

Aug. 29 — Record crowd of 76,712 sees fourth consecutive pre-season victory, 20-13 over Baltimore.

Oct. 3 — Dolphins post first-ever victory over Oakland, 20-13, as WR Paul Warfield catches two TD passes.

Oct. 10 — Dolphins post first-ever victory over New York Jets, 20-6, and QB Joe Namath (93/161 for 1,506 yards and 12 TDs in eight previous meetings), 20-6.

Nov. 22 — Dolphins reverse a 35-0 loss by defeating Baltimore, 34-17 at Orange Bowl as free safety Jake Scott returns punt 77 yards for TD.

Dec. 20 — Dolphins extend winning streak to six games and clinch playoff berth with 45-7 victory over Buffalo at Orange Bowl.

1971

Sept. 1 — Miami obtains LB Bob Matheson from Cleveland in trade for 1972 second-round pick and Matheson later becomes key to the 53 Defense.

Oct. 17 — QB Bob Griese sets NFL record with three consecutive passes for TDs in first quarter of 41-3 victory over New England at Orange Bowl.

Nov. 7 — Dolphins post first-ever shutout, 34-0, over Buffalo at Orange Bowl although Bills gained 364 yards.

Nov. 14 — QB Bob Griese, despite illness, rallies Dolphins from 21-3 deficit to a 24-21 victory over Pittsburgh at Orange Bowl with record

86-yard TD pass to Paul Warfield and record 73-yard punt by Larry Seiple.

Dec. 19 — Record regular-season crowd of 74,215 paid sees Dolphins win AFC East title by defeating Green Bay, 27-6. FB Larry Csonka becomes clubs first 1,000-yard rusher with 1,051 yards, and placekicker Garo Yepremian leads NFL with 117 points.

Dec. 25 — Dolphins win longest game (82 minutes, 40 seconds) in pro football history, 27-24 at Kansas City as Garo Yepremian kicks 37-yard field goal in second overtime of AFC semifinal playoff

1972

Jan. 2 — Dolphins stymie Baltimore, 21-0, for first AFC Championship before 78,629 spectators at Orange Bowl. Colts are scoreless for first time in 97 games and strong safety Dick Anderson returns interception 62 yards for clinching TD.

Jan. 16 — Dallas rushes for 252 yards in defeating Dolphins 24-3 in Super Bowl VI before 81,035 spectators at Tulane Stadium, New Orleans.

April 25 — Dolphins claim 16-year pro QB Earl Morrall, 38, on waivers from Baltimore.

Oct. 1 — Dolphins end season ticket sale at record 69,303.

Oct. 15 — QB Earl Morrall replaces injured Bob Griese (broken right leg, dislocated ankle) at Orange Bowl and finishes 24-10 victory over San Diego for 5-0 record.

Oct. 22 — Garo Yepremian kicks longest field goal (54 yards) of career in 24-23 victory over Buffalo at Orange Bowl.

Nov. 12 — Don Shula becomes first NFL coach to win 100 regular-season games in 10 seasons as Dolphins smother New England, 52-0 with 501 total yards at Orange Bowl.

Dec. 16 — Dolphins achieve NFL's first 14-0 regular-season record and break NFL rushing record with 2,960 yards by defeating Baltimore 16-0 at Orange Bowl.

Dec. 31 — QB Bob Griese comes off bench in 7-7 battle in third quarter after 10-game absence and rallies Dolphins to 21-17 victory at Pittsburgh to repeat as AFC champions.

1973

Jan. 14 — Dolphins cap a perfect season in Super Bowl VII at Los Angeles by defeating Washington 14-7 for NFL's first unbeaten, untied record. A 28-yard TD pass form Bob Griese to Howard Twilley and interceptions by LB Nick Buoniconti and safety Jake Scott are key plays.

April 18 — Dolphins surpass NFL record with 74,961 season ticket sales. Kansas City held old record of 72,855 in 1972.

Sept. 30 — RB Mercury Morris sets single-game rushing record of 197 yards on 15 carries with three TDs (24, 70, 35) in 44-23 win over New England at Orange Bowl.

Nov. 11 — Dolphins shut out Baltimore for fourth consecutive time, 44-0, as CB Tim Foley returns two blocked punts for TDs at Orange Bowl.

Dec. 15 — WR Paul Warfield catches four TD passes (21, 7, 16, 4) from Bob Griese in first half of 34-7 victory over Detroit at Orange Bowl. Dolphins compile best two-year record (26-2) in NFL history.

Dec. 30 — Dolphins rush for 266 yards in defeating Oakland 27-10 for unprecedented third straight AFC Championship at Orange Bowl.

1974

Jan. 13 — Dolphins overpower Minnesota 24-7 in Super Bowl VIII at Rice Stadium in Houston for second consecutive NFL Championship. FB Larry Csonka gains 156 yards on 33 carries as Dolphins outscore three playoff foes, 85-33.

Jan. 20 — Garo Yepremian kicks five field goals for AFC including 42-yarder with 21 seconds remaining for 15-13 victory in Pro Bowl at Kansas City.

March 31 — FB Larry Csonka, WR Paul Warfield and RB Jim Kiick sign $3.3 million package deal in Toronto to play for John Bassett in World Football League.

July 1 — NFL Players Association declares strike, Dolphin Managing General Partner Joseph Robbie charges NFLPA with search and destroy mission.

July 10 — Chicago Tribune Charities cancels July 26 College All-Star Game with Dolphins due to strike.

July 17 — Seven veterans cross picket line: C Jim Langer, S Jake Scott, TE Jim Mandich, LB Bob Matheson, QB Earl Morrall and RBs Don Nottingham and Mercury Morris.

Aug. 14 — Strike ends after seven weeks.

Nov. 17 — Dolphins outlast Buffalo 35-28 at Orange Bowl on 23-yard TD by

Don Nottingham with 19 seconds remaining; third time in season that Dolphins score winning points with less than 20 seconds to play.

Dec. 2 — FB Larry Csonka gains 100 yards for 19th time with 123 yards in 24-3 victory over Cincinnati at Orange Bowl; seventh consecutive win on Monday night TV.

Dec. 15 — Dolphins rally from 24-point deficit to defeat New England 34-27 for 31st consecutive victory (excluding pre-season) at Orange Bowl. QB Earl Morrall passes for 288 yards as Miami closes with 11-3 record.

Dec. 21 — Raiders spoil Dolphins bid for third consecutive NFL Championship 28-26 in AFC semi-final at Oakland on 8-yard TD pass from Ken Stabler to Clarence Davis with 26 seconds remaining.

1975

Sept. 22 — Winning streak at Orange Bowl stops at 31 games after 31-21 loss to Oakland.

Oct. 19 — Dolphins intercept Jets' QB Joe Namath six times in 43-0 victory at New York.

Oct. 22 — World Football League folds after losing $30 million, but three ex-Dolphins still under contract to John Bassett.

Nov. 23 — QB Bob Griese suffers torn tendons in right foot during third quarter of 33-17 loss to Baltimore at Orange Bowl.

Dec. 7 — Third-string QB Don Strock directs 31-21 victory over Buffalo at Orange Bowl for 12th consecutive victory over Bills.

Dec. 14 — Dolphins suffer 10-7 loss in overtime at Baltimore on 31-yard FG by Toni Linhart and miss qualifying for playoffs for first time in six years under Don Shula.

1976

Jan. 22 — Prescription Athletic Turf (grass) approved for Orange Bowl stadium at a cost of $244,500.

March 30 — Seattle selects Dolphin original OT Norm Evans in expansion draft; Tampa Bay selects LBs Bruce Elia and Doug Swift, who retires to enter medical school.

Sept. 26 — Dolphins face QB Joe Namath of New York Jets for last time and post 16-0 shutout at Orange Bowl.

Oct. 17 — WR Howard Twilley, last of Dolphin originals, surpasses 3,000 career yards with eight catches for 104 yards in 20-17 overtime loss to Kansas City at Orange Bowl.

Dec. 5 — WR Freddie Solomon gains 252 yards in three-TD spectacular that includes 79-yard punt return, 53-yard pass play and 59-yard flanker reverse in 45-27 victory over Buffalo Bills at Orange Bowl.

1977

March 14 — Dolphins agree to 10-year lease for use of Orange Bowl with three-year cancellation notice. New lease doubles rent to $45,000 per game, but is less than City of Miami's proposed 10 percent of gross ticket sales.

May 2 — QB Earl Morrall, 43, who spent five seasons with the Dolphins, retires from a 21-year career. Morrall passed for 20,809 career yards and guided the Dolphins through most of undefeated 1972 season.

Sept. 11 — QB Bob Griese, forced to wear eyeglasses because of problems with contact lenses, passes for two TDs in 27-21 pre-season victory at New York Giants.

Nov. 24 — QB Bob Griese becomes first since 1972 to throw six TD passes in a game, and Dolphins set records of 55 points and 503 yards in 55-14 rout on Thanksgiving Day at St. Louis.

Dec. 5 — Rookie RB Leroy Harris gallops 77 yards for longest TD run in Dolphin history, capping 17-6 victory over Baltimore at Orange Bowl.

Dec. 15 — Maxwell Club of Philadelphia names QB Bob Griese as its Pro Player of Year.

Dec. 17 — Dolphins close 10-4 season with QB Bob Griese's record 22nd TD pass and Nat Moore's record 13th TD in 31-14 victory over Buffalo at Orange Bowl.

1978

Feb. 17 — Chuck Connor, 40, becomes Director of Player Personnel after three years scouting for BLESTO. He succeeds Bobby Beathard, who resigned Feb. 7 and became general manager of Washington Redskins.

April 17 — Dolphins acquire RB Delvin Williams from San Francisco 49ers in exchange for WR Freddie Solomon, S Vern Roberson and picks in the first and fifth rounds of 1978 draft.

Aug. 25 — QB Bob Griese suffers torn ligaments in left knee during 24-20 pre-season victory at Tampa Bay, and backup Don Strock guides Dolphins to 5-2 record before Griese returns as starter Oct. 22.

Nov. 5 — A 17-point blitz in first quarter and five quarterback sacks enable Dolphins to upset defending Super Bowl champion Dallas Cowboys, 23-16 at Orange Bowl.

Nov. 12 — Delvin Williams becomes first 1,000-yard rusher of 1978 with 144 yards and two TDs in 25-24 triumph at Buffalo, marking 18th straight win over Bills. Williams sets Dolphin record of 1,258 yards rushing in season.

Dec. 10 — LB Larry Gordon intercepts three passes in 23-6 rout of Oakland Raiders at Orange Bowl to clinch wild-card berth in playoffs.

Dec. 18 — Garo Yepremian ties NFL record with 16th consecutive field goal, capping 23-3 victory over New England and boosting Dolphins to 11-5 record.

1979

Jan. 8 — Howard Schnellenberger, receivers and passing game coach, is named head coach at the University of Miami.

Feb. 22 — FB Larry Csonka, 32, re-signs with Dolphins as a free agent after four-year absence in World Football League (1975) and NFL's New York Giants (1976-78).

Sept. 23 — FB Larry Csonka scores three TDs for second time in career as Dolphins crush Chicago 31-16 at Orange Bowl for 4-0 start.

Oct. 14 — Tony Nathan escapes on record 86-yard punt return for TD as Dolphins defeat Buffalo, 17-7, for 20th consecutive win in series.

Oct. 28 — WR Duriel Harris sets then single-game record of 10 catches for 180 yards in 27-7 rout of Green Bay at Orange Bowl.

Nov. 29 — QB Bob Griese, benched in favor of Don Strock for second straight game, rallies Dolphins to 26 points in second half for 39-24 victory over New England as FB Larry Csonka scores three TDs.

Dec. 9 — QB Bob Griese completes 17 of 22 passes for 229 yards in 28-10 win at Detroit which clinches AFC East title.

Dec. 30 — Pittsburgh overpowers Dolphins with 20-point first quarter in 34-14 playoff victory at Pittsburgh, and Steelers eventually win Super Bowl XIV.

1980

Sept. 5 — Don Shula signs four-year contract through 1983 season and cancels old pact which had one year remaining.

Sept. 21 — QB Bob Griese wins his 100th game, coming off bench and passing for two TDs in fourth quarter for 20-17 victory at Atlanta.

Nov. 9 — Rookie QB David Woodley passes for three TDs and runs for another two TDs in stunning 35-14 upset of defending National Conference champion Los Angeles Rams at Anaheim.

1981

Feb. 5 — Six-time All-Pro guard Larry Little, 35, retires following a 14-year career including 12 years with the Dolphins. He ended with a then-club record 164 starts.

June 25 — QB Bob Griese, the 14th passer in football history to eclipse 25,000 yards, retires following a 14-year career with the Dolphins. He had presided over 101 of the 135 victories in the club's history (101-62-3) and was consensus All-Pro in 1971 and 1977. The six-time Pro Bowl quarterback held records of 1,926 completions in 3,429 attempts, 25,092 yards and 56.2 percent passing accuracy. He guided Dolphins to Super Bowl triumphs in 1972 and 1973.

July 1 — Dolphin linebacker Rusty Chambers is killed in an automobile accident in Hammond, Louisiana.

Sept. 10 — Rookie Tom Vigorito rambles 87 yards for record punt-return TD as Dolphins crush Pittsburgh 30-10 before 74,190 fans, largest Orange Bowl crowd since 1975.

Sept. 27 — Coach and son clash, Shula Bowl I, has Don Shula opposed by Baltimore rookie punt returner David Shula. Dolphins outlast Colts 31-28 for fourth straight win in Baltimore.

Oct. 4 — Wide receiver Nat Moore sets Dolphin record with 210 receiving yards (seven catches) as Miami and New York Jets play to 28-28 tie.

Nov. 8 — Don Shula captures 200th NFL coaching victory when linebacker Bob Brudzinski intercepts pass in overtime and sets up Uwe von Schamann for 30-yard field goal in 30-27 triumph at New England.

Dec. 19 — Dolphins complete sweep of last four games of season and win AFC East title in 16-6 conquest of Buffalo before 72,956 fans at Orange Bowl. Miami posts fourth-best record (11-4-1) in NFL.

1982

Jan. 2 — Dolphins overcome 24-0 deficit but succumb in overtime, 41-38, to San Diego in highest-scoring playoff game in history. Rolf Benirschke ends four-hour struggle with 29-yard field goal. It is only game in NFL where two quarterbacks, Miami reliever Don Strock and San Diego star Dan Fouts, both passed for more than 400 yards. Orange Bowl crowd of 73,735 comprised fourth sellout of season.

Sept. 21 — NFLPA calls players' strike with games not resuming until November 21.

Dec. 12 — In one of the most bizarre incidents in Miami Dolphin history, a work release parolee cleared a space on the snow-frozen New England Patriots' turf that enabled the Patriots to kick a late fourth-quarter field goal and win the game 3-0 before 25,716 fans.

Dec. 27 — The incredible record of not having won in 16 years in the Orange Bowl continued as the Dolphins scored 20 unanswered points in the second half to defeat the Buffalo Bills 27-10.

1983

Jan. 8 — For the first time in nine years, the Dolphins win a playoff game, defeating the New England Patriots 28-13 before 68,842 fans.

Jan. 16 — The Dolphins choke off the San Diego Chargers famed offense and defeat them 34-13 before 71,383 fans. The Chargers were held to a total offense of 247 yards, 203 yards below their league-leading average.

Jan. 23 — A.J. Duhe sets an AFC playoff record with three interceptions, including one for a 35-yard touchdown romp — as the Dolphins defeat the New York Jets for the third time in one season to win the AFC crown 14-0.

Jan. 30 — In Pasadena, California, the Dolphins appear in their fourth Super Bowl, and in spite of leading with only ten minutes to play, they lose 27-17 before a sellout crowd of 103,667 and a TV audience estimated at 115 million. Fulton Walker sets a Super Bowl record with a 98-yard kickoff return for a touchdown, and he returns four kickoffs for a total of 190 yards.

Apr. 26 — The Dolphins select quarterback Dan Marino in the first round of the 1983 draft (27th player overall). The drafting of the former University of Pittsburgh All-America marks the first time in Dolphin history that the club has chosen a QB with its initial draft choice.

June 25 — Starting linebacker Larry Gordon dies of a rare heart disease while jogging in Arizona at the age of 28. Gordon had been the Dolphins' first round draft choice in 1976 out of Arizona State.

Sept. 4 — Led by six quarterback sacks (four by Doug Betters), the Dolphin defense shuts out the Buffalo Bills 12-0 in the 1983 season opener. 78,715 fans in Rich Stadium see four Uwe von Schamann field goals account for all the scoring.

Oct. 9 — Quarterback Dan Marino and wide receiver Mark Duper make their first-ever starts for the Miami Dolphins, with Marino passing for 322 yards and Duper netting seven catches for 202 yards. The offensive explosion produces 971 total yards between the Dolphins and Bills, with Buffalo winning the Orange Bowl encounter, 38-35 in overtime.

Oct. 16 — The Dolphin secondary intercepts six New York Jet passes (three by William Judson in one quarter) to lead Miami to a 32-14 win in the Dolphins' final Shea Stadium appearance. QB Dan Marino completes 17 of 30 passes for 225 yards, 3 TDs and 0 interceptions.

Nov. 28 — Dolphin Owner Joseph Robbie announces the signing of Head Coach Don Shula to a multi-year contract.

Dec. 2 — Bill Arnsparger, the Dolphins' Assistant Head Coach and mastermind of the team's defense, resigns to become the head coach at Louisiana State University. His resignation is effective at the end of the season.

Dec. 14 — Squads for the 1983 Pro Bowl are announced with six Dolphins being named to the squad (four starters), plus four alternates. Earning places on the team are NT Bob Baumhower, DE Doug Betters, WR Mark Duper, QB Dan Marino, G Ed Newman and C Dwight Stephenson. The alternates included LB A.J. Duhe, G Bob Kuechenberg (later added to team), P Reggie Roby, and KR Fulton Walker.

Dec. 16 — With starting QB Dan Marino sidelined for the second consecutive game, relief pitcher Don Strock again steps in to help lead Miami to a 34-14 Orange Bowl win over the Jets. Safety Mike Kozlowski breaks open a close game when he returns two interceptions for touchdowns in a 61-second span in the fourth quarter. WR Mark Duper catches four passes for 71 yards to become the first Dolphin receiver to go over the 1000-yard mark in a single season.

Dec. 27 — The Dolphins name 54-year-old Chuck Studley as their Defense Coach to replace Bill Arnsparger. Studley had spent the 1983 season as defensive coordinator, and then interim head coach of the Houston Oilers.

Dec. 31 — Despite winning or sharing the AFC East title for the 11th time in 14 years, the Dolphins see their season and 1983 end on a disappointing note as the Seattle Seahawks beat them 27-20 in a conference semi-final playoff game in Miami.

1984

March 5 — Miami Dolphin Owner Joseph Robbie announces plans to build a new multi-purpose stadium in north Dade County. Mr. Robbie also announces acquisition of the land and discusses possible stadium funding.

June 24 — Running back David Overstreet is killed in an automobile accident in Winona, Texas.

July 6 — The Dolphins name Joe Abrell to the post of Vice President/Public Affairs.

Sept. 2 — Miami defeats the defending NFC Champion Washington Redskins 35-17 in the season opener at R.F.K. Stadium. QB Dan Marino completes 21 of 28 passes for 311 yards and five TDs while WR Mark Duper catches six balls for 178 yards and two scores.

Oct. 7 — Dolphins beat Pittsburgh 31-7 to move Head Coach Don Shula into third place on the NFL's list for all-time winningest coaches. Shula now has 219 regular season victories.

Oct. 21 — Wide receiver Nat Moore catches a 19-yard TD pass from QB Dan Marino for the 58th touchdown of his Dolphin career. That surpasses Larry Csonka's all-time club record of 57.

Nov. 11 — The Dolphins remain the NFL's only unbeaten team as they improve their record to 11-0 (16 straight regular season wins) with a 24-23 victory over Philadelphia. DE Doug Betters' block of an Eagle PAT with 1:52 remaining in the game seals the win.

Nov. 26 — Miami clinches the AFC Eastern Division title with a 28-17 triumph over the Jets. The Dolphins have now won or shared that distinction in 12 of the previous 15 years.

Dec. 2 — The Dolphins lose a 45-34 decision to the Raiders, but QB Dan Marino breaks the all-time NFL record for TD passes in a season with his 37th. He also shatters Dolphin single game records for most yards passing (470), most completions (35) and most attempts (57).

Dec. 12 — Squads for the AFC-NFC Pro Bowl are announced with eight Dolphins being named to the team including four starters in WR Mark Duper, QB Dan Marino, G Ed Newman and C Dwight Stephenson, plus four reserves in NT Bob Baumhower, WR Mark Clayton, LB A.J. Duhe and P Reggie Roby. G Roy Foster and T Jon Giesler are selected as alternates.

Dec. 17 — Miami ends the regular season with the best record in the AFC (14-2) following a 28-21 victory over Dallas. WR Mark Clayton catches three touchdown passes to give him 18 for the season as he eclipses the all-time NFL mark in that category. Dan Marino becomes the first-ever NFL quarterback to pass for over 5000 yards in a season as he ends up with 5,084. Both Clayton (73/1,389) and WR Mark Duper (71/1,306) surpass prior Dolphin records for receptions and reception yardage in one season.

Dec. 20 — QB Dan Marino is named as the NFL's Most Valuable Player by the Associated Press.

1985

Jan. 6 — The Dolphins defeat the Steelers 45-28 in the AFC Championship Game in Miami to earn a berth in Super Bowl XIX.

Jan. 8 — Joseph Robbie gives the go-ahead to prepare final plans and specifications to construct the new 73,000 seat Dolphin Stadium.

Jan. 20 — The Dolphins drop a 38-16 decision to the San Francisco 49ers in Super Bowl XIX before 84,059 fans in Stanford Stadium in Palo Alto, Calif.

Feb. 15 — Miami names 42-year-old Mel Phillips as its new defensive backfield coach. Phillips comes to the Dolphins after five seasons in the same

capacity for the Detroit Lions.

March 14 — Following a presentation led by Joseph Robbie to NFL owners at the league meetings in Phoenix, Miami is selected as the site for Super Bowl XXIII (1989).

Sept. 15 — The Dolphins register their first victory of the 1985 season as they defeat the Indianapolis Colts 30-13 while racking up a season-high 486 yards of total offense. QB Dan Marino completes 29 of 48 passes for 329 yards while WR Mark Clayton catches eight balls for 106 yards.

Sept. 29 — In a game billed nationally as "Marino-Elway I," Miami's Dan Marino wins this one over Denver 30-26, completing 25 of 43 passes for three TDs and a season-best 390 yards. Veteran WR Nat Moore also produces his top performance of 1985 with the 12th 100-plus yard game of his career. WR Vince Heflin's first-ever NFL TD, a 46-yard catch, proves to be the game-winner.

Oct. 9 — The Dolphins acquire all-pro linebacker Hugh Green from Tampa Bay in exchange for a first and second round draft pick in 1986.

Nov. 10 — Wide receiver Mark Duper, in his first game back after being sidelined with a broken leg, establishes a new Dolphin record by gaining 217 reception yards. In addition, his 50-yard scoring catch from Dan Marino with less than a minute remaining gives the Dolphins a 21-17 win over the Jets and the start of an eight-game winning streak.

Dec. 1 — Owner Joseph Robbie officially breaks ground on the new 73,000-seat Dolphin Stadium.

Dec. 2 — Led by a swarming defense that produces six sacks and three interceptions, the Dolphins administer the only defeat to be suffered by the eventual Super Bowl champion Chicago Bears, 38-24. A season-high Orange Bowl crowd of 75,594 witnesses the Monday night affair.

Dec. 19 — Squads for the AFC-NFC Pro Bowl are announced with four Dolphins named to the team, including two starters. QB Dan Marino and C Dwight Stephenson are selected to start while WR Mark Clayton and G Roy Foster will serve as reserves. It is later determined that the Dolphins' coaching staff will lead the AFC.

Dec. 22 — The Dolphins clinch the AFC Eastern Division championship with a 28-0 win over the Buffalo Bills, thus marking the 13th time in 16 years that Miami has won or shared that title.

Dec. 31 — Owner Joseph Robbie obtains the construction loan and is granted permanent financing for the new Dolphin Stadium.

1986

Jan. 4 — The Dolphins rally from a 21-3 deficit to defeat the Cleveland Browns 24-21 in an AFC divisional playoff game. Miami is led offensively by Tony Nathan's 10 receptions for 101 yards and rookie Ron Davenport's two touchdowns.

Jan. 12 — Despite 20 tackles by LB Bob Brudzinski, the Dolphins commit six turnovers and lose 31-14 to the New England Patriots in the AFC Championship Game before 74,978 fans in the Orange Bowl. It marks Miami's first loss in an AFC title game in six tries.

Jan. 21 — Dolphin C Dwight Stephenson is named the recipient of the NFL's Man of the Year award at a press conference in New Orleans. The award is in recognition of Stephenson's outstanding performance on the playing field and in the community.

Jan. 22 — The Dolphins announce the retirement of Defensive Line Coach Mike Scarry, a member of Don Shula's staff since 1970. Dan Sekanovich, formerly of the Jets and Falcons, is named to replace him.

Feb. 19 — Miami appoints Receivers and Quarterbacks Coach David Shula to the position of Assistant Head Coach. In addition, the club names Mike Westhoff as the Special Teams/Tight Ends Coach.

June 3 — Owner Joe Robbie plants a ceremonial 30-foot Royal Palm tree to begin a million dollar beautification project near Dolphin Stadium.